# IROQUOIA

Christopher Vecsey, *Series Editor*

# IROQUOIA

## The Development of a Native World

WILLIAM ENGELBRECHT

SYRACUSE UNIVERSITY PRESS

First Edition 2003
03  04  05  06  07  08      6  5  4  3  2

The paper used in this publication meets the minimum requirements of
American National Standard for Information Sciences—Permanence
of Paper for Printed Library Materials, ANSI Z39.48–1984.∞™

**Library of Congress Cataloging-in-Publication Data**
Engelbrecht, William E.
Iroquoia : the development of a Native world / William Engelbrecht.—
1st ed.
p. cm. — (Iroquois and their neighbors)
Includes bibliographical references and index.
ISBN 0-8156-2958-3 (alk. paper)
1. Iroquois Indians—History. 2. Iroquois Indians—Antiquities. I.
Title. II. Series.
E99.I7 E534 2002
974.7004'9755—dc21
2002153009

*For Marian E. White, Archaeologist*
1921–1975

**William Engelbrecht** is professor of anthropology at Buffalo State College. His articles have appeared in many journals, including *American Antiquity, North American Archaeologist, Northeast Anthropology,* and the *Bulletin: Journal of the New York State Archaeological Association.*

# CONTENTS

# ILLUSTRATIONS

**Figures**

## Maps

# PREFACE

Few residents of New York State are well informed concerning the rich cultural heritage that is at times literally beneath their feet. Archaeological sites throughout the state are testimony to thousands of years of human occupation. In some areas, the more recent of these can be associated with the historically known Iroquois, consisting in the seventeenth century of the Seneca, Cayuga, Onondaga, Oneida, and Mohawk. One cannot claim a full understanding of the history of New York without an understanding of the development of these nations.

In anthropological parlance, the Seneca, Cayuga, Onondaga, Oneida, and Mohawk are referred to as tribes. In the present study, I use the term *nation* in place of *tribe*. In Canada, native peoples are now commonly referred to as "First Nations." This usage recognizes commonality of language, territory, and culture as the basis for this designation (LaDuke 1992, 55).

As an ethnohistoric work, this study draws on diverse lines of evidence, including archaeology and history. Both sources have their limitations. Archaeology can tell us few specifics about spiritual beliefs, while early historic sources are often incomplete and contain biases. This is especially true of missionary discussions of native beliefs. During the first half of the seventeenth century, French missionaries recorded aspects of daily life of the Huron, a northern Iroquoian Confederacy whose people are assumed to have been culturally similar to the New York Iroquois. Comparable historic documentation for the New York Iroquois does not exist for this period, so at times information from the Huron is used cautiously to flesh out this narrative.

There is no question that the European discovery, exploration, and subsequent colonization of North America profoundly affected Native American cultures. In recognition of this, archaeologists studying the Iroquois have traditionally referred to a late prehistoric or precontact period, followed by a protohistoric or contact period, and then an early historic period. This approach is used sparingly here. While useful for some purposes, this division of the temporal continuum into culture historical periods defined by European presence or absence has the effect of introducing discontinuities where none may exist in terms of the development of native societies.

In a recent book, *War Before Civilization,* Lawrence Keeley criticizes archaeologists for having pacified the past. That is, they have tended to overlook examples of past conflict or to downplay its importance. While many of his examples are drawn from Mesolithic and Neolithic Europe, his observations ring true for northeastern North America. Double—and triple-wall palisades taking tremendous expenditures of energy to construct are said "to define community membership," and earth rings encircling early Iroquoian communities define "ceremonial spaces." This book takes the view that hostilities were a fact of life for Late Woodland peoples in the Northeast, and much of Iroquoian culture is comprehensible as a response to these conditions. This view is also reflected in oral tradition, which records widespread conflict before the advent of the Peacemaker and the formation of the famous League of the Haudenosaunee.

I am indebted to Larry Hauptman, former series editor for Syracuse University Press, who encouraged me to undertake this study, and to Sally Atwater and Irene Vilar, formerly senior acquisitions editors at the press. This study would not have been possible without the previous work of many researchers. Dean Snow recently published a volume entitled *Mohawk Valley Archaeology: The Sites,* which was based on a long-term research project and which is a major source of information on the Mo-

hawk. In 1987, the Rochester Museum and Science Center initiated the Charles F. Wray Series in Seneca archaeology, spearheaded by Martha Sempowski and Lorraine Saunders. Two volumes have appeared in this series, and the third volume is expected shortly. I thank Martha Sempowski for photocopying a draft of their "Summary and Interpretations" from the third volume for me. Jim Tuck's 1971 pioneering study of Onondaga development, followed in 1987 by Jim Bradley's study of Onondaga acculturative change proved invaluable for this study, as did Mary Ann Niemczycki's 1984 study of Seneca and Cayuga development and Peter Pratt's 1976 study of the Oneida. The late William Ritchie, along with Robert Funk, established much of the necessary culture historical framework for this and other studies. I extensively used dissertations by Susan Bamann, Robert Hasenstab, Steven Monckton, Susan Prezzano, and Mary Socci for this study. Over the years, George Hamell of the New York State Museum has provided me with a series of draft manuscripts that have influenced my thinking and interpretations of Native American spirituality. He also read a number of chapters of this manuscript and made many helpful suggestions.

Over the years Charles F. Hayes III, Martha Sempowski, Lorraine Saunders, Brian Nagel, and Betty Prisch, all of the Rochester Museum and Science Center, have greatly facilitated my research. In particular, Martha Sempowski read and commented on a number of chapters of the present work and Charles F. Hayes III read and commented on the entire manuscript.

J. V. Wright, curator emeritus of the Canadian Museum of Civilization, read an early draft of the manuscript and provided many valuable insights. Tim Abel, then a graduate student at the University at Albany, SUNY, and Nancy Herter and Doug Perrelli, then graduate students at SUNY-Buffalo, also read early versions of the manuscript and provided valuable suggestions. Tom Abler of the University of Waterloo read a later version and also provided suggestions. Portions of the manuscript were read by John Hart, Robert Hasenstab, Richard Hosbach, Kurt Jordan, Mima Kapches, Jordan Kerber, Wayne Lenig, Neil O'Donnell, Elizabeth Peña, Daniel Weiskotten, and Tony Wonderley. Peter Pratt reviewed the entire manuscript for Syracuse University Press. The input of all these individuals is gratefully acknowledged.

Many individuals freely answered my questions or shared information during the course of this research. Jack Holland has long provided me with sage advice on lithics and continues to do so. Glenice Guthrie provided information on mortuary practices and evidence of skeletal trauma in the Midwest. Gary Crawford updated me on recent developments in archaeobotany. Thanks for information also goes to James Adovasio, Oscar Bartochowski, Hetty Jo Brumbach, Robert DeOrio, Art Einhorn, Dolores Elliott, Robert Funk, Robert Gorall, Robert Grumet, Robert Hall, Stephen Monckton, Blair Rudes, William Sturtevant, Neal Trubowitz, and Alexander von Gernet. Thanks go also to Deanna Mekarski, a Buffalo State College student who signed up for an independent research project with me while I was on sabbatical and suddenly found herself a library research assistant.

This book was made possible by a sabbatical leave from Buffalo State College. I am grateful to the college and to a number of colleagues there. These include anthropology department chair Jill Nash, as well as Jim Haynes of biology, Greg Stein of geography, Henry Lang and Cynthia Conides of history, and Marjorie Lord and Elizabeth Plewniak of interlibrary loan.

This book is dedicated to Marian White. She hired me to run the Highway Salvage Archaeology program at SUNY-Buffalo back in 1968 when I was still a graduate student at the University of Michigan. I worked with her both in the field and the lab and learned a great deal in the process. She was a professional dedicated to protecting and interpreting the archaeological record. It is hoped that this book will further these ends.

# IROQUOIA

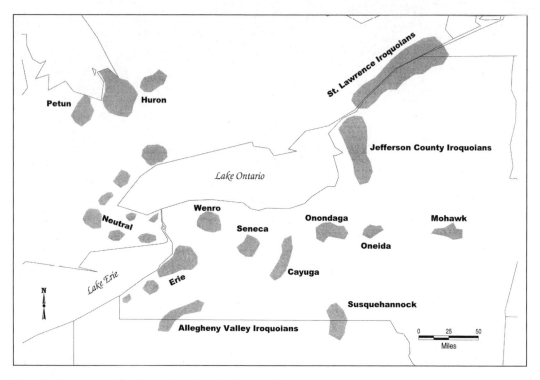

Map 1. Core areas of native nations in the sixteenth century.

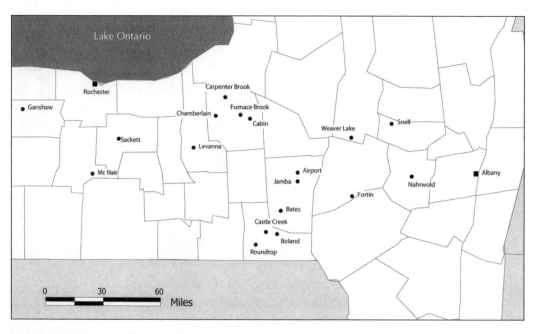

Map 2. Distribution of Owasco sites (c. A.D. 900–1350) mentioned in the text. Modified from Snow 1994b, 25.

# THE ANCIENT ROOTS OF THE IROQUOIS

*Hunting, Fishing, Gathering*

## Introduction

When Europeans first encountered the Iroquois, or Haudenosaunee, each nation consisted of one or more fortified villages. From west to east, Iroquois territory extended almost two hundred miles across what is now central New York State. Core areas of the Iroquois nations were typically separated by twenty to forty miles (see map 1).

This population distribution is taken as typical, and most assume that it has considerable time depth. In fact, this distribution represents a snapshot of Iroquois development at one point in history. Had Europeans encountered the Iroquois two hundred years earlier, not only the population distribution but the political, ethnic, and even linguistic groups they observed would have been different (see map 2 for the distribution of ancestral Iroquois [Owasco] sites mentioned in the text).

This study traces the development of the New York Iroquois over the last millennium. Archaeology, oral tradition, historic documents, linguistics, and any other relevant sources of information are used. Following common practice, the term *Iroquois* refers to the Five Nations (Seneca, Cayuga, Onondaga, Oneida, and Mohawk) while "Iroquoian" is used for additional groups like the Huron, Neutral, and Susquehannock, whose members spoke a language belonging to the larger Iroquoian language family. Each of the Five Nations Iroquois spoke a different, though related, Iroquoian language.

While one cannot trace seventeenth-century Iroquois nations much farther back in time than that, certain elements of Iroquois culture had great antiquity and are shared with surrounding peoples. Techniques of hunting, fishing, and gathering were developed over thousands of years in the Northeast. Along with these techniques the Iroquois maintained a spiritual view of the land and its resources.

These ancient beliefs and practices are discussed in this chapter, along with evidence that even before the introduction of maize farming, intergroup relations were at times hostile. This study argues that both spirituality and warfare are deeply rooted in the cultures of northeastern North America and are key to understanding Iroquois cultural development.

The development of Iroquois culture can be likened to the growth of a great tree, with roots spreading wide and deep. Like an old tree on the edge of a new subdivision, Iroquois culture can be found today if one knows where to look.[1] It is still growing.

## Spirituality

It may seem odd that a book that relies heavily on archaeological data would start with a discussion of Native American spirituality. Spirituality cannot be dug up, mapped, catalogued, or quantified in the manner archaeologists traditionally use to deal with data. For this reason, archaeologists have largely ignored it as a subject. However, even a superficial examination of Native American cultures reveals that spiritual attitudes are integral to understanding traditional ways of life. Taking a strict "stones and bones" approach in reconstructing the past leads to an impoverished perspective.

While we cannot know what people believed a thousand years ago with the same specificity that we can know the shape of their houses or projectile points, traditional accounts, historic records, and the

beliefs of living Native Americans all provide clues. For example, most Native American languages do not have a separate word for religion because spiritual attitudes are not considered separate from everyday life. Modern distinctions between the spiritual and material world do not apply. It seems safe to assume that this was true for the ancestors of the Iroquois.

A number of scholars have commented on ideological commonalities between Native American groups over a broad area (Hamell 1987; von Gernet 1992, 172; Hall 1997). Rituals surrounding the horticultural cycle overlay a worldview common to hunter-gatherers throughout the Americas (Hultkrantz 1979, 144–45; von Gernet and Timmins 1987, 32). In this worldview, humans are not set apart from the natural world, but rather share it with both animate and inanimate entities. The earth itself is alive and nurturing. Rocks, streams, waterfalls, plants, and animals are viewed as sentient and having humanlike qualities (Hewitt 1903, 134). The use of human kin terms to address these beings— "Our Grandmother, the Moon," for example, or "Our Mother" for the earth— reflects this worldview (Hamell 1998, 258).

Typically, hunters performed rituals indicating their respect for their quarry and their thankfulness when successful (Dennis 1993, 38). Rituals are a form of social contract with spirit forces, and failure to observe them results in negative consequences (Hamell 1992, 453). Huron men sometimes cut themselves with flint flakes

---

1. The League is often symbolized as a white pine. Needles on this tree grow in clusters of five, "one for each nation" (Fenton 1978, 103).

so that their blood flowed in order to enlist spirit forces to aid them in the hunt (Thwaites 1896–1901, 12:69–71). Far to the south in Mexico, individuals also drew their own blood, believing that the shedding of blood was necessary for the continuation of life. Such a view may have its roots in a distant hunter-gatherer past.[2]

Bones of animals hunted were deliberately not given to dogs to eat for fear that the animals would not allow themselves to be killed in the future (Thwaites 1896–1901, 44:301, 303; Fenton 1978, 298). This practice was continued by traditional Iroquois into the early part of the twentieth-century (Waugh 1973, 131). Arthur Parker suggested that the reason so many complete projectile points are recovered from Iroquois sites is that they are a form of sacrifice. "The bear is pleased that the instruments of his death are not kept" (Parker 1918, 36).[3]

Among Iroquoians, *orenda* is the spiritual power inherent in existence. According to Hope Isaacs, the Seneca believe that all natural entities have spirits, and hence inherent power or *orenda* (1977, 170–71). Successful hunters had *orenda*. If an animal was successful in escaping from a hunter, its *orenda* was greater (Isaacs 1977, 168). Human-made objects may or may not have

power. Objects acquire power when humans invest them with it through ritual, customarily using sacred tobacco. The degree of power an object has is variable, and relates in part to how it is used (Isaacs 1977, 173).

Iroquois false face masks provide a contemporary example of human-made objects charged with great spiritual power. A block of wood that is to become the mask is removed from a living tree, so that the power inherent in the tree becomes part of the mask. Once the image is formed, it gains power as a representation or icon of the spirit forces it portrays (Speck 1955, 72). Ritual use of tobacco adds to this power, as does the mask's use in ceremonies such as Midwinter, or in curing the sick. When the State Museum in Albany suffered a disastrous fire early in the twentieth century, Iroquois stated that it was because the masks in the collection had not been treated with proper respect. Traditionalists believe that masks "trapped" in museums become restless and agitated, and need to be "fed" or renewed with tobacco and sunflower oil.[4]

We cannot know with certainty what objects recovered from archaeological excavations were seen by their makers as possessing orenda. Effigy pipes depicting humans or animals clearly had spiritual significance. Turtle-shell rattles used in rituals to maintain the proper balance and har-

2. The importance of shedding blood is common to many world religions including Christianity. Among Iroquoians, flint (chert) was viewed as the solidified blood or body of Flint, the younger twin in the story of creation (Moulton and Abler 1991).

3. I am indebted to George Hamell for this reference.

4. *The False Faces of the Iroquois* by William Fenton (1987) offers an extensive treatment of this subject.

mony in the world must also have been held as sacred as well as light, bright, and white objects (Hamell 1996; N. Saunders 1998).

Even objects that today most regard as "ordinary" may have represented spirit forces. For example, we categorize fish nets as inanimate objects, but it is clear that this was not the case for the early seventeenth-century Huron.

> One day, as I was about to burn in the fire the skin of a squirrel, which a savage had given me, they would not allow it and sent me to burn it outside, because of the nets then in the lodge, saying that otherwise the nets would tell the fish. I said to them that the nets could see nothing; they replied that they could, and also that they could hear and eat. "Then give them some of your sagamité," I said. One of them replied to me: "It is the fish that feed them, not we." (Sagard-Théodat 1968, 187)

Huron "talking nets" were part of a world, now largely vanished, in which the distinction between animate and inanimate did not exist. It was a world in which natural and manufactured objects possessed spiritual power, and a world with which humans needed to maintain a proper relationship.

**Warfare and Hunter-Gatherers**

A common misconception about the past is that it was generally peaceful. In no part of the world is this borne out by an examina-

tion of the evidence. Cross-cultural studies of hunter-gatherers indicate that most engaged in warfare (Keeley 1996, 30–31). Indeed, the archaeological record from the Old World suggests that conflict is as old or older than modern humans. The hunting of animals and the hunting of fellow humans are both ancient activities. Regardless of the weapon used, similar skills are needed. Typically males begin their training early.

In North America, spear points lodged in human bone and other forms of physical trauma are observable in even very early skeletal material (Gramly 1988, 88; Milner et al. 1991; Seeman 1992, 46). Kennewick Man from Washington State (more than nine thousand years old) received a spear wound in the pelvis that healed (Slayman 1997). The equally ancient skeleton, from the Grimes Burial Shelter in Nevada, of a sixteen—to eighteen-year-old male indicates that he was killed by an obsidian blade. The tip broke off in his chest (Owsley and Jantz 2000, 58).

At the Lamoka Lake site in central New York (c. 2500 B.C.), William Ritchie found the skeletons of three young males, two with single Lamoka projectile points and one with four projectile points embedded in their skeletons (1932, 116–18, 124–27; 1980, 77). Two of the males had been decapitated and partially dismembered, the right arm of one being found partially charred in a hearth. The skeleton of a female of about forty years of age was also recovered, but the lower legs were missing. Ritchie observed marks near the severed edges of the bones that he suggested were made by a stone axe (1932, 127). At the Archaic Oberlander No. 1 site at Brewerton, New York, two children and two adults (a female and a male), were found buried together in a common grave (Ritchie 1980, 103). The male skeleton was found with a projectile point in his thorax, suggesting that the four individuals were the victims of a raid. The Frontenac Island site in Cayuga Lake yielded a series of adult male skeletons showing both healed and fatal skull fractures, suggesting to William Ritchie, the excavator, a group engaged in warfare (1945, 12–13; 1980, 120). One male skull shows stone knife marks on the frontal bone in an apparently unsuccessful attempt to remove an embedded stone point (Ritchie 1945, 13).

The reason or reasons behind these early conflicts remain obscure. Crossculturally, revenge is a major motive for prestate warfare (Keeley 1996, 115). Once conflict exists in a region, revenge is self-perpetuating (Trigger 1967, 153–55, Abler and Logan 1988, 13). Each side seeks vengeance for past wrongs, a cycle observable in many areas of the world today. Even what we would regard as a natural misfortune could be blamed on a neighboring people, precipitating a raid for revenge.

Given what is believed to have been a low population density among early hunter-gatherers in eastern North America, archaeologists have generally been unsuccessful in making a convincing case for conflict over resources. It is possible that competition arose on occasion over rich resources that were highly localized. Prime fishing spots would be an example of such a "point resource." The New York Archaic sites with skeletons reflecting violence (Lamoka Lake, Oberlander No. 1, and Frontenac Island) were all located at prime fishing locations. Burials with trauma from Archaic shell middens in the mid-continental United States appear to be similarly located, suggesting a connection between conflict and prime fishing spots. This is a hypothesis that could be tested.

Regardless of the reasons for intergroup conflict, the forests and fishing spots of ancient North America were not safe places. Males were hunters, fishermen, and warriors. Enemies could be anywhere. The descendants of these early hunters, the Iroquois, faced similar enemy threats (Fenton 1978, 298). How the Iroquois and their ancestors dealt with the spiritual forces and the human enemies that were a part of their world is a recurrent theme in the following pages.

*Weapons*

The spear preceded the bow and arrow in North America. Spears could be thrown (javelins) or used as thrusting spears. The spear thrower or atlatl gave added force to the throw. It is not clear when the bow and arrow was introduced into the Northeast since no preserved wooden parts have been found. Estimates are based on the size of the stone projectile, arrow points typically being smaller than spear points. Meadowood points (c. 1000–500 B.C.) have been suggested as possible arrow points, though John Blitz argues for a later diffusion of this technology to the Northeast around A.D. 600 (1988, 132).[5] It is possible that both spear thrower and bow and arrow were in use by some groups for a time as they were in the recent past by the Inuit and Aleut. The bow and arrow may not have been uniformly used in the Eastern Woodlands until around A.D. 700 (Nassaney and Pyle 1999, 245).

It is widely assumed that the triangular Levanna point of the Owasco culture (c. A.D. 900–1350) functioned as an arrow point. Over time, large triangular Levanna points decrease in size and shift from an equilateral to isosceles shape (Ritchie 1980, 278). The decrease in size and weight would seem to reflect the evolution of a more aerodynamically efficient arrow point, in contrast to earlier spear points that were larger and heavier (Seeman 1992, 42; Bradbury 1997, 226). Small triangular arrow points on Iroquois sites are referred to as Madison points. Robert Kuhn has demonstrated that change in the length to width ratio of these points can be used for relatively ordering sites within an area and for cross-dating sites between areas (1996).

Technologically, the bow and arrow offers several advantages over spear throwers including greater accuracy and range. A quiver of arrows is much easier to carry than a comparable number of spears.[6] While clearly of benefit while hunting, such advantages become critical in warfare (Seeman 1992, 42; Bradbury 1997, 226). Warriors who did not adopt this technology would have been placed at a disadvantage. The widespread distribution of small arrow points is most efficiently interpreted as an effect rather than a cause of warfare.

Archaic and later sites in the Eastern Woodlands typically contain a variety of heavy chipped and ground stone tools, including axes (celts), adzes, choppers, and pestles. Stone axes were sometimes hafted by inserting an axe into a sapling, which then grew around the artifact (Lafitau 1977, 71). Axes and adzes were used for woodworking, choppers for butchering or even hide scraping (Ritchie 1980, 62), and pestles for pounding nuts. Some of these tools served a secondary function as weapons of war. For example, at the late prehistoric Norris Farm #36 cemetery in west-central Illinois, ground stone celts appear to be responsible for many of the penetrating skull fractures observed (Milner et al. 1991, 583).[7]

---

5. J. V. Wright (1994, 60–62) suggests that Meadowood points were used as arrow points, with bow and arrow technology having diffused from a Middle Paleo-Eskimo culture.

6. The Huron made quivers out of dog skin (Sagard-Théodat 1968, 154).

7. Keeley (1996, 50) points out that both European Early Neolithic axes (c. 5000 B.C.) and highland New Guinea axes functioned as weapons of war in addition to their woodworking function.

*The Forest*

A commonly held image in need of revision is that eastern North America was covered by unbroken virgin forest before European settlement. Europeans coming from regions that had been clear-cut may have thought the environment untouched, but long human presence in the Northeast had affected the distribution of plant and animal communities even before the establishment of Native American horticulture (Moeller 1996, 61). While separating the effects humans had on ecosystems from those of climatic change remains an issue, the environment in which Native Americans lived is increasingly viewed as an environment that Native Americans altered, both consciously and unconsciously (White 1984, 181; White and Cronon 1988, 417).

Early Europeans in the Northeast recorded that both forests and grasslands were burned. Fires were set in the early spring and sometimes in the fall (Day 1953; H. Lewis 1980; Russell 1983; Dennis 1993, 33, 36). In 1632, Gabriel Sagard-Théodat wrote of the Huron area, "The country is full of fine hills, open fields, very broad meadows bearing much excellent hay, which is of no use except to set fire to as an amusement when it is dry" (Sagard-Théodat 1968, 90).

Actually, the firing of dead grass in open areas in early spring was more than an amusement: it was important in the management of the ecosystem. These fires leave the ground surface blackened, causing greater heat absorption and promoting earlier growth while the damp or still frozen soil protects the root systems (H. Lewis 1980). Such areas provide good browse for deer and elk. Dead, unburned grass does not rejuvenate as quickly. Repeated burning of open areas each spring expands such areas, not only promoting new growth for herbivores but improving visibility for hunters. A series of fires set in a circle was sometimes used to circumscribe game when hunting.

At present, the distribution and extent of past grasslands in New York is unknown. Grass produces biogenic silica (phytoliths), which may be preserved in soil profiles. The search for these minute particles has the potential for establishing the duration and extent of such grasslands (Wykoff 1988, 225). Such data, coupled with knowledge of settlement patterns, could provide useful information on past human use and modification of the environment.

Within a forest, variability in natural conditions promotes species diversity. However, the most dynamic variable affecting species diversity in a forest are human-set fires (H. Lewis 1980, 77). George Loskiel, an eighteenth-century observer of Iroquois burning, wrote, "These fires run on for many miles" (in Dennis 1993, 33). The distribution of fire-tolerant trees, including oaks, black walnuts, and chestnuts, increased as a result of human-set fires, and this in turn increased forest productivity (Swan 1970; Delcourt et al.

1998, 276). While acorns must be processed before they can be eaten by humans, white-tailed deer, elk, and other animals are not similarly limited. Occasional forest fires from either human or natural causes would create forests free of understory growth, providing easier and quieter passage for travelers or hunters. How widespread and frequent human-set forest fires were in the Northeast remains uncertain (Russell 1983). Negative effects of repeated burning of the same area of forest would be a decrease in the quantity of available mast and firewood.

The ideal habitat for deer is not deep woods but a mixture of cover such as might be found at the edge of forests and swamps, including brush and young trees (Socci 1995, 106). Abandoned villages and fields, as well as burned-over areas providing second growth, allow deer to thrive (Sauer 1971, 285). The distribution of bluestem grass (used for lining storage pits) was probably increased by human forest clearance and the maintenance of open areas through burning (Swan 1970).

## Hunting

Deer were the most important source of meat in the diet and are the predominant mammalian remain on Iroquois village sites (Socci 1995, 107). Though fall and early winter hunting were most important, seasonality studies based on antler growth indicate that deer were taken year round (Snow 1995a, 167–68).

A successful hunter enjoyed great prestige. It is assumed that men and a few women established hunting camps, while old people, pregnant women, and children stayed in the village (Fenton 1978, 298). Seventeenth-century accounts of the Iroquois suggest that the village was nearly abandoned during the winter hunt (Thwaites 1896–1901, 54:117; Gehring and Starna 1988, 4; Abler 1970, 33). In the hunting camps, women helped butcher the game and dry the meat. Both men and women carried it back to the village in pack baskets with the aid of a burden strap passed over the forehead. John Witthoft argued that this strap "was both a magical and a spiritual binding, to overcome the animals' ability to retaliate, and a decorative binding intended to please and flatter the spirit of the dead animal" (1953, 13; see fig. 55). The role of Iroquois women as bearers of venison is reflected in Iroquois cosmology in the account of Sky Woman carrying a heavy load of venison from her husband's house back to her village. Harmen Meyndertsz van den Bogaert observed Mohawk houses with forty or fifty quarters of venison that had been cut up and dried (Gehring and Starna 1988, 21). Some of this meat could also have been transported by canoe.

Before the establishment of horticultural villages, the entire band presumably lived together most of the year. Maximum band aggregation is believed to have occurred in warm-weather months. In fall and early winter, families would relocate to hunting camps. Deer were then at their fattest. Lean, semistarved deer at winter's end would not have provided comparable food value (O'Shea 1989, 64). At such times bones may have been pounded and boiled to extract any available marrow. Our typical modern diet is too high in fat, so we tend to be unaware that fat is critical for both energy and metabolism (Speth 1983).

Iroquois hunting camps have not been systematically studied by archaeologists, who have concentrated instead on village sites. Therefore, it is not clear if the hunting camps of the Iroquois and their immediate ancestors differed from those of earlier peoples. Presumably knives used in butchering would be common to both, and possibly the equipment for making stone tools: hammerstones and antler billets for initial percussion and smaller cylindrical antler flakers for pressure flaking (Ritchie 1980, 278).[8] End scrapers, presumably used for hide scraping, are common on Iroquois village sites, but their frequency on hunting camps is unknown, leaving open for further archaeological study the question of where most hide processing was done.

Analysis of deer bone on Mohawk sites indicates that lower limb and foot bones are most frequently represented. This pattern suggests that these bones were brought back to the village with the hide, while the remainder of the deer skeleton was left where the deer was butchered

(Socci 1995, 117). On some sites, the presence of all deer skeletal elements suggests that whole deer carcasses were brought back to the village, the animal presumably having been killed nearby (Guilday 1973, 330).

Deadfalls and snares were used by Iroquoians in hunting deer, and it is probable that these methods have considerable antiquity. Samuel de Champlain observed that many deer were taken with snares (Grant 1907, 299). Partridge and turkey were also taken by snares, probably by older men around the village (Fenton 1978, 298). Women may have used snares to capture birds and small animals in their fields.

In late October 1615, Champlain participated in a deer hunt with some twenty-five Huron men. Two converging lines of stakes eight to nine feet high were constructed over a ten-day period. At the apex of this open triangle was a small enclosure. Every two days for the next thirty-eight, the men fanned out and frightened the deer into the enclosure, where they were killed. A total of 120 deer were taken, which suggests an average of between 8 and 9 deer taken on each drive. Champlain notes that the fat was saved for winter (Grant 1907, 297–99).

Deer hides were an extremely important, possibly critical resource (Gramly 1977). Clothing was made of deerskin, and it is estimated that six were needed for a man's outfit while eight were required for a woman, including her skirt (Gramly 1977, 602). Moccasins were made of deer hide,

8. A flaker of bear bone from the Cabin site [Onondaga] showed evidence of an arrow wound (Tuck 1971, 43).

and deer skin provided ground cover for sleeping as well (Thwaites 1896–1901, 31:83; Socci 1995, 108).

In addition to meat and hides, deer provided sinew for sewing, and bone and antler for tools (Pratt 1976, 19). Deer bone awls, needles, and husking pins are found on sites along with antler flakers (Pratt 1976, 19). Bone *beamers* (scraping tools for removing hair from the hides of deer and other animals) are also found (Ritchie 1980, 287). These are often made of deer foot or pelvic bones or bear leg bones. Deer mandibles were used for removing maize kernels from the cobs (Waugh 1973, 40; Snow 1995a, 167–68).

Elk (*wapiti*) is frequently found on Iroquois sites but in limited quantity (Socci 1995, 119–20). It was probably taken opportunistically while hunting deer. The hides of elk and deer were probably used similarly. A variety of smaller mammals, including rabbit, woodchuck, muskrat, porcupine, and squirrel, were also hunted.

The environment of the New York Iroquois provided a good habitat for bear (Socci 1995, 92). Both bear meat and fat were prized. Bear grease was rubbed on the skin and hair, and the Iroquois said that it prevented lice (Socci 1995, 86). Bear robes were used in winter as clothing and bedding. Bear teeth were perforated and worn. These uses of the black bear were sufficient to make it an important prey of Iroquois hunters. Bear typically were hunted in winter when they were hibernating or when they could be chased through deep snow,

the hunters having the advantage of snowshoes (Morgan 1962, 377).

While bear meat was eaten as food, the bear hunt was about more than subsistence. Bears were held in special reverence by the Iroquois (Socci 1995, 88). Bears are the most humanlike of animals in the northern hemisphere, and shamanic rituals relating to the bear are found throughout the circumpolar region. Bear meat was eaten by members of a war party as a symbolic representation of a captive (Socci 1995, 86–87). A feast of bear meat might appease the Iroquois spirit-being who demanded a human sacrifice (Fenton 1978, 316; Goddard 1984, 230–31). Bear meat was also eaten at the Iroquois Ohgi:we: (Feast of the Dead).

Rituals surrounding the bear are reflected at two sites investigated by William Ritchie (1947; 1950). At the Carpenter Brook site (Owasco), some two hundred ceramic vessels were recovered along with animal remains—predominantly bear—especially of the cranium and foot (Ritchie 1947). Whole pots containing bear meat were cast into the stream, which today is at least five feet lower than in Owasco times (c. A.D. 900–1350) because of drainage relating to construction of the Erie Canal. Throwing bear skulls into the water or tying them to a tree in order to protect the skulls from dogs is one way northern people show respect to the spirit of the bear (Hallowell 1926).

The ritual represented at Carpenter Brook could also be a predecessor of the

Iroquois Ohgi:we: (Feast of the Dead), in which a drum was thrown into a cemetery at the conclusion of the ritual (Fenton and Kurath 1951, 152; Ritchie 1947, 68–69). This part of the ceremony was called "Carry-out-the-Kettle" (Fenton and Kurath 1951, 158). In Onondaga, the same term is used for both "drum" and "kettle" (Fenton and Kurath 1951, 150), and Father Joseph Lafitau refers to a drum made from a skin stretched over a cooking pot (1974, 150).

The beaver was appreciated both for its meat and for its pelt. An average male weighs in at fifty-five pounds, making the amount of meat not inconsiderable (Scheele 1950, 7). Beaver were hunted in winter, when the animal could be found inside its lodge and the fur was at its best (Thwaites 1896–1901, 42:203; Socci 1995, 55). Beaver incisor teeth were hafted and used as woodworking tools.[9]

As a consequence of the European fur trade, beaver became a very important resource to seventeenth-century Iroquois. Even by the mid-sixteenth century, there was an increase in beaver bone on Onondaga and Mohawk sites (Bradley 1987, 54; Snow 1995a, 160, 169). Paradoxically, European trade materials form only a very minor portion of the archaeological record at these sites. Another archaeological enigma is the low incidence of beaver remains on late sixteenth—and early seventeenth-century Seneca sites (Martha Sempowski, personal communication). Perhaps beaver were butchered where they were taken, rather than in the village, or were disposed of in some manner so that dogs could not eat them.

In addition to deer-skin clothing and robes made of bear or beaver pelts, fur robes were made of squirrel, wolf, panther, otter, marten, and raccoon (Pratt 1976, 18; Socci 1995, 49, 54). Ethnohistoric accounts indicate that otter skins were frequently used, but the lack of otter bones on sites suggests that the flesh was not eaten and just the pelts were brought back to the village. The interpretation that otters were not eaten agrees with a Seneca oral tradition explaining why otters, along with panthers, mink, fishers, and other long-bodied or long-tailed animals are not good to eat.[10] The otter and other water animals are sometimes associated with sickness, calling for healing rituals by members of the Iroquois Otter Society (Tooker 1964, 103).

For a shaman, wearing a fur robe made from an animal pelt was a step in the transformation into that animal (Parker 1923, 4; Mathews 1981, 17). One can acquire the power of an animal in part by impersonating it. This was especially appropriate in the case of animals that were felt to possess great power like the panther (cougar or

---

9. Bradley (1987, 229n. 6) argues that the crooked knife, a wood-working tool, was a Native American innovation which replaced the beaver incisor after 1655.

10. Hewitt (1903, 239–40), Parker (1923, 68) and Hamell (1998, 264).

Fig. 1. Bone awl from the Seneca Cameron site, fashioned from a bear *os baculum* (penis bone). Length: 12.7 cm. From Wray et al. 1991, 228. Courtesy Rochester Museum and Science Center.

mountain lion) or bear. Effigy pipes of individuals with associated wolf or bear heads are probably surviving material manifestations of this belief system (Mathews 1981, 16–17). Even if one were not a shaman, by wearing an animal's skin or teeth one could potentially possess some of that animal's power.

Male bear and raccoon both have a bony element, an *os baculum,* in their penises. A bear *os baculum* modified into an awl was recovered from the Seneca Cameron site (Wray et al. 1991, 228; see fig. 1) and another made into a projectile point was recovered from the Thurston site (Pratt 1976, 133). At Adams, a male burial contained eleven raccoon *os baculae.* This selective use of bear and raccoon skeletal elements suggests the transference or management of the animal's potency to the tool or individual associated with the object.

The passenger pigeon was once a major resource for the Iroquois. Huge flocks nested in the spring, and by late April young passenger pigeons were fat and vulnerable. They were then dislodged from their nests with long poles. They were also taken with snares and nets. They were eaten fresh as well as rendered into oil or

dried and smoked at the nesting sites and then packed back to the village. Passenger pigeon remains have been recovered from archaeological sites, but they are probably underrepresented as a species, since the incompletely ossified bones of the squabs were not likely to be recovered (Thwaites 1896–1901, 42:97; 43:153; 56:49–51; Fenton 1978, 297–301; Socci 1995, 136–39; Orlandini 1996).

Ducks, geese, and other birds were hunted and eaten. Many Iroquois villages were located near wetlands, and hunting migratory waterfowl was a seasonally important activity. Turkeys were said to be common among the New York Iroquois (Fenton 1978, 297; Bradley 1987, 13; Socci 1995, 112, 140). Beads were manufactured from hollow bird bones, but often fragile bird bone is not well preserved. Frog bones likewise are often poorly preserved, although they have been recovered from a number of sites in New York (Ritchie and Funk 1973, 114, 161, 186, 210, 219, 235, 290, 329). Ethnohistoric sources indicate that frogs were eaten (Waugh 1916, 134–38; Socci 1995, 155).

The Iroquois showed respect to many of the animals they had killed by not feeding them to dogs. Among hunting peoples of the Northeast, Frank Speck observed, "It is their belief that the game animals are sensitive to ill-treatment of the parts left over after the flesh had been eaten. The spirits of the animals resent in particular the ignominy of seeing their bones fought over, crunched, and devoured by dogs" (Speck 1925, 64; quoted in Kerber 1997, 89). Historic accounts from Canada most commonly mention beaver bone as being specially protected from dogs (Kerber 1997, 88). This agrees with a recent faunal analysis of Mohawk sites that indicated that few beaver bones were gnawed by dogs (Socci 1995, 56). Fish, deer, moose, birds, and porcupine bones were also protected, but the bones of other animals were reportedly thrown to the dogs (Kerber 1997, 88). Dogs ultimately scavenged many animal bones. Analysis of faunal remains from Iroquois sites indicates that many bones were devoured by dogs after having been discarded (Guilday 1973, 329), a process observed worldwide (Schiffer 1987, 70). In addition to bones, dogs will scavenge human waste.

The discovery of Archaic dog burials indicates a long-standing relationship between dogs and humans. Dogs were the only animal domesticated by Native Americans in the Northeast before the introduction of animals domesticated in Europe. No breeds native to the Northeast exist today, as native dogs interbred with dogs introduced by Europeans (Kerber 1997, 87). As Cantwell observed, dogs "are intermediate between the forest, the world of animals, and the camp, the world of man"

(1980, 491). This makes them an ideal mediator or messenger between these worlds.

An important early function was probably as a watchdog, alerting the occupants of a site to possible intruders. This function would have continued in later times, alerting residents of longhouses to the presence of human or animal strangers. Conversely, dogs might also accompany a scouting party to pick up the scent of an enemy (Kerber 1997, 88). The role of dogs in hunting has been questioned (Strong 1985, 32; Schwartz 1997), but early Europeans among Iroquoians noted their use for this purpose (Sagard-Théodat 1968, 100, 226). Champlain in 1603 noted that the Huron had many dogs for hunting and that they slept next to their dogs (Kerber 1997, 87).

## Fishing

While the faunal data recovered by archaeologists indicates that the hunting of large animals was of major importance, historic records stress the importance of fishing (Bradley 1987, 120). In light of these records, fish appear to be underrepresented in the archaeological record. There are several reasons for this.

In general, fish remains are more fragile than mammalian remains, so they are less often recovered. Fish were cooked and eaten whole, which also contributed to the loss of fish bone from the archaeological record (Brumbach 1986, 46; Socci 1995, 152). On sites where appropriate recovery techniques are used, fish remains are generally recovered. Also, recurrently occupied camps at prime fishing localities point to the importance of this activity.

Spearing large fish like sturgeon and pike when they spawn in lake shallows or streams was probably a practice of great antiquity. Spearing fish can be thought of as a land-based technique transferred to aquatic resources (Cleland 1982, 763, 774). Sturgeon, which can weigh up to three hundred pounds, spawn in spring (Cleland 1982, 767). Fish were speared using barbed bone points fixed to a shaft. Ritchie suggests that multipronged leisters were also used (1980, 278). By Middle Woodland times (c. A.D. 1), harpoons with detachable heads were supplanting spears (Cleland 1982, 774). The detachable harpoon head permitted the harpooner to play the fish on the line, which improved the chance of landing the fish (Cleland 1982, 774). In the mid-seventeenth century, Jesuits at Onondaga observed, "Eels are so abundant in the Summer that a man can harpoon as many as a thousand in one night" (Thwaites 1896–1901, 42:97; Bradley 1987, 120).

Angling represents another ancient technique, and both bone and copper fishhooks have been recovered from Archaic sites in the Great Lakes area. Bone fishhooks were made from bird bone or flat sections of mammal bone (see fig. 2). At the Lamoka Lake site (c. 2500 B.C.) in New York, bone fishhooks were recovered along with needlelike implements that may have been used in making and repairing nets (Ritchie 1932, 102–4; Cleland 1982,

769). At the Owasco Castle Creek site, a trot line was recovered with nineteen dropper lines, each with a hook made from two hawthorn spines. The line was made from Indian hemp (Ritchie and Funk 1973, 166; Ritchie 1980, 278).

Fish weirs consisting of lines of converging stones are found in many streams in New York. They are similar in principle to the converging lines of stakes constructed for deer hunting observed by Champlain. Fish were channeled into the apex where they were speared or trapped in a fish basket or box (Beauchamp 1905, 148–49; see figs. 3 and 4).

Stone weirs are difficult to date, but a wooden fish weir along the Atlantic coast is dateable to 2500 B.C. (Fiedel 1987, 102). In 1656, Claude Dablon observed that Oneida weirs "catch at the same time the Eels, that descend, and the Salmon, that always ascends" (Thwaites 1896–1901, 43:261; Brumbach 1986, 40). Regular maintenance of these facilities by cooperative work groups was no doubt required.

Nets are rarely preserved in the archaeological record, but we have indirect evi-

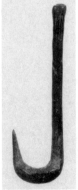

Fig. 2. Bone fishhook from the Seneca Cameron site. The length is about 4 cm. From Wray et al. 1991, 232. Courtesy of the Rochester Museum and Science Center, Rochester, N.Y.

Fig. 3. Fish weir on Tonawanda Creek, Tonawanda Indian Reservation, in the 1950s. Photo courtesy of the late Richard McCarthy.

dence of their existence from net weights, notched pebbles used to weigh down the nets. Net weights are common at the Archaic Lamoka Lake site (c. 2500 B.C.), indicating the early use of nets (Ritchie 1932, 89). Actual fragments of net made from Indian hemp fiber and attached to notched pebble weights were recovered at the Morrow site in Ontario County, New York, a Meadowood site dated to the sixth century B.C. (Ritchie 1980, 186). Among historically known peoples of the Great Lakes, both males and females were involved in net manufacture. Women made the fiber and cordage that men then used to make the nets (Beauchamp 1905, 147–48; Cleland 1982, 763).

In 1644 Johannes Megapolensis, Jr., wrote that "when [Mohawk men] want to fish with seines, ten or twelve . . . will go together and help each other, all of whom own the seine in common" (Megapolensis 1857). In 1687 at Mackinac, Henri Joutel

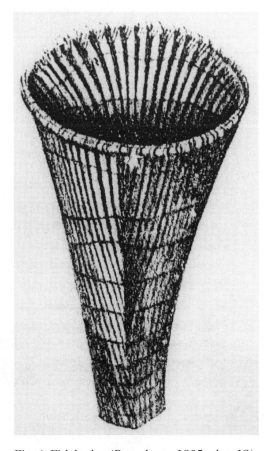

Fig. 4. Fish basket (Beauchamp 1905; plate 19).

observed gill nets two hundred fathoms long and two feet deep with cedar-wood floats (Cleland 1982, 762). These were sometimes set at a depth of thirty fathoms. This use of gill nets probably did not occur until the Late Woodland period (Cleland 1982, 777). The Huron netted fish in winter by passing a net under the ice with poles (Thwaites 1896–1901, 42:71–72; Grant 1907, 331–32). The use of nets in harvesting fish, like the use of deer drives in hunting, required cooperation between groups of men.

Unlike seine nets, which are typically used close to shore, gill nets are set in deep water, which requires canoes. Unlike more northerly peoples who had access to birch bark, the Iroquois used either elm bark canoes or dugouts (see fig. 5).

Pehr Kalm describes the construction of an elm bark canoe (1966, 363–65). Scant attention has been paid to watercraft; instead writers on the Iroquois have stressed their use of trails in travel. But the proximity of all Five Nations to lakes and rivers and the historic importance of fishing would have encouraged the regular use of watercraft in both subsistence activities as well as travel and transport.

Fishing occurred year round but was especially important in the spring. Spring is the time of year when hunting is least productive, owing to the lack of fat and generally poor condition of deer and other prey, so spring fishing does not present a scheduling conflict with hunting. At other times of the year, older men fished while younger men went hunting (Fenton 1978, 297; Ritchie 1980, 278; Richter 1992, 200–201).

On Lake Ontario, fish are generally inaccessible except when spawning in shallow water in either the spring or fall (Cleland 1982, 766). Data from Ontario suggest that fall-spawning species in Lake Ontario were not intensively exploited by Iroquoians (Wright 1998, xiii). Excavations at the Archbald site near the mouth of Oak Orchard Creek on Lake Ontario in New York revealed a multicomponent fishing station (Bigelow et al. 1987). Spring- and summer-spawning species were well represented, unlike fall- and winter-spawning species. The small size of the many net

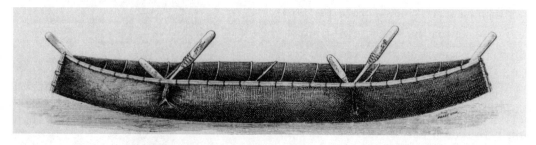

Fig. 5. A twenty-five-foot-long canoe made from a single piece of red elm bark. The rim is of white ash and the thin ribs of ash are spaced approximately one foot apart. It is estimated this canoe could carry two tons (from Morgan 1962).

weights suggests the use of shallow-water seines, rather than deep-water gill nets. The general absence of bone fish hooks and the high fish species diversity also points to net fishing rather than angling as the major procurement strategy.

Fish caught in the fall could be stored for winter use, either by drying in the sun or smoking (Thwaites 1896–1901, 51:203; Socci 1995, 146). The Huron sometimes boiled fish for oil, skimming it off and storing it in gourds (Sagard-Théodat 1968, 186). Colder temperatures in the late fall retard spoilage of smoked fish or permit freezing. Smoking fish for winter use requires considerable labor expenditure in gathering firewood, constructing drying racks, keeping fires going, and turning the fish (Cleland 1982, 779).

When visiting the Oneida in late December 1634, Harmen Meyndertsz van den Bogaert observed houses with seventy or more dried salmon (Gehring and Starna 1988, 13). He also encountered Oneida women trying to sell dried and fresh salmon in Mohawk country, but he remarked that the fish smelled bad (Gehring and Starna 1988, 6).[11]

Among the Huron, certain shaman were believed to be able to induce fish to be caught in nets (Trigger 1990b, 38). The Huron avoided throwing fish bones into the fire, for fear that the spirits of these fish would warn their fellows not to get caught (Sagard-Théodat 1968, 186–87). Like the treatment of animal bones, it was a sign of respect.

*Gathering*

A recent study of plant remains from Huron sites by Stephen Monckton indicates that wild plants were clearly more significant in the diet than historic documents suggest (1992, 12). The lack of emphasis on gathered plants foods in these documents may be due to a bias on the part of male European observers who were more interested in native hunting, fishing, and farming practices, pursuits with which they were already familiar.

Monckton analyzed soil at sites using flotation, a water separation technique useful for recovering seeds and other small remains that in the past escaped the attention of archaeologists. He discovered that strawberries, blackberries, raspberries, and other fleshy fruits were particularly important, but pin cherry, plum, elderberry, and black nightshade were also commonly represented (1992, 44–45). Raspberries were the most commonly identified plant remain from Seneca graves at the Adams and Culbertson site (Wray et al. 1987, 135; 1991, 144). The species was probably black raspberry, as red raspberry is now believed to be a European introduction (Wray et al. 1991, 144).

These fleshy fruits could be spread in flat baskets or bark trays and dried by the fire or in the sun to be used later (Waugh

11. Peter Pratt (personal communication) suggests that rancid salmon may have been considered a delicacy, as was rancid salmon oil among some Northwest Coast groups.

1916, 126; Sagard-Théodat 1968, 237–38; Fenton 1978, 298–99; Monckton 1992, 45, 78). Berries could also be preserved by mashing and forming small cakes that were then dried (Waugh 1916, 127). Consumption of dried fleshy fruits during winter provided vitamin C and was probably important in preventing scurvy (Monckton 1992, 86).

A variety of trees provide edible sap, including yellow birch, hickory, butternut, and red and silver maple (Pendergast 1982, 49). Historically, maple sap was important as a beverage and a sweetener (Fenton 1978, 298; Pendergast 1982, 28). Sugar maple is one of the dominant tree species on the Allegheny Plateau, to the south of the core areas of the Iroquois nations. In historic times, both men and women left the village in early spring to harvest maple sap. The sap was collected in large bark tubs (see fig. 6). Maple sap can be reduced to syrup by boiling, evaporation, or removing ice from frozen sap (Pendergast 1982, 21–22). Further reduction leads to maple sugar. While there is no evidence that Native Americans produced large quantities of maple sugar at the time of European con-

tact, it seems likely that maple sugar was discovered by Native Americans, rather than by Europeans unfamiliar with making sugar from tree sap (Pendergast 1982, 27, 55).

Traditional Iroquois observe a number of ceremonies of thanksgiving, including Thanks-to-the-Maple in late February or March and the Strawberry Festival in June (Wallace 1972, 50–51). The Iroquois calendar contains both a sugar moon and a strawberry moon (Snow 1994b). Both ceremonies and calendrics argue for the importance and antiquity of these resources (Waugh 1916, 125–28; Pendergast 1982, 30; Monckton 1992, 83).

Nuts were processed by crushing and throwing into boiling water, where the nut meats and oil could be skimmed off (Sauer 1971, 181–82). This procedure is far more efficient than cracking and picking out nut meats (Munson 1988, 11). Nuts have the advantage of being storable and are high in protein and calories. Historically, hickory nuts were most important, but walnut, beech, chestnut, and acorns were also gathered (Waugh 1916, 122–25; Parker 1968, 99–102). White oak acorns have less tannin than red oak acorns, and so were prob-

Fig. 6. Bark sap tub (from Morgan 1962).

ably more sought after, but both are edible after boiling (Sagard-Théodat 1968, 108; Finlayson 1998, 241).

The inner bark of a variety of trees, including black ash, white pine, hemlock, and elm was used in times of famine. In addition, medicinal teas were brewed from various conifer leaves and bark (Monckton 1992, 86). Jacques Cartier's men were cured of scurvy during the winter of 1535–1536 by brewing such a tea (Cook 1993, 79–80).

The New York Iroquois possessed an extensive knowledge of medicinal plants, but they had to be gathered with respect. In 1912, Frederick Waugh was told, "Plants can make themselves invisible when they wish" (Herrick 1995, 35).

Through a detailed knowledge of the plant and animal species in their environment and the skill and technology to secure these resources, generations of Native Americans maintained a balance with the environment of the Eastern Woodlands. A temporary decrease in the availability of one resource could be made up by increased reliance on other species. Rituals were observed in order to maintain the proper relationship between humans and the spiritual forces felt to govern these resources.

Evidence of fighting suggests that a comparable reciprocal balance between neighboring human groups did not always exist. What was lacking was the vision and the rituals to make enemies into neighbors with a common purpose.

## ❧ 2 ❧

# FARMING AND FIGHTING

**Beginnings**

The origin of corn (*Zea mays*) and the origin of the Iroquois are closely linked in traditional narrative. While the good-minded or right-handed twin is born in the usual manner from the daughter of Sky Woman, Flint, the evil-minded or left-handed twin, is born through his mother's armpit, thereby killing her. From her grave grew maize, beans, and squash, or "the three sisters" (Witthoft 1949, 80; see fig. 7).

Palcobotanical investigations indicate that the adoption of these plants by the ancestors of the Iroquois was a gradual process. Farming never replaced hunting, fishing, and gathering. Rather, it required additional tasks for both men and women and it provided an additional source of storable food. An expanded subsistence base ultimately permitted the growth of larger communities, but it did not bring more peaceful relationships. The construction of palisades around many early farming communities indicates intergroup

Fig. 7. "From the body of the old woman grew their food." This 1936 sketch by Jesse J. Cornplanter appears in his book *Legends of the Longhouse*. Reprinted by permission of HarperCollins Publishers, Inc.

FROM THE BODY OF THE OLD WOMAN GREW THEIR FOOD

22

hostilities and some human skeletal remains suggest sacrifice. Just as the sacrifice of the daughter of Sky Woman was needed to bring forth the crops that sustained the Iroquois, ancient Iroquoians must have believed human sacrifice to be necessary for their well-being.

Dates from Ontario indicate that a small form of Eastern Eight-Row or Eastern Complex maize was grown along the Grand River as early as the sixth century A.D. (Crawford et al. 1997). This maize is similar to early varieties grown in the Southwest, suggesting its diffusion from there, although diffusion of maize from Mesoamerica at some point is another possibility. Phytolith analysis of the carbonized residue on ceramic vessels provides evidence for maize in New York at a slightly later period (Hart et al. n.d.). Residues can now be dated by accelerator mass spectrometry (AMS), and phytoliths (small silica bodies derived from plant cells) can be identified as to species.

The archaeological culture in New York dating from A.D. 900 or 1000 until about A.D. 1350 is termed the Owasco (Snow 1995a, 52–54). During the Owasco, at least two varieties of maize were grown: flint (*Zea mays indurata*) and flour corn (*Zea mays amylacea*) (Ritchie 1980, 279). Additional varieties known to have been grown historically by the Iroquois include sweet corn (*Zea mays saccharata*), popcorn (*Zea mays everta*), and a pod corn (*Zea tunicata*), an early sacred variety sometimes known as "grandfather corn" (Parker 1968, 43; Heidenreich

1971, 173; Barreiro 1989, 13). Frank Speck states that the Iroquois cultivated fifteen to seventeen varieties of maize (1955, 39).

By A.D. 1300, a way of life including the cultivation of maize, beans (*Phaseolus vulgaris*), various species of the *Cucurbita* genus (pumpkins, squashes, and gourds), sunflower (*Helianthus annus*), and tobacco (*Nicotiana rustica*) appears to have been well established in the Iroquoian area (Kuhn 1994b, 74–77; Smith and Crawford 1997, 26). The Mesoamerican triad of maize, beans, and squash spread separately into the Northeast from the Midwest. Squash came first, followed by maize and then beans. One by one, these cultigens were added to a hunting and gathering way of life, each addition increasing the importance of horticulture as an adaptation, but never completely replacing wild food resources.

Critical to an understanding of the beginnings of farming is the recovery of actual plant remains, especially seeds. The use of flotation has resulted in the recovery of large quantities of charred plant remains from sites along the Mississippi River Valley and its tributaries. Since the 1980s, advances in radiocarbon dating have allowed individual seeds or carbonized plant fragments to be directly dated, using AMS dating. The combination of improved recovery and the ability to date very small individual specimens has revolutionized our conception of the origins of farming in the Midwest.

Sunflower, native to western North

America, spread east and was grown four thousand years ago in the Midwest. Even earlier, a variety of cucurbit native to the East may have been cultivated. Starchy seed plants we now regard as weeds—sumpweed, chenopod, little barley, marsh elder, maygrass, and erect knotweed—were also grown along floodplains of the Midwest, some undergoing changes indicative of domestication. This occurred prior to the introduction of maize into the Midwest some two thousand years ago (Smith 1989; Monckton 1992, 9; Prezzano 1996, 11).

Recent evidence suggests that the growing of cucurbits, especially gourds, may have great antiquity in the Northeast, although the possibility remains that these plants were gathered from the wild. Remains of cucurbit recovered from Maine have been dated to more than five thousand years ago (Petersen and Asch Sidell 1996) and others recovered from the West Branch of the Susquehanna River to about 5400 B.P. (Hart and Asch Sidell 1997). These dates are similar to early dates from the Mississippi Valley. The extent of pre-maize plant domestication in the Northeast is at present unclear; more intensive archaeobotanical investigations using flotation are needed.

The seeds, flesh, and blossoms of *Cucurbita pepo* could have been a food source, but the plant's major uses were probably as a short-term container, fishnet float, or rattle (Hart and Sidell 1997, 530; Perkl 1998, 280; Fritz 1999). Gayle Fritz argues that the use of gourds as net floats spread from the Gulf Coast (1999). The use of gourd rattles by shamans extended from North America southward into Amazonia (Prentice 1986; George Hamell, personal communication).

By A.D. 900, cucurbits, chenopod, little barley, and sunflower were being grown with maize in the West Branch of the Susquehanna River basin (Hart and Asch Sidell 1996). Evidence from the Boland site along the Susquehanna River indicates horticultural village life there by A.D. 1000. In Europe, the time between A.D. 900 and A.D. 1200 is known as the Medieval Warm Period or neo-Atlantic climatic episode. It has been suggested that a similar warm period in New York facilitated the spread of farming, although this remains to be demonstrated (Hasenstab 1990, 16).

John Hart argues that for maize to have been successfully established as a crop in the Eastern Woodlands, gene flow between maize populations would have been necessary, in part because small isolated maize populations are subject to decreases in yield as a result of inbreeding depression (1999b). Crossing two varieties can result in increased vigor (heterosis). While knowledge remains uncertain about the human behavior resulting in the movement of maize between populations in the Northeast, it should be noted that similarities in ceramic style over broad areas suggest contacts between populations during the time it is believed maize was becoming established as a crop.

After A.D. 900, we have evidence for the growing of maize and cucurbits along

New York rivers near good fishing spots (Tuck 1978, 325; Prezzano 1992, 431; Kuhn 1994b, 74). At the early Owasco component of the Fortin site on the floodplain of the Upper Susquehanna, abundant fish bones were recovered, along with carbonized maize. A small pile of net weights recovered from a feature suggests that they were attached to a discarded net (Funk 1993, 236, 269).

Maize is a plant of tropical origin and can be distinguished isotopically from other food sources used by the Iroquois. The consistent presence of maize in the diet can be confirmed by isotopic analysis of the skeleton. Analysis of skeletal remains from the Snell site, A.D. 1000–1300, indicates significant quantities of maize in the diet of the inhabitants of this Owasco community (Vogel and van der Merwe 1977). Analysis of human bone from southern Ontario indicates a dietary shift toward increased maize consumption around A.D. 650–1250, though maize did not contribute more than 50 percent of the diet (Schwarcz et al. 1985; Katzenberg et al. 1995; Crawford et al. 1997). The figure of less than 50 percent maize intake is lower than the estimate of 65 percent that Heidenreich arrived at (1971, 163) for the Huron through a consideration of historical accounts (Monckton 1992, 5).

Analysis of bone indicating the importance of maize to Owasco populations is complemented by dental analysis. An increased incidence of dental caries commonly accompanies the shift to farming. Owasco skeletons reveal an increased inci-dence of tooth decay over that of earlier populations, suggesting an increased reliance on carbohydrates in the diet (Ritchie 1980, 276). Dental decay is rare among earlier, prehorticultural populations of New York, although their teeth generally show heavier wear.

Corn soup and cornmeal mush are easier to eat than foods generally available to nonfarmers, which is advantageous to children who are being weaned or to adults with dental problems. However, corn soup by itself is not a nutritionally adequate substitute for breast milk unless animal fat or fish are added (Hosbach 1999).

At first glance, pressure on local resources does not appear to have been a factor in the increased emphasis on farming, although this remains to be demonstrated. Resources available from hunting, fishing, and gathering appear to have been more than adequate to meet the subsistence needs of small, scattered populations.

One advantage of maize is that it is a storable resource, and harvesting a sufficient quantity allows populations to live in one place most of the year. Large storage pits of maize have been found on some early sites, one containing probable fragments of bluestem grass, a mold-resistant species that probably was used to line the pit.[1] At the Alhart site in western New

1. Ritchie (1973, 232–33) reported this on the Bates site. Bluestem (*Andropogan gerardi*) was widely used by Native American farmers on the Eastern Great Plains as lining for storage pits. It is believed to have mold-resistant properties (Ritchie 1980, 280).

York, George Hamell found pits lined with bluestem grass overlain by sheets of bark (personal communication). Such linings would help keep the pits' contents dry and separate from the surrounding soil (Ritchie and Funk 1973, 323–24).

When excavated today, typically all that is left of a storage pit lining is a circular stain around the edge of the feature. After use, pits were filled with refuse (Ritchie and Funk 1973, 166–67). Although they are often referred to as refuse pits, this was a secondary and final function. Scattered charred plant remains found in such pits generally represent accidentally burned food discarded with other refuse (Monckton 1992, 62).

The location of early Owasco sites near good fishing spots is no coincidence. Late spring fishing would tie populations to these locations, promoting the seasonal sedentism by the inhabitants needed for planting activities. As in the Midwest, river floodplains provided a natural environment for growing many plants (Prezzano 1992, 431). If males were fishing and women were planting, the two sexes could carry out complementary economic activities in the same location. Spring fishing was also important from a dietary standpoint, as spawning anadromous fish contain large fat reserves, which were needed (Brumbach 1986; Speth 1983). Nutritionally, fish are an excellent source of protein as well as vitamins and minerals, but they are lacking in carbohydrates (Cleland 1982, 768).

Returns from farming and fishing are essentially unrelated. Fish resources are highly predictable, while weather conditions are not. Fish resources can thus serve as a buffer against a bad crop year, rendering the inhabitants of early farming and fishing settlements less vulnerable in the face of crop failure (O'Shea 1989, 65–66). Even after horticulture was long established among the New York Iroquois, fishing remained of major importance. Before beans were grown, fish would have provided critically needed protein as well. It is possible that spring and summer fishing and farming base camps persisted along the Mohawk River flats through the fourteenth century (Wayne Lenig n.d.).

The bean (*Phaseolus vulgaris*) was apparently the last of the Mesoamerican triad to be cultivated in the Northeast. Bean varieties adapted to colder climates may have been slow to develop (Tuck 1978, 325). Two-thousand-year-old beans have been identified from the Southwest, making that area the likely source of beans in the Eastern Woodlands (Watson 1988, 47). Beans generally do not appear in the East until around A.D. 1000, and even after that they are scarce in the archaeobotanical record (Watson 1988, 46). Beans, like corn, store well when kept dry. While squash must be cut into strips and dried for storage, it too will keep for some time if kept dry. In Huronia, Jean de Brébeuf wrote that "squashes last sometimes four and five months" (Thwaites 1896–1901, 10:103). The practice of parching corn to dry it makes it more liable to accidental charring and preservation; this is not the case for either beans or squash, which may be why these species are probably underrepresented archaeologically (Monckton 1992, 81).

Beans dated to A.D. 1000 from the Roundtop site in the Susquehanna Valley were thought to be the earliest in New York, but recent dating of a specimen and associated material by AMS indicates that the Roundtop beans actually date to around A.D. 1300 (Hart 1999a; Hart and Scarry 1999). Roundtop, initially occupied around A.D. 1000, was a multicomponent site, and the beans discovered there came from a feature associated with a later occupation. As it now stands, the earliest dated beans in New York and Ontario were grown long after the introduction of maize (Hart and Scarry 1999).

Maize is deficient in two amino acids: lysine and tryptophane. Since beans supply these, maize and beans together provide a good dietary combination (Kaplan 1973, 76). However, a heavy dependence on maize without a protein complement such as beans, fish, or meat creates a risk that children will develop the nutritional diseases of pellagra or kwashiorkor. An alternative source of lysine is the Jerusalem artichoke or Indian potato (*Helianthus tuberosus*) (Kaldy, Johnston, and Wilson 1980, 355; Hasenstab 1990, 12), which frequently grew on its own in Iroquois corn fields (Parker 1968, 106).[2]

Sunflowers were probably grown as a source of oil. Both sunflower oil and bear grease were rubbed on the skin and hair.

Both were also mixed with pigment for face and body painting (Thwaites 1896–1901, 37:105; Grant 1907, 284, 318; Monckton 1992, 3). Today, the Iroquois anoint wooden masks with sunflower oil. Maize and sunflowers require similar growing conditions, so it is no coincidence that they are found growing together (Bodner 1999).

## Field Clearing and Its Effects

Clearing fields was traditionally a male activity (Parker 1968, 21). Trees were killed by removing bark around the trunks and burning dry brush stacked at their bases. Large dead trees were left standing, their bare branches letting in adequate sun for crops planted below. A reflection of this practice survives in a prayer included in the ceremonial of Midwinter, asking that these branches not fall on children (Parker 1968, 22).

Fire was used to clear brush before planting, a practice that increased soil fertility through the addition of ash (Heidenreich 1971, 182–83).[3] However, long-term burning has a detrimental effect (Heidenreich 1971, 183). It is commonly assumed that old fields were regularly burned over (Heidenreich 1971, 182–83; Starna et al. 1984, 201), but Robert Hasenstab cautions that there is little ethnohistoric evidence for this practice (n.d.).

---

2. Jerusalem artichoke is also a good source of potassium (Kaldy et al. 1980, 354).

3. Given the beneficial effect of ashes on crops, one wonders if it is coincidence that ashes are used in healing ceremonies by members of curing societies.

A reference to burning in the *Jesuit Relations* may have been to the firing of grasslands (Thwaites 1896–1901, 12:155).

Throughout this discussion, the term *horticulture* is used to refer to a farming system using a hoe or digging stick in contrast to *agriculture,* which makes use of the plow. In the absence of plows, horticulturalists are free to form irregularly shaped garden plots, working around boulders or fruit-bearing plants and nut trees. Useful plants, like groundnut (*Apios americana*), purslane (*Portulaca oleracea*), raspberry, and strawberry, could have been protected and their growth encouraged without deliberate planting. Birds could have been the means of spreading seeds of these plants to the disturbed soils of garden plots. Many "wild" resources could therefore have been gathered near or in cultivated fields (Monckton 1992, 92). Large quantities of both corn and purslane pollen in three lakes on the Niagara Escarpment in Halton County, Ontario, are interpreted as the result of washing purslane plants in those lakes (Turton, Brown, and Finlayson 1998, 119).

It is quite possible that inhabitants increased the frequency of nut and other useful trees in the Eastern Woodlands by selective forest clearing or weeding around young saplings (Cowan 1985, 219–20). When Champlain passed through a recently abandoned area near Lake Ontario, he observed many nut trees and remarked that the trees looked as if they "had been set out for ornament" (Grant 1907, 288). Isolated fruit or nut trees between garden

plots would develop larger crowns, which would then produce a larger crop (Cowan 1985, 219–20). An additional benefit to isolating a tree in the middle of a clearing is that it would be less accessible to squirrels than one in a forest and would provide a greater yield. Whether immediately adjacent to a cleared field or in its midst, such trees would benefit from reduced competition from other species and would have an advantage in propagation once a field was abandoned.

Some trees may even have been planted. Wykoff has studied the distribution of black walnut as reflected in early records (1991). This species generally has a more southerly distribution, which suggests that its concentration in the core areas of the Five Nations is the result of deliberate planting. Its soil and moisture requirements are similar to those of maize (Wykoff 1991, 13). Another example in New York is the pawpaw, where isolated populations correspond with the former presence of Iroquoians (Wycoff 1991, 14; Keener and Kuhns 1997). A tradition recorded by a French Jesuit—that warriors brought back pawpaws to Onondaga after fighting the Erie between 1654 and 1656—supports the theory that pawpaws were deliberately planted (Thwaites 1896–1901, 43:259).

The degree to which the distribution of modern vegetation may have been affected by Iroquois practices remains to be assessed. Jim Pendergast argues that the bladder-nut shrub (*Staphylea trifolia*), used for pigment, is a good indicator of St.

Lawrence Iroquoian archaeological sites (1994). The hawthorn often invades newly cleared land, and the diverse species of this genus (*Crataegus*) may stem from land clearance by Native Americans (Soper and Heimburger 1982, 170; J. V. Wright 1998, xiii).[4] Hazelnut trees also grow in disturbed soil.

Charred remains of hickory and black walnut were the most common floral specimens from the Carman site, a Cayuga village dating to the late 1500s (Allen 1998). Today, hickory and black walnut abound in the woods in the vicinity of the site. Presumably these trees are descended from those exploited by Carman site inhabitants. In Ontario, Wilfrid Jury noted the association of Iroquoian villages with American chestnut trees (Wykoff 1988, 110).

Like fish, gathered wild plants provided an important buffering mechanism when crops failed to meet expectations. Horticulture altered the environment in a way that encouraged the growth of useful wild plants (Monckton 1992, xii). An eighteenth-century naturalist observed that hemp (*Apocynum cannabium*), used for twine and cordage, grew well on old corn fields (Kalm 1966, 277).

It is widely assumed that wild plants were more important in the diet of hunter-gatherers than in the diet of later horticulturalists in the Northeast. Given the

4. The hawthorn fruit is bitter but has a very high vitamin C content. J. V. Wright (1998, xiii) suggests it may have been eaten with other dried fruit for its vitamin content.

favorable environment for wild plants created by swidden farming, this may not be the case. This is another assumption that can be tested with better methods of recovery and analysis.

Abandoned fields were also important for the habitat they provided deer and other animals (White and Cronon 1988, 419). "Garden hunting" of small game favoring brushy habitats, such as rabbits and quail, probably occurred regularly, even though the bones of such animals tend to be sparsely represented in archaeological collections, at least in part because of a lack of appropriate recovery techniques. An exception is the recently excavated Hubbert site, an early fifteenth-century Iroquoian site near Barrie, Ontario (Thomas 1997). Squirrels were probably also killed in and around the fields, as historic sources state that they damaged the corn (Heidenreich 1971, 179; Kalm 1935, 115–16). Socci reports that squirrel bones are frequently found on Iroquois sites, and a burned squirrel femur from the Mohawk Elwood site suggests cooking and consumption (Socci 1995, 49, 51).

Research undertaken in the Crawford Lake area northwest of Hamilton, Ontario, suggests that oak and pine often grow on abandoned swidden fields (Monckton 1992, 59; Finlayson 1998, 58, 62). Oak trees provide mast for deer. Uniform stands of old pine trees found growing near Iroquoian village sites have been interpreted as abandoned fields, colonized by pine. One such stand was observed in an early survey between Quaker Bridge and

Onoville in southwestern New York (Day 1953, 338).[5]

## Planting and Harvesting

As farmers, the Iroquois were clearly aware of soil quality in choosing a location for both their villages and their fields. The siting of Iroquois villages evinces a clear preference for soils suitable for corn cultivation (Hasenstab 1990, 124–25, 132). The Iroquois preferred moist loam or sandy loam soils high in lime content. The lime content of soils is important because nitrogen-fixing bacteria found in beans grow best in moist, limy soils (Hasenstab 1990, 96, 150; 1996, 21; 2001, 454, 459). This nitrogren then served as fertilizer for maize. Robert Hasenstab has hypothesized that the Iroquois may have learned to identify these soils through the use of plant indicator species that favor such conditions, such as the yellow lady slipper (1990, 150).

Fields were not necessarily immediately adjacent to the village. In 1677, Wentworth Greenhalgh noted that the Seneca town of Ganondagan had "a good store of corne, growing about a mile to the Northward" (O'Callaghan 1849, 13). In areas of varied topography, Iroquois farmers may have pursued a strategy of planting areas of variable drainage. By so doing, crops in poorly drained areas would do better in dry years, while in wet years those in

well-drained areas would thrive. Snow suggests this was the case for some seventeenth-century Mohawk sites (1995a, 366, 371).

Whether or not Native Americans used fish as fertilizer is currently debated. Tisquantum (Squanto) is credited with teaching the English at Plymouth this method, but Lynn Ceci argued that he learned this practice from Europeans (1975). However, recent work on Cape Cod suggests that Native American corn hills on poor or older soils were fertilized with fish (Mrozowski 1994; Currie 1994). The location of early horticultural settlements near good fishing spots make this method at least a possibility.

In an important but as yet unpublished paper, Hasenstab questions the widely held assumption that the Iroquois regularly abandoned garden plots and cleared new ones (n.d.). Robert Carneiro described such a slash-and-burn or swidden system for the rapidly leached soils of the tropics (1956), and archaeologists then applied it to the temperate forests of the Northeast. The assumption that soil exhaustion inevitably results from long-term corn cultivation may also stem from the unfortunate colonial New England practice of repeatedly planting corn without crop rotation or interplanting legumes (Cronin 1983, 150, 169).

If maize and beans are planted together on soils with adequate lime content and moisture, the soil will not be depleted, especially if crop residues are returned to

---

5. See Finlayson (1998, 139) for a reference to a similar stand near the Draper site in Ontario

the corn hill (Mt. Pleasant 1989, 36; Hasenstab n.d.). Moreover, if fields were not repeatedly burned over, as is commonly supposed, and if fish were used occasionally for fertilizer, such additional measures would have increased the long-term productivity of a field.

Light soils were important for good drainage in a village. Good drainage would have retarded rot, both of structures and of produce stored in pits (Vandrei 1987, 12–13). Sites located on very well-drained soils (sand or gravel) are generally characterized by numerous storage pits (Hasenstab 1990, 125). Light soils also would have eased digging efforts associated with village construction.

Areas that remained frost-free for the longest periods would have been desirable. In the fall, areas of intermediate elevation provide such frost-free zones and are referred to as thermal belts (Hasenstab 1996, 21). Cool air drains downhill, warding off frost. Gibson noted Oneida sites tended to be located in this zone (1971) and Smith has noted a similar phenomenon for Ontario Iroquois sites located along the Niagara Escarpment, where farmers claimed that the growing season was extended for two weeks (1987, 57). I have noted a similar placement of Iroquoian sites on the edge of the Tug Hill plateau near Watertown, New York. Local residents there were well aware of cold air drainage extending the growing season.

Planting too early would subject crops to the risk of killing frost. To avoid this danger, it was said planting should occur "when the white oak leaves are the size of a red squirrel's foot" (Fenton 1978, 301). Ceci has suggested that the constellation of the Pleiades was widely associated with winter and frost in the northern hemisphere (1978, 306). The Pleiades appear in fall in the eastern horizon, are directly overhead at midwinter, and disappear in the spring. If they could be seen in the spring, there was still the possibility of frost damage to crops.

Insect infestation appears to have been a concern of northern Iroquoian horticulturalists (Starna et al. 1984, 205). In recent times, seed corn was soaked in "corn medicine," which may have inhibited both insect and bird pests. One ingredient was hellebore, which has insecticidal qualities. Other ingredients apparently caused crows eating "doctored" seed corn to behave erratically, frightening other birds (Parker 1968, 26; Starna et al. 1984, 205).[6]

While digging sticks probably were used when planting seeds, hoes must have been used in "hilling" up earth around the corn plant. Seneca and Onondaga have terms for both "digging stick" and "hoe" (Hamell n.d.). Waugh illustrates a wooden digging stick or spade (1973, 159, plate 1, figure a), but the only illustration of an Iroquois hoe is that made by the Jesuit father

6. Chief Jacob Thomas states that phragmites was a common ingredient in this medicine, and that bottle-brush grass (*Hystrix patula*) was used occasionally (Thomas 1994, 61).

Claude Chauchetière in 1686 at Mission du Sault (Kahnawake) (fig. 8).[7]

Corn hills were formed two to five feet apart (Waugh 1973, 14–15; Ritchie 1980, 280; Starna et al. 1984, 201). This practice may have had the effect of protecting the crops from frost damage early in the growing season, when cold air stayed close to the ground between the hills (Heidenreich 1971, 184). Corn hills also facilitated drainage in wet areas (Watson 1988, 45) while they conserved moisture under dry conditions (Hasenstab n.d.).

A traditional Native American garden plot was very different from the large, single-crop fields of modern agriculture. Beans and squash were planted with corn, and the bean vines grew up the corn stalk.[8] Nitrogen-fixing bacteria on the roots of the bean plant returned to the soil some of the nitrogen that maize had taken out (White and Cronon 1988, 419–20). The large leaves of cucurbits that were grown between the corn hills shaded the ground, reducing weed growth and evaporation (Perkl 1998, 280). In addition, by absorbing lime into their tissue, squash plants recycled leached lime back to the surface (Hasenstab n.d.). The diversity of a swidden plot mirrored that of plants in the surrounding natural environment (Dennis 1993, 32; see fig. 9).

Iroquois women worked together planting, cultivating, and harvesting the crops, directed by a senior woman, a clan matron (Fenton 1998, 23). Women who were related to one another through their mothers would have lived together, and it was they who probably worked together and gave one another support as needed.

Fig. 8. "On travaille aux champs," by Claude Chauchetière, S.J., 1686. Chauchetière manuscript. Jesuit archives, Gironde, France.

7. George Hamell (n.d.) notes the similarity of the implement drawn by Chauchetière to an Anasazi digging implement at the National Museum of the American Indian in New York City. He suggests the possibility that this implement diffused with the cultivation of maize. He further notes the resemblance of these implements to field hockey sticks or shinny sticks and suggests their evolution from hoe prototypes. While something resembling an ice hockey stick is observable in early seventeenth-century Dutch winter landscapes, I would venture that these hoes were prototypes for ice hockey sticks as well.

8. Parker (1968, 27) says beans and squash were planted in every seventh hill. There are other references in Eastern North America to beans being planted in every hill (Hasenstab n.d.).

Fig. 9 "Three sisters." Painting by Ernie Smith. Courtesy of the Rochester Museum and Science Center, Rochester, N.Y.

The Iroquois kinship system extends the term "sister" to parallel female cousins, which includes daughters of sisters. By a further extension, these "sisters" who worked together referred to the maize, beans, and squash that grew together as the "three sisters, our supporters," another example of the extension of human kin terms to nonhuman but animate aspects of the Iroquois cosmos (Fenton 1978, 301; Herrick 1995, 19). All these "sisters," both human and nonhuman, nurtured one another and the community.

Children who were still nursing were carried back and forth to the fields (Engelbrecht 1987, 17). In open areas, clear of underbrush as a result of burning, there was less danger from a surprise raid, although this was still a concern. Heidenreich cites several references in the *Jesuit Relations* to female casualties in the fields (1971, 215). A woman working in the fields with two or more young children would have had difficulty running back to the village with them in the event of a raid. Parker wrote, "Too many babies meant danger when raids occurred" (1967, 75). Scaffolds were sometimes erected in fields in eastern North America on which old women sat to ward off crows and other animal predators. These structures could have served a secondary function as watch towers for enemy raiders while women worked in the fields (see fig. 10).

Historic literature suggests that the Ontario Iroquois constructed isolated cabins near agricultural fields (Warrick 1984, 18). Among the Onondaga, the Jesuits reported visiting outlying cabins, but it is not clear whether or not they were adjacent to fields (Thwaites 1896–1901, 42:127, 157; 52:165; Tuck 1971, 3). The extent to which the New York Iroquois established separate structures adjacent to their fields remains to be determined.

Fig. 10. Iroquois field. Courtesy of the New York State Museum and Science Service.

## Lithic Technology

In general, Late Woodland stone tool as-semblages show an abundance of what ar-chaeologists refer to as expedient tools, flakes used for a variety of functions. The flakes were struck off cores of different shapes that did not undergo much initial preparation (Parry and Kelly 1987). Some-times an anvil was used to smash a core and produce flakes. They were then used until dull and then discarded. Some flakes were resharpened or made into other kinds of tools.

There is a concomitant reduction over time in formal tools, that is, specialized chipped tool types (Smith and Crawford 1997, 25). Chen Shen sees the shift from specialized to generalized stone tool pro-duction in the Princess Point culture of Ontario as paralleling an increasing re-liance on horticulture (1997). As long as people have ready access to lithic sources, it becomes less necessary to invest effort in carefully preparing cores or preforms and curating them (Braun 1988, 24).

The study of lithics on Iroquois sites has been neglected, so comparative data on the frequency of different formal stone tools is generally lacking. The impression is that points are the most common formal stone tool, and that their number increases on sixteenth- and early seventeenth-century sites (Pratt 1976, 144; Bradley 1987, 41). End scrapers, drills, and ovate bifaces also occur. At the Adams site (Seneca), a hafted large oval biface was re-covered, the wooden handle being pre-served by its close associated with a brass gorget (Wray et al. 1987, 98; see fig. 11).

## Warfare

The appearance of fortified villages during the Owasco period is often taken as an indi-cation of the beginning of organized con-flict between groups (Ritchie 1980, 281; Gramly 1988, 91). Since the appearance of

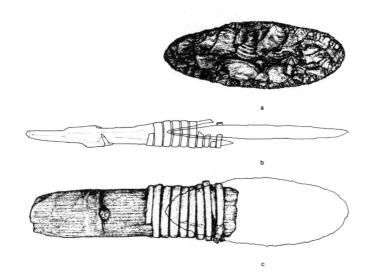

Fig. 11. Hafted chert biface with splint binding from the Adams site (Seneca). Length of a: 11.5 cm. From Wray et al. 1987, 100. Courtesy of the Rochester Museum and Science Center, Rochester, N.Y.

fortifications closely follows the inception of maize horticulture, some direct connection between farming and large-scale conflict in the Northeast is generally assumed. However, as mentioned in chapter 1, most hunter-gatherers engage in hostilities. What is missing from the archaeological record of hunter-gatherers in the Northeast is not evidence of violence, but rather of settled fortified villages.

Hunter-gatherers moved seasonally or at least semiannually, precluding the construction of elaborate palisades or longhouses. Group size may have fluctuated, depending on the seasonal availability of resources. With maize farming and food storage, a more sedentary life allowed for the formation of palisaded villages consisting of longhouses (Trigger 1976, 1:119–39). These palisaded villages do not mark the beginning of hostilities in the Northeast, but they provided increased security, especially for women, whose pri-

mary activities centered on the village and the immediate surrounding area.

The new way of life placed new demands on male labor: clearing fields and building longhouses and palisades. Were these new time and energy commitments made possible by the increased productivity of female horticultural activities as well as the increased efficiency of the bow and arrow in hunting?[9] For by the time of palisaded villages, the bow and arrow was the preferred weapon for warfare.

When we speak of increased sedentism during the Late Woodland period, we are really speaking of increased sedentism for portions of the population: females, children, and old people (Nancy Herter, personal communication). Hunting, fishing,

9. Michael Glassow (1972) argues that increased efficiency of the bow and arrow facilitated the shift to farming and maintenance activities in the Late Basketmaker culture of the Southwest.

warfare, trade, and diplomacy frequently took males far from the village. Women sometimes accompanied men, especially hunting or fishing. If fear of warfare operated to restrict female mobility, it also served to focus female gathering and horticultural activities near the safety of the village.

Economic factors leading to conflict among horticulturalists in New York have been suggested, such as competition for good farmland or deer hides (Ritchie and Funk 1973, 362–67; Gramly 1977). However, given a relatively small early farming population, intergroup competition over these resource seems unlikely. Some have hypothesized that Mississippian economic systems played a role in Iroquoian warfare, but hard evidence for this idea is lacking as well (Dincauze and Hasenstab 1989; Hasenstab 1990).

Arthur Parker relates various traditional explanations for Iroquois warfare, including the often overlooked tradition that the Iroquois conducted distant raids to acquire new varieties of maize or other vegetables (1968, 42). Pawpaws were acquired in this fashion, and it is possible that black walnuts were as well. It is even possible that the successful establishment of maize horticulture was facilitated by raiders who brought back new varieties of maize, but this is speculation. In short, a convincing economic reason for fighting among early horticultural populations in New York has not yet been advanced.

Witthoft suggested that success in war gave men the prestige that before the

adoption of horticulture had been provided by the role of hunter (1959, 32–36). There are two problems with Witthoft's suggestion, however. First, it implies that before horticulture, fighting was infrequent. This is unlikely, and successful fighters among hunter-gatherers would have gained prestige. Second, hunting remained an important male economic activity after the advent of horticulture. In historic times a successful hunter was greatly admired (Trigger 1976, 1:146; Fenton 1978, 315; Abler and Logan 1988, 6). The desire for revenge and the acquisition of prestige are not mutually exclusive. Both motives for fighting probably continued among farming populations from a hunter-gatherer past.

Daniel Richter has argued for the importance of the "mourning war" among Iroquoians (1992, 32–38). Women would urge male kinsmen to go to war to capture a traditional enemy, who was then either symbolically or actually adopted into the group to replace a deceased individual. The deceased's name was then "requickened" in the captive. If the captive was incorporated into the group, he or she was expected to assume the social role of the deceased. Requickening ceremonies affirmed for the living that the "spiritual potency embodied in the departed's name had not disappeared" (Richter 1992, 32).

There is an additional possible reason for fighting among early farmers. The maintenance of balance and harmony in the world is an important unifying principle in Iroquoian thought (Herrick 1995,

15). Crops are subject to a variety of hazards, including drought, frost, and insect infestations. A harvest in jeopardy may have been taken as a sign that balance needed to be restored with spirit forces. In similar situations, farming cultures around the world have turned to a drastic measure: human sacrifice (Davies 1984, 213).

## Corn and Blood

In Mesoamerica, agricultural fertility was felt to be linked to human sacrifice and the shedding of blood. The Aztecs even conducted ritualized "Flowery Wars" for the purpose of capturing warriors for sacrifice. Capturing an enemy for later sacrifice was considered more desirable than killing an enemy on the field of battle, and warriors who did so gained great prestige. The warrior sacrificed in the plaza or on the top of the temple platform was encouraged to cooperate in the ritual, so that his "religious exaltation" hopefully "triumph[ed] completely over the weakness of the flesh" (Wissler and Spinden 1916, 55).

Mississippian cultures, located along the Mississippi River and its tributaries including the Ohio River, were contemporaneous with the Owasco culture in New York as well as with various Postclassic cultures in Mesoamerica, such as the Toltec. Mississippian ceremonial centers were characterized by large earthen platform mounds fronting on a plaza. Although generally smaller and less architecturally complex than large Mesoamerican centers, the general plan of Mississippian centers is similar. With the exception of an obsidian scraper from the Spiro site in Oklahoma, which came from Hidalgo, Mexico (Barker et al. 2002), direct contact between these two regions remains to be demonstrated. Owasco sites lack the monumental features and large populations of the Mesoamerican or Mississippian cultures, so the development of the Owasco culture is typically seen as occurring independently of their influence.

Although the nature of any connection between Mesoamerican and Mississippian cultures or Mississippian and Owasco cultures is unclear, all these cultures shared important domesticates: maize, beans, and squash. All three also practiced human sacrifice. Like Mesoamerican warriors, Iroquois warriors sought prisoners (Thwaites 1896–1901, 1:271; Richter 1992, 36). Warfare was a spiritual act. The emphasis was not on killing in battle, as was common in Europe, but rather on bringing a prisoner back for either sacrifice or adoption. Bruce Trigger has suggested that for the Hurons, the sacrifice of prisoners was linked to crop success, game abundance, and the continuation of the natural world (1985, 99; 1990b, 52).

In the Iroquois account of the origin of corn mentioned in the beginning of the chapter, Flint pierces his mother's armpit at birth, thereby sacrificing her. From her body grew maize, beans, and squash. This account implies a connection for Iroquoians between sacrifice and crops. The role of Flint in killing is also implied by his association with crystals and ice, the latter

fatal to crops. Surprisingly, Floyd Lounsbury (1982, cited in Hall 2000:247)
pointed out that the Cherokee spirit force
Tawiskala (Flint, Ice) sounds the same as
the first part of Tlahuizcalpantecuhtli, the
Mesoamerican deity associated with the
Dawn and Frost.

A Mesoamerican-like connection between blood and corn is reflected in the
Iroquois Little Water Ceremony. The traditional origin of this medicine involved
cutting a magical corn stalk that exudes
human blood (Curtin and Hewitt 1918,
274; Wilson 1959, 306). Perhaps this tradition was suggested by the red maize
plant, which contains the pigment anthocyanin. The anthocyanin in the cells of the
stem are red and can stain one's hands
when the cells are crushed. Reddish varieties of maize are common in tropical environments, where this pigment offers
protection from solar radiation.[10]

In the Southeast, Cherokee oral tradition attributes the origin of corn to Selu,
the corn maiden. Robert Hall (2000) notes
the similarity of her name to the Aztec
(Nahuatl) word *xilotl,* meaning "tender ear
of green maize," and to Xilonen, Green
Corn Goddess, providing further linguistic
evidence for a connection between
Mesoamerican and eastern North American beliefs surrounding corn. Perhaps the
idea of sacrifice to ensure crop success
spread into the Eastern Woodlands from
Mesoamerica with the spread of maize.
The Mexican seeds may have come with in-
structions in case of emergency!

## Arrow Sacrifice

While the most widely reported form of
sacrifice in Mesoamerica involved removal
of the heart, various other forms were practiced, including decapitation and arrow
sacrifice. Among the Aztecs, arrow sacrifice
was associated with the corn goddess,
Chicomecoatl, and with Xipe Totec, a fertility god also associated with warfare (Hall
1997, 87–88). In the Aztec year One-
Rabbit, corresponding generally to 1506,
Moctezuma ordered a man sacrificed by arrows in order to prevent the possibility of
famine. The Aztec calendar followed a
fifty-two-year cycle, and in the previous
years of One-Rabbit, there had been
famine (Hall 1997, 86).

Striking similarities exist between the
sacrifice of the Skiri Pawnee of Nebraska
and Mesoamerican ritual (Hall 1997,
86–94). The Pawnee occasionally sacrificed an individual to the Morning Star to
ensure crop success (Weltfish 1965, 106).
When there was to be a ceremony, a warrior deliberately set out to capture someone for the sacrifice. At the appropriate
time in spring when the Morning Star rose,
the one to be sacrificed mounted a wooden
scaffold. Following initial rituals, all the
men and boys shot arrows at the victim
(Weltfish 1965, 114). The individual was
then placed face down on the earth (Hall
1997, 91, 101). "In the way of the Morn-

10. I am indebted to Ricardo J. Salvador,
Phil Stinard, David Weber, and Edward Coe for this
information.

ing Star, death and life, war and fruitfulness were one process" (Weltfish 1965, 115).

The Midwest provides both artifactual and skeletal evidence suggesting a similar ritual. An engraved shell bowl from the Spiro site in Oklahoma has been interpreted as representing arrow sacrifice (Phillips and Brown 1984, plate 165; Hall 1997, 90; see fig. 12).

An early Late Woodland site in Illinois contained the burial of a male, face down, with six Koster Corner Notched points in the skeleton (Perino 1973, 149). Direct dates for this burial are not available, but Koster Corner Notched Points appear around A.D. 500–700 (Nassaney and Pyle 1999, 256). At the Eiden phase (c. A.D. 1000–1200) cemetery at the Pearson site in north-central Ohio, two individuals were interred in a face-down extended position, one skeleton being found with five projectile points and the other with two (Stothers and Abel 1989, 122).

Skeletons with multiple arrows encountered during excavations in the Northeast are generally interpreted as examples of "overkill," an expression of hatred for the enemy. This was practiced on the Great Plains and can be inferred archaeologically in other parts of the world (Keeley 1996, 102). It is also possible that skeletons associated with large numbers of arrow points represent arrow sacrifice.

At the Owasco-period Sackett site, four males, ranging in age from nineteen to fifty, were found with multiple arrow points embedded in their skeletons (Ritchie 1936, 57–65). One skeleton had

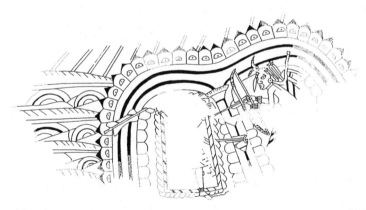

Fig. 12. Engraved shell bowl depicting arrow sacrifice from the Spiro site, Oklahoma. The petals in the border each contain a stylized eye, believed to represent stars. From Philip Phillips and James A. Brown, *Pre-Columbian Shell Engravings from the Craig Mound at Spiro, Oklahoma,* paperback edition, part 2, plate 165. Peabody Museum Press. Copyright 1984 by the president and fellows of Harvard College.

three arrow points, one had six, and two had eleven. Of the points from Sackett, William Ritchie, the excavator, observed, "From the fact that about half the arrow points are broken, and the tip of one unrecovered head was taken from among the bones of Burial 39, it seems likely that some of the arrows were repeatedly reused" (1936, 61). Ritchie also noted the following: "It will readily be seen that the majority of the missiles (65.6 percent) had entered the bodies from the front and sides, in two cases from slightly to the rear, and apparently at nearly right angles to the long axis of the body, which suggests that the victims were standing upright when shot, probably fastened to a post or a tree of small diameter" (1936, 61).

Ritchie noted two parallel examples. On Staten Island, the skeletons of three adult males were associated with twenty-three stone and bone points, some of which were broken. Alanson Skinner wrote, "Taking into consideration the number of arrows which must have been embedded in the bodies of the warriors, it is perhaps probable that the majority of the projectiles were driven into the victims at close range after death" (Skinner 1909, 15). The available triangular points suggest a Late Woodland date (Jacobson 1980, 38, 39). In Niantic, Connecticut, a double burial of two male skeletons contained fifteen and six points respectively. There were four triangular quartz points, and the remaining points were bone (Rogers 1935, 2–3).

In a footnote in a later publication, Ritchie mentions the discovery by avoca-tional archaeologists of the skeleton of a male with thirty-eight Levanna (Owasco period) triangular arrow points in his thorax (1947, 73). The skeleton was found at the McNair site south of Rochester in a pit four feet deep. A nearby site in West Sparta excavated by one of the same individuals revealed a skeleton with multiple projectile points embedded in it (see fig. 13). [11]

Further east, excavations in the early 1950s by avocational archaeologists Clyde Olson and Leo Maclean at the multicomponent Weaver Lake site in Herkimer County revealed two male skeletons with projectile points embedded in their bones. The first was associated with seven triangular points and two conical antler points, while the second was associated with nine triangular points, a point tip, and a conical antler point.[12]

The skeleton of a male with six Lev-

11. Examination of records and artifacts at the Rochester Museum and Science Center relating to the McNair site revealed a total of forty-seven projectile points recovered from the thorax and the immediate vicinity, rather than the thirty-eight mentioned by Ritchie. Peter Pratt suggested to me that William Ritchie may have considered nine of the points to have been intrusive. The field notes of the late Joseph Quinlan at the RMSC indicate that he excavated another grave in the same general area with five triangular points (Section II, Burial 2, of a fifty-acre lot in West Sparta, Livingston Co.). The RMSC has a bag of seven points, presumably from the latter grave, labeled "found in bone" which are illustrated in figure 13.

12. The field notes of Clyde Olson and Leo Maclean were written up by Donald Lenig in an unpublished manuscript and were provided by his son, Wayne Lenig, who also told the author about the site.

Fig. 13. Projectile points embedded in human bone, West Sparta site, also known as Dansville Flats and Wray site #206. Courtesy of the Rochester Museum and Science Center, Rochester, N.Y.

anna (Owasco) points, one embedded in the third thoracic vertebra, was recovered from the cemetery at the Orchid site in Fort Erie, Ontario, across the river from Buffalo (Granger 1976, 11). There is also an arrow-riddled skeleton of a male burial from the Long Point site. The number of complete projectiles is not given in the report, but three point tips are mentioned as being embedded in bone. This site is located along the west side of Conesus Lake and contains both Iroquois and Owasco material (Wright 1950, 75).

To summarize, those skeletons with multiple points identified as to gender are all male. Many of the examples assignable to a cultural period are Owasco (c. A.D. 900–1350). The intact nature of the skeletons, with the exception of the Long Point

individual, indicates that all these individuals were buried after their death, not left on the ground or dismembered. In some cases, point tips were recovered, suggesting projectiles were pulled out of the body, presumably to be used again. This evidence, coupled with the number and diversity of points used, implies that multiple archers were involved.

In addition to possible ideological beliefs, shooting a victim with arrows, like other forms of torture, may have prepared young males psychologically for their role as warriors. Mary Jemison relates how her second husband, Hiokatoo, tied prisoners to trees and had young boys shoot them with arrows until they died (Seaver 1975, 115). Although her account provides historical evidence of the practice, Jemison gave no rationale other than her husband's warlike nature.

More than a hundred years earlier, the Jesuits recounted a curious incident during a drought in Huronia. When the efforts of a Huron shaman failed to produce rain, he blamed this on a cross beside the Jesuit's door. Some Huron threatened to pull the cross down, while "some young people, having made another [cross] and having placed it on the ridge of a cabin, began to shoot at it as at a target with their bows and arrows" (Thwaites 1896–1901, 10:37, 39). While this could be interpreted as merely an insult to the Jesuits, it could also be seen as a symbolic form of arrow sacrifice designed to bring rain.[13]

Echos persist of an ancient connection between drought, warfare, and arrow sacrifice. In the recent past, the Thunder Ceremony was scheduled at Six Nations Reserve in Canada when rain was needed. Considered a male ceremony, a "war dance" in the context of this ceremony is considered to be a "rain dance." A tradition concerning the origin of this ceremony relates how a hunter was instructed by the Thunderers to shoot a snake with twelve red willow arrows (Shimony 1961, 162, 165).

A concern with crop fertility commonly resulted in arrow sacrifice in Mesoamerica and in Nebraska among the Skiri Pawnee. Such may also have been the case among early farmers in the Northeast. Wykoff has argued that the Northeast suffered a drought toward the end of the thirteenth century and into the early fourteenth century—the end of the Owasco period (1988). At present, solid evidence is lacking to connect drought and arrow sacrifice in the Northeast, but it suggests an avenue for further research.

## Decapitation and Scalping

As mentioned previously, decapitation was another form of sacrifice in Mesoamerica. In the Midwest, decapitated skeletons have been found as well as depictions of warriors holding trophy skulls. Similarly, Iroquois sites have yielded both skeletons without skulls and skulls without skeletons. At the Oneida Marshall site (c. A.D. 1630–1650), for example, a male skeleton was found minus the skull (Pratt 1976, 137). The skull of a middle-aged male, presumably from the California Ranch site (early Seneca), bore an artificially thinned and polished temporal portion of the left zygomatic arch, suggesting that it was carried by a thong as a trophy skull (Sublett and Wray 1970, 22).[14]

Worldwide, the custom of taking the head of a fallen enemy is very common. As Keeley notes, "The head of a vanquished foe was an unequivocal token of the indi-

---

13. Images of St. Sebastian shot with arrows must have struck a familiar note among Catholic converts who witnessed arrow sacrifice.

14. Two Seneca lacrosse legends recount how victors decapitated losers (Vennum 1994, 312–16), reminiscent of the sacrifice of losing ball players in Mesoamerica.

vidual that had been overcome" (1996, 100). It is also an added insult to an enemy who believes that this mutilation negatively affects the soul or spirit of the deceased (Keeley 1996, 100). More than a trophy, it imbues the victor with the spiritual power of the deceased. Taking heads and scalping were a form of soul capture (George Hamell, personal communication).

In oral tradition, the cannibal sorcerer Thadoda:ho was said to have dishes and spoons made from the skulls of his enemies (Beauchamp 1922, 4). Such utensils have not been found archaeologically, but ritual items made from human skulls have been found. Rattles made from cut human skulls have been recovered from a number of Iroquoian sites.[15]

Scalping was more common than decapitation among the historic Iroquois (Scheele 1950, 68) but may be thought of as a functional equivalent. Victorious warriors far from the village would not be limited in the number of scalps they brought back. The scalp, like an animal pelt, still retained its animacy and power.

15. Human skull rattles have been recovered from a Crawford Lake satellite site in Ontario (Finlayson 1998 1:244); from Adams [Seneca] (Wray et al. 1987, 45–46); and from Diable [Oneida] (Pratt 1976, 19). Items identified as human skull gorgets have been recovered from Tram [Seneca] (Wray et al. 1991, 56); from Kelso [Onondaga] (Tuck 1971, 76); and from Atwell [Onondaga] (Bradley 1987, 216–17n. 23). George Hamell suggests these also may have been rattles. What may have been either a human skull gorget or rattle was also recovered from Otstungo [Mohawk] (W. Lenig n.d.).

*Torture and Cannibalism*

The French Jesuits were not shocked at the fact that the Iroquois practiced torture, as judicial torture was widely practiced in Europe at the time, often by religious establishments such as the Spanish Inquisition. What shocked them was the participation of women and children (Thwaites 1896–1901, 31:45; 40:133–35).

Among the Iroquois, as in Mesoamerica, prisoners generally accepted their fate and played out their assigned role. One might think it preferable to die on the battlefield than to be slowly tortured. Why then did captive warriors of the Iroquois submit rather than fight to the death? There was always the chance of escape or possible adoption, but spiritual beliefs concerning the afterlife and cultural conditioning may have played an even greater role (Snyderman 1961, 588). Among the Huron, warriors killed in battle formed a band of their own in the afterlife, separate from those of other Huron (Thwaites 1896–1901, 10:145; 39:29–31). Those who committed suicide were excluded from the village of souls (Trigger 1990b, 122). Perhaps anxiety over permanent separation from loved ones outweighed the transitory agony of torture (Scheele 1950, 103). Among the Huron it was considered bad luck for the torturers if the captive was able to maintain his composure. By going to their deaths bravely, captives continued to wage symbolic warfare (Trigger 1990b, 60).

Scattered human bone, sometimes cut

and burnt, has been recovered from both Owasco and Iroquois sites and is typically interpreted as evidence of cannibalism. One such site is Sackett (c. A.D. 1130), the same Owasco site having arrow-riddled skeletons. At the Onondaga Bloody Hill site (A.D. 1400–1450), a large cooking pit with the disarticulated skeletal elements of a middle-aged male is interpreted as evidence of cannibalism (Tuck 1971, 113–14; Sublett and Wray 1970, 17). Strong arguments for cannibalism likewise can be made for remains from the Seneca Alhart (Wray et al. 1987, 248) and Cameron sites (Wray et al. 1991, 207–9). Human bone has also been found in the middens of the Oneida sites of Buyea and Olcott (Pratt 1976, 19).

Whereas the bones of game animals like bear, deer, and beaver were treated with respect so as not to offend the spirits of these animals, the flesh and bones of enemies were fed to the dogs (Thwaites 1896–1901, 46:45; Scheele 1950, 75). However, the Iroquois were afraid of the souls of their victims, and they made noise after the sun went down on the day the victims died so as to frighten these souls away (O'Callaghan 1849, 13; Scheele 1950, 46).

In some cases, alternative explanations for scattered human bones are possible. The secondary burial of individuals, such as occurred in the Huron Feast of the Dead, called for gathering up the bones of the deceased and reburying them. During this process, some bones might be lost and scattered. Among the Huron, individuals who died a violent death were burned or buried immediately, and the body of a witch was cremated (Thwaites 1896–1901, 39:31; 14:35–37). The bones of a person who died outside of Huronia were brought back to be buried (Thwaites 1896–1901, 11:131). The flesh was stripped from Huron individuals who died by drowning or freezing and the skeletal elements were thrown into a ditch in the cemetery (Thwaites 1896–1901, 10:163–65, 273; Tooker 1964, 132). It is possible that similar practices existed among the New York Iroquois, accounting for some scattered or burnt human bone.

Despite these considerations, the evidence suggests that in the past the Iroquois practiced cannibalism, at least on ritual occasions. Oral tradition speaks of it. Thadoda:ho, the Onondaga sorcerer, was said to eat humans. Ingesting a portion of the sacrificed captive symbolized the absorption of that individual's spiritual power (Richter 1992, 36). If the captive had been particularly brave, one might gain some of his bravery by eating his heart (Thwaites 1896–1901, 10:227; Abler and Logan 1988, 5). In Mesoamerica the victim often represented a deity, so this rite contained aspects of Christian communion. The sacrificed warrior became a messenger to the gods.

The Iroquois torture pattern had certain traits in common with human sacrifice in Mexico. These included cardiac emphasis, death by a knife, eating of the victims, and perhaps dancing and the use of a platform (Knowles 1940, 215). Knowles ventured the opinion that these practices did not have great time depth for the Iroquois, but evidence of both arrow sacrifice and cannibalism during Owasco times suggests the opposite (1940).

Offerings to the sun played a role in both cultures as well. Aireskoi was the Huron term for the spiritual force equated with both the sun and war. The Jesuits recorded the following: "Aireskoi, we sacrifice to thee this victim, that thou mayst satisfy thyself with her flesh, and give us victory over our enemies" (Thwaites 1896–1901, 39:219).

The similarity of details between prisoner sacrifice in Mesoamerica and the Eastern Woodlands strengthens the argument for elements of a shared belief system, even though this practice is not uniformly distributed between these areas (Rands and Riley 1958).

## Dog Sacrifice

Historic accounts indicate that dogs were eaten at feasts such as those dedicated to the Mohawk war god, Agreskoué (the Huron Aireskoi) (Waugh 1916, 133; Fenton 1978, 316). Sagard thought dog tasted "rather like pork" (Sagard-Théodat 1968, 226). References to dog being eaten are almost always in ritual contexts (Kerber 1997, 89). Like bear meat, dog meat symbolized the flesh of captives (Fenton 1978, 316; Socci 1995, 78).[16] Butchering marks

on disarticulated bone are interpreted as evidence of dog consumption.[17]

In 1636 a Jesuit missionary referred to the sacrifice of a white dog among the Huron "to make a feast with it and to seek information by it" (Thwaites 1896–1901, 8:125; Kerber 1997, 90). During the eighteenth century, the New York Iroquois sacrificed white dogs by strangulation (Beauchamp 1922, 184). There was a special breed of dog for this purpose. The sacrifice occurred during the calendrical ceremonies of Midwinter and Green Corn. After being strangled, the dog was suspended from a pole and then later taken down and burned with tobacco.[18]

In the late seventeenth and early eighteenth centuries, the white dog sacrifice was used as a substitute for human sacrifice (Knowles 1940, 214; Tooker 1965, 195–96). Later, it was used to communicate with the Great Spirit and to remove evil from the community (Morgan 1962, 216–17). Toward the end of the nineteenth century at Onondaga, a white basket containing tobacco was burned as a substite for the dog (Beauchamp 1922,

16. A revival of the White Dog ceremony in 1799 involved eating the animal. Consumption of this sacrificed dog was compared to Christian communion (Wallace 1972, 206).

17. However, it should be noted that in terms of faunal identification, fragmentary remains of dog, coyote, and gray wolf are generally so similar as to be indistinguishable (Socci 1995, 76).

18. I suggest that wolf/dog effigy pipes (see fig. 16) may be a symbolic representation of similar beliefs, involving communication and maintenance of a relationship with spirit forces. Additionally, Noble (1979, 83) suggests that such pipes may be symbolic of the sun, as was the white wolf in Iroquoian cosmology.

156; Tooker 1970, 152–53). Now offerings of tobacco are thrown into a fire.

Iroquois spiritual practice evolved as their world changed, moving in this context from the sacrifice of humans to that of white dogs, white baskets, and finally tobacco: Today, failure of the maize crop is not a threat. In the present day, the Iroquois stress giving thanks to the Creator and the Iroquois Thanksgiving Address provides a reminder that we share this planet with many other species.

# SPIRITUALITY AND THE INDIVIDUAL

## Health

From birth, Iroquois were part of a network of relationships that included both humans and spirit forces. The spiritual power or orenda inherent in existence could be harnessed for either good or evil. Sometimes evil forces were released that harmed human beings (Herrick 1995, 40). To maintain one's health and good fortune, harmony had to be maintained with spiritual forces and with the individuals in one's community (see fig. 14).

In historic times, if an infant survived to either the Midwinter or Green Corn ceremony, it would be publicly named (Wallace 1972, 52). Lineages had a stock of names, and bestowing one of these on an individual emphasized continuity of the group. An individual was a member of a nuclear family as well as a matrilineage, though males also had obligations to their father's lineage, the *agadoni* (Fenton 1998, 27–28, 32). Kinship relations, gender, and age largely shaped social roles

Fig. 14. Clay pipe bowl effigy, front view, perhaps from the Pompey Center site (Onondaga, c. A.D. 1640). The height is approximately 3.6 cm. Drawing by Gene Mackay, photograph by Jack Williams. Courtesy of the Rochester Museum and Science Center, Rochester, N.Y.

within a community, and a child learned these while growing up.

Illness was seen as a result of an imbalance with spirit forces, with other individu-

47

als, or between one's body and soul. Thus failing to observe proper conduct, or causing envy or hatred in others was seen as a source of illness (Herrick 1995, 66). Dreams were seen as either resulting from contact with the spirit world or reflecting the desires of one's soul (Wallace 1958; 1972, 60–75; Hamell 1998, 258). Failure to act out dreams, either actually or symbolically, could lead to illness. "To lose touch with or deny the desires of the soul could cause it to revolt against the body" (St. John 1987, 136–37).

Witchcraft might also be suspected in cases in which no other causes for illness could be determined. At the Burke site (Onondaga) a small rock-filled feature located within a longhouse was found to have a face effigy at the bottom, carved from a human patella (Bradley 1987, 211 n. 25). Bradley suggests this may reflect witchcraft (see fig. 15).[1]

Presumably it was fear of witchcraft that led residents of the Maynard/McKeown site in Ontario (St. Lawrence Iroquoian) to place diseased human teeth in pits in the longhouse (Wright and Wright 1993, 6). In many cultures, hair or nail parings from an individual may be used to cast a spell, so these are carefully disposed of. The teeth may have been hidden in pits for the same reason.

1. Herbert Kraft (1972) found a sandstone pendant at the base of a pit at the Miller Field site in New Jersey. He cited Speck (1931, 43) to the effect that the Delaware ceremonially buried masks to dispose of them "lest the effects of neglect of the mask be handed down."

Fig. 15. Face effigy made from a human patella, Burke site (Onondaga). From Bradley 1987, 33. The length is about 3.6 cm.

Shamanic specialists existed among the Iroquois who sought to determine the cause of illness and effect a cure. Over time, a healing function was extended to medicine societies (Grim and St. John 1987, 128).[2] These preserved many of the ancient shamanic rituals of the hunter-gatherer past (St. John 1987, 135). Some of these rituals were incorporated into calendrical ceremonies like Midwinter and

2. Names of medicine societies include the Society of Medicine Men (Shake the Pumpkin), the Company of Mystic Animals, the Little Water Medicine Society, the Little People Society (Dark Dance), the False Face Society, the Husk Faces, the Towii'sas Society, and the Ohgi:we: Society (St. John 1987, 135–36).

Green Corn for the health and well-being of the entire community. If an individual were cured by a society ritual, he or she typically joined that society. Ritual paraphernalia included masks and rattles made from bark, gourds, horn, or turtle shell.

Village farmers typically engage in community-wide ceremonial events that focus on planting and harvesting crops. Iroquois calendrical ceremonies begin and end with a thanksgiving address to the Creator and the spiritual forces that support and renew life (St. John 1987, 134). Elements of these ceremonies include dancing, drumming, a bowl game, and tobacco invocations (St. John 1987, 134).

## Toward an Archaeology of Spirit Forces[3]

Owasco and Iroquois sites have yielded a variety of objects that can be interpreted in light of what we know of the Iroquois belief system. When interpreting an object, it must be remembered that all objects, whether natural or human-made, were felt to possess spiritual power. This spiritual dimension of the material world is often not explicitly addressed when discussing material recovered from archaeological sites.

Chunks of graphite and hematite on sites are thought to have been used as pigments (Wray et al. 1987, 123). Men painted their faces blue, black, or red. Blue was equated with well-being, black was the color of war or mourning, and red could mean violent death or life (Hamell 1992, 456–57; Snow 1994b, 93). The Iroquois commonly painted diagonal red stripes on equipment used in warfare, hunting, and ceremonies (Fenton and Dodge 1949, 191, 192), and they may have painted themselves in this manner as well. In the Upper Great Lakes region, it was common for the hair and face of deceased individuals to be painted red (Hall 1997, 34).[4] In the Seneca region, hematite was available from the Genesee River Gorge and is well represented on the Adams site, where it is most commonly associated with the graves of young and middle-aged males (Wray et al. 1991, 127).

Some small, sharply pointed bone objects identified as awls may have been used as tattooing needles. Some cases of Iroquois tattooing were recorded by seventeenth—and eighteenth-century artists. Geometric designs as well as clan emblems were tattooed on faces and other visible parts of the body (Fenton 1998, 24; Einhorn and Abler 1998). A few Iroquois women had "a little branch of foliage traced along the jaw" to prevent or cure toothache (Lafitau 1977, 35). There is a painting of the grandfather of Joseph Brant from 1710 showing him with blue tattoos (Fenton 1978, 310). While the specific meaning of these tattoos eludes us today, it seems likely that the designs held a spiritual meaning for the wearer, perhaps conferring

---

3. This subtitle was inspired by Robert Hall's book, *An Archaeology of the Soul.*

4. This was the observation of Nicholas Perrot in the latter half of the seventeenth century.

protection or reminding the wearer of a guardian spirit or animal medicine society. Bodily decoration was a material manifestation of the spiritual world.

Dancing was one way in which people gave thanks. Deer phalanges or "toe" bones with a hole in one end are often found on Owasco and Iroquois sites. Sometimes the toe bone was ground into a cone shape. These are believed to have been fringe jangles or "tinklers," which would have created a soft, rattlelike sound when an individual danced (Ritchie 1980, 289; Bradley 1987, 41–42; Wray et al. 1991, 240). When European metal became available, the Iroquois manufactured brass cones that replaced these artifacts.[5]

Discs made from antler, stone, and potsherds (fragments of ceramic vessels) become common on early seventeenth-century sites, often associated with the graves of women and children (Sempowski and Saunders n.d.). These were probably associated with the game of "deer buttons" or the bowl game. The former made use of eight deer buttons or bones scattered by hand while the latter made use of six peach pits shaken in a bowl (Beauchamp 1905, 180; Blau 1967). The two sides of the discs were of different colors, and scoring was based on how many of the same color appeared after being shaken or scattered. Deer buttons was played for recreation, especially by women and girls. The bowl game was associated with healing rituals and major ceremonies. Depending on the context, it can be viewed as a symbol of the struggle for crops to attain maturity or more generally as the struggle between the good and evil twins of Iroquois tradition for control of the earth.[6]

Charms were objects seen as having orenda and could be used for both good and evil (Herrick 1995, 87). These were often kept in medicine bundles of otter skin or the skin of other long-bodied or long-tailed animals. Charms were used for protection from illness or for healing. Parts of spiritually powerful animals were often used as charms. Various manufactured artifacts probably also had protective or curative functions.

Large quartz crystals known as Herkimer diamonds are particularly common on Mohawk sites and were used as charms in medicine bundles (Snow 1995a, 212). While found in the Mohawk area, quartz is not naturally occurring at these sites. Quartz crystals have a widespread association with shamanic divination and healing

---

5. It is also possible that the cone-shaped deer phalanges were used in the cup-and-pin game (Tuck 1971, 135; Ritchie 1980, 289; Bradley 1987, 213n. 41; Wray et al. 1991, 288), although Culin (1975, 549) offers only one ethnohistoric reference (Father Louis Hennepin) to Iroquoian use. At the Nodwell site in Ontario, deer phalanges have a statistically significant occurrence as a pair in pits, suggesting their possible use as toggles on either end of a lashing cord or belt (J. V. Wright, personal communication).

6. Frank Speck (1955, 83) quotes William Fenton on the idea that the bowl game can be seen as a struggle between the Good and Evil Twins. Blau (1967) presents a detailed description of the bowl game and its associated symbolism.

in the Northeast (Hamell 1983, 13–14; N. Saunders 1998, 231). As a material manifestation of light, crystals are seen as having life-giving and health-promoting properties, as do all light, bright, and white objects (Hamell 1996, 51).

Projectile points from earlier cultures are not uncommon discoveries on Iroquoian sites. In some cases, these may have functioned as hunting charms. At the Tram site (Seneca), the grave of an elderly male contained four pre-Iroquoian points (Wray et al. 1991, 105–8). Pre-Iroquoian points were also found in at least six male graves at Dutch Hollow and thirteen such points were found within the general village area (Ritchie 1954, 67). At Schoff (Onondaga), pieces of a four-thousand-year-old slate knife were found in the village debris (Tuck 1971, 103). Pre-Iroquoian points also are found stuck in the foreheads of old wooden masks representing Stone Giants.[7]

Jim Tuck found three miniature pots associated with a miniature pipe at the Cabin site (Owasco) (1971, 40).[8] Minia-ture artifacts such as these may have functioned as tokens in a dream-guessing rite or may have been used as charms. Iroquoians believed in spiritually powerful "little people," and miniature objects associated with them provided skill to whoever owned them (Tooker 1964, 121; Kapches 1992, 78). Miniature objects also appear in Iroquois origin traditions. In one version, Sky Woman falls to earth with a miniature mortar and pestle, a small pot, and a soup bone (Fenton 1998, 42).

Some small pots are crudely made, and archaeologists commonly refer to these as toy pots, or children's practice pots. The presence of red ocher on some Huron specimens suggests the possibility that they held pigment (Pratt 1976, 105). It is also possible that small pots were used for medicines and even witchcraft. Beauchamp relates a story from Albert Cusick in which witches drink blood from a small pot "not larger than a tea-cup" (1922, 63).

Particular animal bones may have served as hunting charms or talismans. The curved last segment of the finger and toe bones of some animals (distal phalanges) are known as claw cores. Bear claw cores have been found on Seneca sites, especially in burial contexts. As Kenton observed, "They sometimes wear on the bottom of their garments little ornaments made from bears' claws, that they may more easily kill these animals, and not be hurt by them" (Kenton 1927, 1:237, quoted in Ritchie 1954, 67).

The use of beads, pendants, and pins increased during the mid-sixteenth cen-

7. Ritchie (1954, 68) refers to these in the Rochester Museum and Science Center and the State Museum in Albany. Perhaps the Iroquois thought these points had been made by Stone Giants. "By contrast with their own small triangular arrow points, these much larger and heavier pre-Iroquoian points would tend to suggest to the Iroquois a greater bodily size and strength for their unknown makers" (Ritchie 1954, 68).

8. Tuck illustrates these miniature pots (1971, 38 plate 6). Other miniature pots that Tuck illustrates in his book are found on p. 110 (plate 29) and p. 143 (plate 35).

tury. Beads were commonly made of hollow bird bone. Animal teeth were also used, especially the canines of bear, elk, wolf, dog, and fox. In addition to their decorative function, these items had a spiritual dimension. Bear teeth were said to be an effective charm for drawing riches (Thomas 1994, 32). Bear molars sometimes had one root removed, making them look like a human foot.[9]

Beads and pendants might also be made from fossils, shell, stone, wood, antler, or from the epiphyseal cap of a bear or deer femur (Tuck 1971, 160; Bradley 1987, 41–42; Wray et al. 1991, 237). These items were either sewn onto clothing or worn as necklaces, bracelets, or ear ornaments. Early European descriptions and paintings indicate that earlobes of both men and women were pierced for ornaments.

Small faces in stone, clay, antler, and other materials are frequently found on sites of the sixteenth and seventeenth centuries and may be a reflection of the growth of medicine societies (Wray et al. 1991, 59; Ritchie and Funk 1973, 367). Beauchamp noted that among the Onondaga of the early twentieth century, the possession of a small stone face indicated membership in the False Face society (1922, 37). Alternatively, at Onondaga and at Six Nations Reserve in Ontario they are given to individuals in the context of the dream-guessing rite (Shimony 1961, 183; Fenton 1987, 502). Wearing small false faces was said to protect against witchcraft (Thomas 1994, 31).

George Hamell has argued that for native peoples in the Great Lakes area, exotic lithics, shell, and copper were viewed as spiritually powerful substances having life-enhancing and life-restorative power (1983; 1987; 1992). They were viewed as gifts from powerful beings (Underwater World Grandfathers) able to transform themselves into panthers or serpents (see figs. 16 and 17). These substances are often

Fig. 16. Clay pipe bowl effigy from the Fugle site (Seneca, c. A.D. 1605–1625). Incised lines on the bowl can be viewed as a continuation of the serpent's body. The maximum width of the bowl is about 3.1 cm. Drawing by Gene Mackay, photograph by Jack Williams. Courtesy of the Rochester Museum and Science Center, Rochester, N.Y.

9. These are found at Adams (Wray et al. 1987, 161) and at Barnes (Tuck 1971, 159). Wayne Lenig (n.d.) suggests that these foot effigies made from teeth may have had a similar symbolism to the rare pipe foot effigies.

Fig. 17. Ring bowl pipe from the Dutch Hollow site (Seneca). Were the horizontal lines on the pipe bowl viewed as serpents, as is probable for figure 16? Courtesy of the Rochester Museum and Science Center, Rochester, N.Y.

Fig. 18. Clay pipe bowl effigy from the Dann site (Seneca c. A.D. 1660–1675). The height of the face is about 3.8 cm. Drawing by Gene Mackay, photograph by Jack Williams. Note the round red glass beads inlaid as eyes. The same word in Huron was used for eye and glass bead (Tooker 1964, 112). Courtesy of the Rochester Museum and Science Center, Rochester, N.Y.

found in graves, further strengthening their association with ritual and their role in the spirit world (Bradley 1987, 42, 179; Hamell 1983; 1987; 1992). Early European glass beads and metal were equated with these native materials and used in similar fashion (see fig. 18).[10]

The curative and life enhancing nature of glass, metal, and shell beads to the Iroquois would have enhanced their function as items of personal adornment.

The whelk and quahog could be fashioned into white and purple shell beads, respectively. Discoidal beads predominated, but various shapes are found (Bradley 1987, 172). There was an abundance of marine shell discoidal beads at the Seneca Adams site, many found in association with brass, which helped to preserve them (Wray et al. 1987, 137). Flat, round, perforated crinoid stem beads may have served as prototypes for discoidal marine shell beads (Kuhn and Funk 1994, 82). George Hamell argues that white shell

10. An early example of this may be the zinc-lead alloy recovered from the eleventh-century Boys site in Ontario. The small metal sheet was originally thought to be native silver, but analysis by Dr. Michael Spence suggests it is of Norse origin (J. V. Wright 1994, 50).

"was a ritual metaphor for light and life" (1996, 51).

Ceramic effigy faces and pipes have been recovered with shell inlay eyes. It is possible that some flat shell discs were used as inlays around the eyes of wooden masks, though this remains to be demonstrated (Mackay 1989, 55, 57; Hall 1997, 25). What may be brass eyes for wooden masks have been recovered from the early seventeenth-century Seneca sites of Fugle and Dutch Hollow (Sempowski and Saunders, in press). Later, in 1687, a member of the De Nonville expedition against the Seneca observed a mask with metal eyes made from a kettle (Thwaites 1896–1901, 63:289; Fenton 1987, 77).

## Tobacco and the Spirit World

Methods of communicating with guardian spirits and the spirit world take many forms. As mentioned earlier, dreams are one way in which contact with the supernatural is achieved. Communication with and sometimes transformation into this spirit world is also enhanced through achieving an altered state of consciousness (von Gernet 1992, 172). Native tobacco (*Nicotiana rustica*) is stronger than commercial varieties grown today and can produce dissociative states. A major advantage of tobacco over other hallucinogens is that it is not as potentially dangerous (von Gernet 1992, 178).

The Iroquois smoked both tobacco and *kinnikinnick*. The latter is a mixture of plant substances, and it is probable that it

was the substance smoked in the earliest pipes more than three thousand years ago (Hall 1997, 158–59). Very early pipes are tubular in form, perhaps evolving from the shaman's sucking tube. More than sixty different plant substances were smoked, some of which could produce altered states of consciousness (von Gernet 1992, 175).[11]

In a recent paper, Gail Wagner and Gayle Fritz argue that a West Coast variety of tobacco, *Nicotiana bigelovii*, spread east of the Rockies along major river routes (n.d.). They identify it at 100 B.C. in Illinois, a time when materials such as obsidian, grizzly bear teeth and other western materials are also moving east. They identify this same species of tobacco at later Mississippian sites. *Nicotiana bigelovii* was also grown by Plains Indians at the time of contact. While the relationship of this species to *Nicotiana rustica* remains unclear, the cultivation of tobacco appears to date as early as A.D. 700 or 800 in the Northeast (Fecteau 1985, 79,81,164; von Gernet 1992, 178–79).

On certain occasions, tobacco is thrown directly into a fire. Since this usage is essentially invisible in the archaeological

11. There is no evidence that marijuana (*Cannabis sativa*) was smoked by Native Americans prior to European contact. It was probably first grown in the Northeast by the French at Port Royal in 1606 (Rousseau 1966, 95). While burning *Cannabis* was used as an incense by some Old World cultures, it was not smoked in the Old World until the diffusion of smoking technology from the New World (Alexander von Gernet, personal communication).

record, the presence of pipes is taken to indicate use of tobacco and related plants. Most pipes were made of clay that was formed around reeds or twisted cordage that then burned away when the pipe was fired. In 1664 Boucher observed that Iroquois men made pipes (Kuhn 1996, 32), and the assumption is that this held true for the Owasco culture as well. Some pipes of stone were also manufactured (Ritchie 1953, 10).

Sagard stated that Huron men glued broken clay pipes together with blood drawn from their arms with a sharp stone (probably chert). Pipes, blood, and chert all had spiritual significance to Iroquoians. The Huron saw chert (flint) as the dried blood of Flint, the younger twin in the story of creation. Given the availability of alternative adhesives, it seems likely that human blood, drawn with the dried "blood" of Flint, was the culturally preferred choice for mending pipes, which were spiritually charged objects.

Pipes and smoking assisted humans in maintaining a proper relationship to the spirit world. Rising smoke served as a medium of communication (Hewitt 1928, 537, 544; Mathews 1978, 158–63; Bradley 1987, 123). Owasco pipe bowls, often barrel-shaped or conical, generally form an obtuse angle with the stem. Over time the standard shape changed so that bowl and stem more often form a right angle. Later Owasco pipe bowls sometimes contain human or animal representations (Ritchie 1953, 10).

Many of these figures may have repre-

Fig. 19. Ceramic wolf effigy from the Dutch Hollow site (Seneca). Smoke may have come out of the hollow eyes. The maximum length is about 12 cm. Drawing by Gene Mackay. Rochester Museum and Science Center, Rochester, N.Y.

sented the guardian spirit of individual smokers (Brasser 1980, 97; Hamell 1998, 272). The image faced the smoker, an example of what has been referred to as "self-directed" art (Brasser 1980; Brown 1997, 476). In other words, rather than a decorative display for others, the image had meaning and was meant for the person using the pipe. As one smoked and looked at the staring effigy, it would have come alive to the smoker (see fig. 19).

Effigy pipes became increasingly common after the fifteenth century, and more than half of animal effigies are birds (von Gernet and Timmins 1987, 37; see figs. 20–22). This may be related to commuication with the Sky World and the dissociative state produced by the tobacco that can produce the sensation of flight (von Gernet and Timmins 1987, 38–39). Similarly, effigies of otters, beavers, frogs, or toads may relate to communication with the Under Water World and reflect a perception of swimming (Brown 1997, 474). Perhaps the rare "boat" pipes (see Bradley 1987, 62, plate 4) also symbolize movement or journey of the soul. While in an altered state, the smoker may feel a merging of his soul with his guardian spirit, represented by the effigy. The smoker is temporarily transformed.

One animal of great spiritual significance to the Iroquois was the panther (*Felis concolor*), also known as the cougar, mountain lion, or puma (Hamell 1998, 129). Its former range was essentially the same as the white-tailed deer, its chief prey. Depictions

Fig. 21. Owl effigy pipe from the Marsh site (Seneca). The owl has metal eyes. The maximum length is about 14 cm. Courtesy of the Rochester Museum and Science Center, Rochester, N.Y.

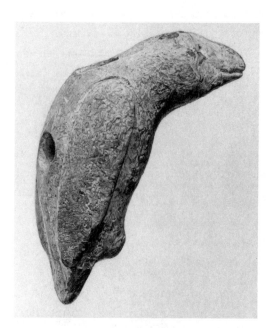

Fig. 20. Bird effigy from the Power House site (Seneca). The pipe bowl is stone. The maximum height is about 10.2 cm. Drawing by Gene Mackay. Courtesy of the Rochester Museum and Science Center, Rochester, N.Y.

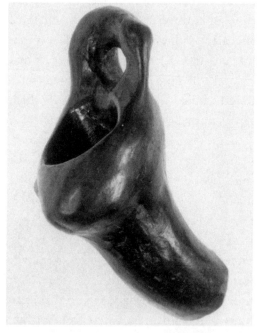

Fig. 22. Long-necked bird (heron?) effigy pipe from the Boughton Hill site (Ganondagan, Seneca). The maximum height is about 5 cm. Courtesy of the Rochester Museum and Science Center, Rochester, N.Y.

of panthers occur on seventeenth-century pipes and combs (see fig. 23).

At night, a panther's eyes are reflective, like the metal inlay eyes on historic panther effigy pipes. Represented in art, these panthers probably represent personal guardian spirits or animal medicine societies (Hamell 1998, 258).

Human effigies on pipes may represent either false face beings or shamans (Mathews 1976; Noble 1979, 83–84; Brasser 1980, 97; see figs. 24–27).

In either case, there would be an asso-

Fig. 24. Human effigy pipe, Otstungo site (Mohawk). Height of face: 7 cm. Drawing by Gene Mackay. Photo courtesy of Dean Snow.

Fig. 23. Panther effigy from the Marsh site (Seneca). The pipe bowl is stone. The maximum height is approximately 13.9 cm. Drawing by Gene Mackay. Courtesy of the Rochester Museum and Science Center, Rochester, N.Y.

Fig. 25. Human effigy pipe, Richmond Mills site (Seneca). The height is about 6.5 cm. Drawing by Gene Mackay, photograph by Jack Williams. Courtesy of the Rochester Museum and Science Center, Rochester, N.Y.

Fig. 26. Human effigy pipe bowl, Nichols Pond site (Oneida). The height is approximately 2.8 cm. From Wray et al. 1991, 59. Drawing by Gene Mackay. Courtesy of the Rochester Museum and Science Center.

kadons, "He looks both ways," an Onondaga firekeeper and chief whose pictograph consists of human heads looking in opposite directions (Fenton 1950, 62; Noble 1979, 85). Pipes with both a human and animal image probably represent human transformation into an animal form (Mathews 1981, 14; see fig. 28).

The small number but wide distribution in time and space of multiple image pipes argues for their use by religious specialists (Mathews 1981, 19).

Some effigies incorporate the entire bowl, and I suggest that these effigies are metaphors for the Iroquois cosmos. The effigy turtle pipe from the Indian Hill site (see fig. 29) is an example, the imagery

ciation with healing. Dual image or Janus pipes may reflect concepts of dualism (good/evil, male/female) or transformation (Mathews 1978, 180; 1981, 13). Alternatively, they may represent Dehat-

Fig. 28. Effigy pipe with human face toward smoker with possible panther behind the human effigy, the stem forming the panther's long tail, MacArthur site (Seneca c. A.D. 1500–1525). The maximum length is about 12.4 cm. Drawing by Gene Mackay, photograph by Jack Williams. The artifact is in the New York State Museum. Courtesy of the Rochester Museum and Science Center, Rochester, N.Y.

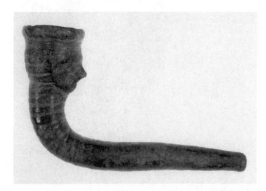

Fig. 27. Pinch-face effigy pipe from the Power House site (Seneca). The maximum length is about 13.5 cm. Courtesy of the Rochester Museum and Science Center, Rochester, N.Y.

suggesting the earth as "turtle island." The "Mother of Nations" pipes (see fig. 30) are similar in the treatment of the effigy. While they are popularly thought to represent Jikonsahseh, the first woman inspired by the Peacemaker, in a more general sense they may represent the earth herself.

If some pipes symbolize the Iroquois world in microcosm, then four-cornered "coronet pipes" (see fig. 31) could represent the four cardinal directions. When looked at from above, coronet pipes form a circle within a square, reminiscent of the Mississippian "cross in circle" motif said to symbolize either sacred fire or the earth and the four cardinal directions. Similarly, the edge of trumpet pipe bowls (see fig. 32) could symbolize the world's rim while

Fig. 30. "Mother of Nations" pipe from the Boughton Hill site (Ganondagan, Seneca). The maximum length is about 16 cm. Courtesy of the Rochester Museum and Science Center, Rochester, N.Y.

pipe rim effigies could represent supernatural world rim dwellers, represented also by Iroquois wooden masks.

**Death**

The Iroquois say "an infant's life is as the thinness of a maple leaf" (Fenton 1978, 314), an apt description of the generally high mortality rate of infants in premodern

Fig. 29. Turtle pipe bowl effigy, Indian Hill site (Onondaga, c. A.D. 1663–1682). The height is about 5.5 cm. Drawing by Gene Mackay, photograph by Jack Williams. Courtesy of the Rochester Museum and Science Center, Rochester, N.Y.

Fig. 31. Coronet pipe from the Dutch Hollow site (Seneca). Drawing by Gene Mackay. Courtesy of the Rochester Museum and Science Center, Rochester, N.Y.

Fig. 32. Trumpet pipe from the Factory
Hollow site (Seneca). Courtesy of the
Rochester Museum and Science Center,
Rochester, N.Y.

societies. According to the *Jesuit Relations,*
when a Huron infant died it was buried
along a path so the soul of the infant could
enter a passing woman and be reborn
(Thwaites 1896–1901, 10:273). The burial of infants within Huron longhouses and
along the central corridor of Neutral longhouses further supports the idea that the
location of infant burials was important in
determining the rebirth of the soul
(Kapches 1976; Lennox and Fitzgerald
1990, 455). The relative paucity of infant
skeletons represented in the archaeological
record may be due both to poor preservation of these fragile remains and to their
placement.

Pits containing the skeletons of multiple individuals are associated with early
Iroquoians in Ontario and western New
York. Each of those ossuaries is interpreted
as representing a single ceremonial event in
which individuals who died previously are
reburied with one another. Owasco and
early Iroquois sites in central and eastern
New York are not associated with such ossuaries and rarely have formal cemetaries.
The cemetery associated with the Owasco
Sackett site appears to have been the exception rather than the rule. In the Mohawk
area, it is not until the early seventeenth
century that cemeteries are located close to
villages. Before that time, most individuals
were buried away from the village, and for
the most part the location of these burial
areas is unknown (Snow 1996, 171).

Individuals buried in Owasco or early
Iroquois settlements were often interred in
former storage pits and associated objects
are infrequent. Children were sometimes
interred with ceramic vessels and adults
have been found with pipes (Ritchie and
Funk 1973, 360; Ritchie 1980, 296; Prezzano 1992, 384). From the occasional personal ornaments found with skeletons,
William Ritchie inferred that the deceased
were buried fully clothed and probably
covered with a robe or mat (Ritchie 1980,
296). Despite over a century of archaeological investigation, little is known of the
mortuary customs of the New York Iroquois before about A.D. 1550 (Tuck 1978,
332).

Most of our information on Iroquois
burials during the latter half of sixteenth
century comes from the Seneca region.
Few burials have been excavated among
the Onondaga, Oneida, and Mohawk during this period (Pratt 1976, 34, 140, 145).

It is possible that the deceased were placed on scaffolds (Pratt 1976, 34, 145). In Hewitt's "Iroquoian Cosmology," the first man to die in the sky world is placed in a burial case in a high place (1903, 146).[12] Iroquois oral tradition contains the story of a vampire skeleton who comes to life and eats people. This event is given as the reason for discontinuing scaffold burial (Wallace 1972, 99–100).

In cases where the dead were buried, it was apparently some distance from the village, making the later discovery of these graves less likely. This practice is traceable back to the Owasco period (Ritchie 1980, 321). An Iroquois example of this practice occurs in connection with the Schoff site (Onondaga), where a few burials were found about a mile to the east of the site (Tuck 1971, 101). The dead may have been buried at some distance in an effort to separate the spirits of the dead from the living, for even recently it was believed that spirits had the power to harm the living (Tuck 1971, 101; Shimony 1961, 228).

Dean Snow states that in the period between A.D. 1580–1614, cemeteries become associated with villages in the Mohawk area (1995a, 197). Peter Pratt dates this shift to the 1630s in the Oneida area with the appearance of cemeteries adjacent to the Thurston site (1976, 129, 132). In his visit to the Oneida in 1634, van den Bogaert noted that above a chief's grave "stood a large wooden bird surrounded by paintings of dogs, deer, snakes, and other

animals" (Gehring and Starna 1988, 7). Occasionally, post molds have been found in association with Seneca burials, and it is possible that these represent grave markers (Wray et al. 1991, 167, 185, 375).

The Bloody Hill site (Onondaga, c. A.D. 1420) contains several historic graves that probably relate to the Weston site (c. A.D. 1682–1696) occupied more than 250 years later. This is probably not coincidence. Surface traces of occupation or oral tradition may have indicated to the Onondaga that this was a place of their ancestors. Dean Snow notes a number of instances in the Mohawk area where village cemeteries were reused at a slightly later period (1995a, 179, 226, 386). In these cases, old people may have wished to be buried with former family members and friends.

Many grave goods are found in burials of the late sixteenth and early seventeenth centuries. Among the Seneca, males were more likely to be buried with grave goods than females (Wray et al. 1987, 175, 226). These graves often contained weapons, pipes, and minerals. In particular, pipes tend to be associated with males (Martha Sempowski, personal communication). Pottery vessels are buried with males, females, and children (Wray et al. 1987, 85). Some seventeenth-century Mohawk graves have produced pottery vessels containing food remains (Peter Pratt, personal communication). George Hamell has suggested that pottery vessels may also have served as the "ohgi:wi:" (Feast of the Dead) drum used during the deceased's fu-

12. This is the Onondaga version.

neral (personal communication). Female burials often include iron hatchets (Wray and Schoff 1953, 58).[13] Combs probably functioned as hair ornaments and are more often associated with women and children than with men in Seneca graves (Wray 1963, 42). There is an increase in the frequency of rattles in early seventeenth-century Seneca graves, especially those of young females and immature individuals (Sempowski and Saunders n.d.).[14] The graves of children contained large quantities of glass, shell beads, and other items of adornment (Wray et al. 1987, 176; Richter 1992, 81).

In discussing grave goods from the Dutch Hollow site (Seneca, c. 1605–1620), William Ritchie cautioned against the automatic equation of grave goods with the economic or social roles of the liv-

13. This may reflect the role of females in gathering firewood.

14. Historic and ethnographic accounts document the use of snapping-turtle rattles, but archaeologically turtle shell rattles are represented by the box turtle (Fenton 1987, 67–69). Today, box turtles (*Terrapene carolina*) are found in New York only along the Lake Erie plain in the southwestern corner of the state (Wycoff 1991, 16). Fenton (1978, 318) notes that box turtle rattles are used today in the woman's *thowi.sas* ceremony, while Speck (1955, 82) notes that small snapping turtles (*Chelydra serpentina*) or painted turtles (*Chrysemys picta*) were also used in the Woman's Dance chant. While dried corn kernels were often used inside rattles, if small pebbles were used one might infer the presence of bark rattles archaeologically from a cluster of small pebbles.

ing (1954, 61). As part of the dream-guessing ritual, which had a healing function, individuals would be presented with a variety of objects. "A dying man may be seen surrounded by awls, scissors, knives, bells, needles, and a thousand other trifles, from the least of which he expects to obtain health" (Thwaites 1896–1901, 43:265, 267). Might some of these items have been buried with the individual if he died?

Grave goods were meant to accompany the souls of the deceased into the afterlife. It is clear that these objects were viewed as having a spiritual essence or soul. As Sagard commented regarding the Huron, "For they imagine and believe that the souls of these kettles, tomahawks, knives, and everything they dedicate to them, especially at the great festival of the dead, depart to the next life to serve the souls of their dead, although the bodies of these skins, tomahawks, kettles, and everything else dedicated and offered remain behind and stay in the graves and coffins along with the bones of the deceased" (Sagard-Théodat 1968, 172).

It is this belief that lies behind the widespread practice in the Americas of breaking the object placed with the deceased. The spirit of these "killed" objects is then free to accompany the soul of the deceased. In particular, pipes associated with burials frequently have a single break in the stem, suggesting the object was snapped in two before being placed in the grave. When native people were asked why so many European goods were placed in graves, they responded that the next world was not well supplied with European goods, as they were new (Thwaites 1896–1901, 6:125, 129–33, 177, 211).[15]

In burials, the cut, front portions of animal jaws are sometimes found in association with the skeleton. These are all that remain of fur robes of wolf, bear, and dog, typically associated with males (Ritchie 1954, 7–8, 27; Wray et al. 1987, 44, 150–51, 269, 274, 295; Hamell 1998, 271–72). Mythically, these specially prepared skins "retain their animacy and transformative potency, and those that also retain their teeth may cry out in anger or snap and bite to protect their wearer" (Hamell 1998, 272). Smaller jaws of various mustelids (weasel, fisher, marten, and otter) are also found in graves and probably are what remain of medicine pouches. Historically, mustelids are associated with shamans, and were not hunted for meat but for their animate nature and power as robes and medicine pouches (Hamell 1998, 269).

In burial contexts, especially on Seneca sites, a wide variety of beads have been found that were apparently strung together into necklaces. Included in these necklaces were bear and wolf canines. Bear claw cores are often found associated with the head or chest of an infant or child burial (Wray et al. 1991, 230; Pratt 1976, 133). In a number of Seneca burials, including three graves at the Tram site, artifacts depicting a heron or

some other long-necked bird have been recovered (Wray et al. 1991, 174).[16]

From the Seneca Tram site, a bone effigy face or maskette encircled by a serpent was made to be worn upside down so that it would appear right side up to the wearer looking down at it (Wray et al. 1991, 59; fig. 33).[17] This is similar to a bone human effigy face recovered from the Onondaga Atwell site that has a hole in the chin, again apparently meant to be worn upside down so that it could be viewed by the wearer looking down at it (Bradley 1987, 65, plate 5a). Like effigy pipes, these provide another example of "self-directed" images. Such art is typical of shamanic practice, where the spiritual world is re-created in the material one (Brown 1997, 476).

Antler figurines appear to have been suspended so that they faced away from the wearer (Wray et al 1991, 218–23). This suggests their use as protective charms

16. Fenton (1940, 227) suggests that the Deer, Beaver, and Heron clans were introduced by Huron captives in the 1650s. If so, then the Heron related material probably does not represent clan affiliation, though the bear and wolf material might. Van den Bogaert mentions a swan, a crane, and a pigeon as being used in medicine bundles (Gehring and Starna 1988, 5) and Shimony (1961, 287) refers to a bird wing as a hunting charm.

17. Tom Abler suggested to me that this might be an image of Thadada:ho?, the legendary Onondaga sorcerer who had snakes for hair (see fig. 51). Sempowski suggests that "helmet" pipes (see fig. 25) represent shamans with snake skins wrapped around their head, in the manner of Mohawk shamans described by van den Bogaert (Sempowski n.d.; Gehring and Starna 1988, 10).

15. The Jesuit Le Jeune was told this by a Montagnais.

copper, early European goods are often found in graves, especially those of children. At the Seneca Cameron site, most shell, brass, or glass beads in graves were associated with children (Wray et al. 1991, 229, 349). The placement of these substances in the same context strengthens the

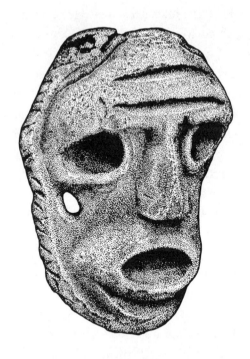

Fig. 33. Face effigy from the Tram site (Seneca). Length: 3.6 cm. Courtesy of the Rochester Museum and Science Center, Rochester, N.Y.

(Ritchie 1954, 67). These figurines are most often recovered from the burials of infants and children on late sixteenth—and early seventeenth-century sites that also exhibit increased infant and child mortality (Wray et al. 1991, 223, 391–92; Saunders and Sempowski 1991, 19; Snow 1995a, 266). The fact that many show evidence of having been rubbed supports Arthur Parker's view that they were worn by living individuals to warn of danger (Saunders and Sempowski 1991, 19). Few such figurines have been found on sites dating after 1650 (Mandzy 1994, 142; see figs. 34–36).

Like marine shell and earlier native

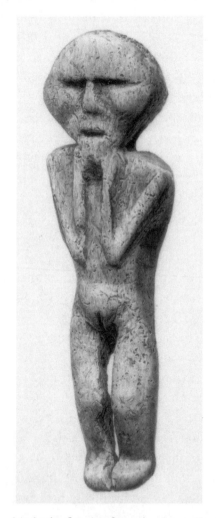

Fig. 34. Antler figurine from the Genoa Fort site (Cayuga). The height is approximately 4.6 cm. Drawing by Gene Mackay, photograph by Jack Williams. Courtesy of the Rochester Museum and Science Center, Rochester, N.Y.

argument that early European goods were analogues to native copper and marine shell (Bradley 1987, 110). That these substances occur in burial contexts in all Five Nations suggests both regular contact and

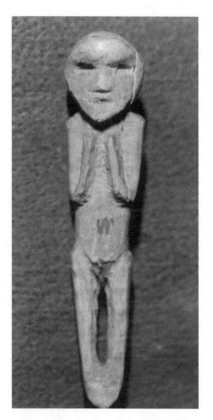

Fig. 36. Bone figurine from Wagner's Hollow site (Mohawk). Height: 6.3 cm. Photo courtesy of Dean Snow.

a shared ideology. This is in marked contrast to earlier localism (Dennis 1993, 63).

Between 15 and 20 percent of the graves excavated at the Adams and Culbertson sites contain marine shell, a major increase from earlier sites in the Seneca region (Sempowski 1989, 84–86). Parker recounted a Seneca tradition to the effect that shell assisted one in gaining entry into the spirit world (Parker 1923, 74–76; Ceci 1989, 67). Shell beads, like fossilized tears,

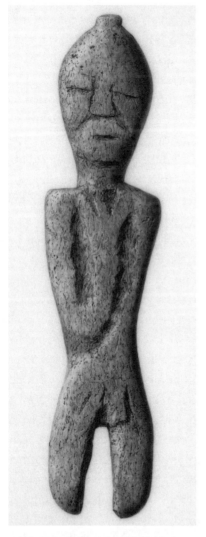

Fig. 35. Antler figurine from the Genoa Fort site (Cayuga). The height is about 5.5 cm. Drawing by Gene Mackay, photograph by Jack Williams. Courtesy of the Rochester Museum and Science Center, Rochester, N.Y.

18. The idea of equating shell beads with tears comes from the late Lynn Ceci.

remain behind as mute testimony to the loss of loved ones.[18]

The practice of making rich burial offerings operated against individuals accumulating large quantities of trade goods. Unlike Europeans, Iroquoians did not seek to amass great wealth (Trigger 1990a; Warrick 1996, 16). Those with abundant trade material were expected to offer these on the death of a kinsman. Most glass trade beads recovered from burials appear not to have been in circulation for a long period, suggesting that rather than being old "hand-me-downs," glass beads in graves were relatively new. From a nonnative perspective, their use as burial offerings can also be seen as a mechanism for "consuming" otherwise indestructible objects.

Occasionally, normally perishable organic material is preserved by being in contact or close proximity to copper or brass material. The copper salts that leach out of copper or brass are toxic, preventing the bacterial growth that would normally break down organic material (Wray et al. 1987, 125; 1991, 136). At the Adams site (Seneca), the insides of tubular brass beads preserved fragments of reeds. It is thought that a long, relatively narrow, thin sheet of brass was wrapped around a reed core and then cut. This inference is supported by the fact that brass beads in a string tend to be of uniform diameter, but varying length (Wray et al. 1987, 49, 195).

Brass beads preserved strips of rawhide and twisted fiber cordage, both of which were used to string beads on necklaces (Wray et al. 1987, 126, 127; 1991, 330).

At Adams, eight thin strips of rawhide were bound together to form a tassel (Wray et al. 1987, 127). Also at Adams, a row of brass beads was found strung side by side, rather than end to end (Wray et al. 1987, 52). This method of stringing is unusual for early beads, but it foreshadows later stringing of shell beads in wampum belts. Coastal groups strung tubular metal beads in a similar fashion to form bandoliers (Brasser 1978a, 86).

On the Seneca Tram site, two rows of tubular beads were found near the wrist of an individual (Wray et al. 1991, 151). These shell beads were strung side by side in the same manner as the brass beads found on the earlier Adams site (Wray et al. 1991, 151). Though they functioned here as a bracelet, rather than as a belt or bandolier, they constitute the earliest example of wampum beads strung in belt fashion.

Martha Sempowski sees change in mortuary behavior in the large early Seneca sites as reflecting rituals designed to integrate individuals into the society, especially the Condolence ritual. The Condolence Council required a dual division of the group, with the "clear-minded" side (moiety) comforting the mourners. The responsibility of one group to the other gave everyone a prescribed role to play and a place in the system. There is a shift to an increasingly western orientation of the bodies, which probably relates to the belief that the soul of the deceased journeyed to the west (Wray et al. 1991, 170). This shift in burial orientation with the head toward the west appears to have been a widespread phenomenon in the Northeast toward the end of the sixteenth century (Axtell 1981, 116). Many graves at Adams also exhibit evidence of burning (Wray et al. 1987, 169). This may have occurred as a result of burning corn as part of the mortuary ritual observed by the Jesuits in the 1650s among the Onondaga (Thwaites 1896–1901, 43:265–69).

Dogs are sometimes found buried with individuals, and there is a tendency for the relative ages of humans and dogs buried together to be similar: infants with puppies and adults with mature dogs (Wray et al. 1991, 67).[19] Early accounts suggest that dogs were widely viewed in North America as spirit guides for the human soul to the afterworld (Strong 1985, 36; Schwartz 1997). According to Sagard, the Huron believed that the souls of dogs followed a nearby path to that of human souls along the Milky Way (Sagard-Théodat 1968, 172).

19. Nahrwold No. 1: Ritchie and Funk 1973, 278; Adams and Tram: Wray et al. 1991, 67; Cameron: Wray et al. 1991, 240; Ripley: Green and Sullivan 1997, 8.

## ❧ 4 ❧

# THE HOUSEHOLD

## The Extended Family

Traditionally, Iroquois trace descent through the female line. This means that children, both male and female, are members of their mother's matrilineage. Matrilineages are grouped together into larger descent groups called clans, usually named after an animal such as Wolf, Bear, or Turtle. Members of the same clan claim descent from a common ancestor, though typically they are unable to trace their precise relationship. Clan members avoid marrying one another.

The extended family lived in long bark-covered structures called longhouses (see fig. 37).

Women of the same matrilineage or clan segment shared the same structure along with their husbands and children. When a man married, he moved out of his mother's (or sister's) longhouse and into the one in which his wife was living.[1] His-torically, the senior woman was the ultimate household authority within the longhouse (Fenton 1998, 27). The longhouse formed a microcosm of the community and has come to symbolize Iroquois society. Matrilocal residence has the effect of moving men around, physically splitting up brothers and other male relatives. This is a pattern that tends to prevent disputes between groups of related males and provides instead for the mobilization of large groups of men, some of whom are not closely related (Snow 1996, 166). Aggression is directed toward more distant communities not a part of the marriage/alliance system. Cross-culturally, matrilocal residence is associated with external warfare and the importance of women in subsistence (C. Ember and M. Ember 1996, 6).

In everyday life, the strict matrilocal pattern of residence was not always followed (Quain 1961; Richards 1967; Warrick 1996, 12). This was probably especially

---

1. An exception to matrilocal residence may have been that of a chief or sachem who remained within his mother's longhouse after marriage. George Hamell (personal communication) suggests that the Onondaga version of Iroquois origins (Hewitt 1903) serves as a charter for this exception. In this tradition, Sky Woman goes to live in the longhouse of the Sky World Chief.

Fig. 37. Reconstructed longhouse at Tawiscaron, Ridgeway, Ontario, now destroyed. Photo courtesy of Dean Snow.

true during the sixteenth and seventeenth centuries, when many non-Iroquois were incorporated into Iroquois society and took up residence in longhouses. In some cases, it was membership in the same clan that determined residence in a longhouse rather than close biological ties.

## Origin and Function of the Longhouse

The ancient bark-covered structures the Iroquois once built are long gone.[2] Modern visitors to an undisturbed village site will find little surface evidence that a com-

2. The term for bark house in Seneca, *ganasote*, is cognate with the place names of Canastota, N.Y., and Conestoga, Pa. (see Beauchamp 1905, 106). George Hamell (personal communication) wonders whether the Conestoga wagons were named simply for their place of manufacture or also for the wooden, arched framework that supported the wagon's canvas covers.

munity was once there. While the posts framing a longhouse decayed long ago, traces of them in the form of a dark stains or post molds sometimes remain in the subsoil. On average, these range between five and ten centimeters in diameter (Prezzano 1992, 260). By removing the topsoil or plow zone from a large area of a village site, archaeologists are able to plot the location of these post molds, and hence the layout of longhouses. In a few rare cases, we have the layout of most of the community.

Longhouses recovered at Boland, an eleventh-century site in the Susquehanna Valley, are similar to the later, well-known longhouse form (Prezzano 1992). Post molds found at the Owasco Castle Creek and Sackett sites, originally thought to represent oval or circular lodges, are now generally regarded as portions of longhouses (Snow 1980, 313; Trigger 1981; Prezzano 1988; 1996, 11; Bamann et al. 1992). On the basis of new radio carbon dates for a series of Owasco sites, John Hart (2000) has recently argued that large longhouses do not appear until the thirteenth century.

In addition to construction efficiency, there are advantages to having a household with many members. Iroquois patterns of hunting, fishing, trading, and warfare took men far from the village for extended periods, leaving women, children, and old people behind to carry out other activities, a situation that encourages the formation of both matrilocal residence and extended families (Pasternak, Ember, and Ember 1976; Trigger 1978c; Harris 1979, 97). In an extended household, many individuals can cooperate in a task, or a variety of tasks can be performed at the same time as needed (Wilk and Rathje 1982, Coupland and Banning 1996, 2–3). Groups of related women cooperated in planting, harvesting, processing, and storing the crops in their longhouses (Quain 1961, 250; Parker 1968, 22–24).

Despite these economic and social advantages, from a Western perspective a traditional longhouse sacrifices both privacy and ease of use (Blanton 1994, 32). Locating the doors only at either end of most longhouses creates limited access to the interior. Individuals living toward the center of a longhouse had to pass by other families living closer to a door. More doorways could have been incorporated easily into longhouse design, and some very long longhouses did have side entrances. Having more doorways would not have negated the economic or social advantages of longhouse life.

There are two advantages to having limited access to longhouses. First, a limited number of doorways reduced drafts in winter. Initial entry to a longhouse was into an unheated storage area, which served a secondary insulation function. One then entered another doorway to the living area. Second, there is a defensive advantage for a number of families to move together into a single house with limited access (Rowlands 1972, 456; Warrick 1996, 18). While most villages were protected by a palisade, not all were. Additionally, there was always the possibility that an enemy might gain entry into a village in a surprise attack.[3] Rather than many individuals defending numerous single-family structures, a small number of individuals positioned at the doors could defend an entire longhouse. This would have been especially important at times when many warriors were absent from the village.

## The Structure

While longhouses were the domain of women, it was a group of men working together who built them. Houses of up to 400 feet long and 15 to 22 feet wide were built by layering bark over vertical posts set in the ground. J. V. Wright has argued that

3. The *Jesuit Relations* (Thwaites 1896–1901, 29:253) of 1646 contain an account of two Huron sentries who fell asleep and were killed by Iroquois warriors. Abler (1970, 28) notes that there are a number of accounts in the *Jesuit Relations* of enemy warriors gaining entry into villages.

white cedar would have provided the best vertical posts, as it grows straight in dense stands and is relatively rot resistant (1995, 18).[4] When cedar trees die they can be easily harvested. Cedar stands are abundant in the eastern Iroquois area, and cedar post remains have been recovered from the Kelso (Onondaga) and Garoga (Mohawk) sites (Prezzano 1992, 240).

It is possible to estimate the number of posts required for longhouse construction. Wright conservatively estimates some 255 wall posts for a seventy-four-foot-long structure (Wright 1995, 15). Some post molds are V-shaped in profile, indicating that the vertical posts were pointed at one end. It is sometimes assumed that these were "screwed" into the ground in spring when the soil was soft (Ritchie 1980, 282), but after experimentation, J. V. Wright concludes this was unlikely.

Large internal support posts tend to be flat-bottomed, rather than pointed, and holes certainly were dug before the posts were placed in them (Tuck 1971, 31). After experimentation, Sohrweide concluded that most posts were set in place after a short pilot post had been hammered into the wet ground several times in order to achieve the desired depth (n.d.). Stones are sometimes found along the edges of

post molds, apparently serving as wedges (Tuck 1971, 31; Ritchie 1973, 302–3). At Otstungo (Mohawk), Snow observed that the builders of a longhouse cut into a slight slope in order to achieve a flat floor (1995a, 126).

The width of longhouses tended to be standardized, ranging between five and seven meters (Prezzano 1992, 270). Susan Prezzano examined the floor plans of sixty-three New York Iroquois longhouses and found the average width to be 6.5 meters (1992, 269), slightly less than the average width of longhouses in Ontario (Dodd 1984, 270).

The length of longhouses varies considerably, even for contemporaneous structures on the same site. Length is understood to be a function of the number of families (Tuck 1971, 30; Kuhn et al. 1997). Length doubles from the Owasco to Iroquois periods. The Onondaga territory contained the longest houses yet discovered in the Five Nations. Tuck noted a 334-foot-long house at Howlett Hill (c. A.D. 1380) and a 410-foot-long house at Schoff (c. A.D. 1410) (1971, 79, 96). Seneca structures appear shorter than those on Onondaga sites for any given period (Niemczycki 1984, 92). It is not known whether this difference in length is a result of sampling problems or of a possible difference in social or political organization. Very long longhouses probably housed members of a clan segment, rather than lineage, as it is unlikely that all female residents of a three-hundred-foot longhouse were closely related biologically.

---

4. George Hamell (personal communication) cautions that because of its linear growth, cedar does not have the advantage of natural "forks" or "crotches." Using cedar, one would either have to use "forks" formed by sturdy lateral branches or one would have to "saddle notch" the top of the cedar post to receive a load-bearing horizontal member.

A trend toward longer houses in the thirteenth and fourteenth centuries appears to be associated with increases in the size of the population in general and the community in particular (Tuck 1978, 328; Warrick 1996, 16). Clustering of populations in larger communities in the Mohawk Valley in the mid-fifteenth century also correlates with longer longhouses in that region (Snow 1995a, 46).

It is assumed that the longest structures in a village were inhabited by chiefs and their families. Such houses were used for political meetings as well as ceremonies (Thwaites 1896–1901, 10:181; Kapches 1993, 156; Warrick 1996, 11, 19; Tooker 1970).[5] The 334-foot-long house at Howlett Hill (Onondaga) was probably used in this manner (see fig. 38). Over a football field in length, such a monumental structure must have impressed visitors as well as reinforced the power of any chief living within (Kapches 1993, 156).

The structure at Howlett Hill contained an additional door on the west side, exactly 167 feet from each end (Tuck 1971, 79). Side doors on very long houses also occur in Ontario.[6] In addition to being convenient for residents living toward the center of this structure, it would have permitted visitors direct access to the area where political councils or ceremonies were being conducted (Kapches 1994b).

The most important calendrical ceremonial observance of the Iroquois today is that of Midwinter. This took place at a time in the annual cycle when all members of a longhouse would have been in residence. Anyone familiar with weather in upstate New York would agree that this would not have been a good time to schedule an outdoor ceremony. Very long longhouses provided the community with ritual space analogous to the ceremonial square ground in the Southeast or plazas in Mississippian and Mesoamerican societies.[7]

Toward the end of the fifteenth century, the average length of longhouses decreases (Prezzano 1992, 271). This trend continues into the sixteenth century (Warrick 1996, 19). Gary Warrick hypothesizes that this is related to clan segments becoming important in village politics rather than matrilineages (1996, 21). While membership in a longhouse matrilineage is precisely determined, membership in a clan segment provides for more flexible "packaging" of individuals.

Occasionally, archaeologists find post molds suggesting that the end of a longhouse wall was inside a structure. When

---

5. Another critical variable for ceremonies may actually be greater width. J. V. Wright (1974, 52, 307) argues that House 10 at Nodwell functioned as the place for public gathering because of its greater width and greater square footage, even though House 8 was longer.

6. Moyer (no. 4) (Wagner, Toombs and Reigert 1973) and Draper (nos. 4, 6, 10, 11) (Finlayson, 1985, cited in Kapches 1994b).

7. Tooker (1960) argues that calendrical ceremonies such as Midwinter were not as important as shamanic rituals to earlier Iroquois. Witthoft (1949, 20) argues that longhouses are replaced by outdoor ceremonial grounds as one moves south.

Fig. 38. Structures at
Howlett Hill. Post molds
are marked by stakes.
From Tuck 1971, 82.

these post molds overlap hearths or storage pits, they are believed to represent the former ends of longhouses that were extended in length later.[8] Among the Iroquois, the phrase "extending the rafters" came to mean not only the addition of new individuals to a longhouse but also the addition or adoption of new groups into Iroquois society.

Distinguishing a house extension from a house contraction would be difficult, but the latter possibility should be kept in mind. Fluctuations in the number of surviving female children in a lineage or clan segment could cause the length of a longhouse to be obsolete within a generation.

The ends of longhouses are frequently difficult to recover archaeologically, apparently because the posts were not driven as

deeply into the subsoil as side wall posts. They did not need to be, as they were not weight-bearing (Latta 1985, 48). Because of this construction, it is possible that longhouse expansion and contraction was more frequent than is represented in the archaeological record. Lafitau notes that the ends were used for storage in winter, but were opened for ventilation in summer (1977, 21). It is possible that what was opened was a porchlike addition. These porches had low, flat roofs, and on hot summer nights people slept on mats on the porch roofs (Lafitau 1977, 19–22). How common these additions might have been on New York Iroquois longhouses is not clear.

Most early longhouses had rounded ends. Later Mohawk structures retained the rounded end while houses of the other nations became more square-ended (Tuck 1971, 159; Ritchie and Funk 1973, 363). In particular, many historic Seneca structures had squared ends (Prezzano 1992,

8. Examples of longhouse extensions include Garoga, House 5 (Funk 1973, 319, 331) and Howlett Hill, House 2 (Tuck 1971, 85).

276). Doorways were at the ends with a width of about two-and-one-half feet.[9]

At the ends of a few houses, archaeologists have observed a row of post molds that may represent a wind baffle to protect the doorway (Whitney 1970, 3; Funk 1973, 319; Pratt and Pratt 1998). Alternatively, in some cases this row may mark the actual curved end of the longhouse, rather than a flatter end expected by some excavators (Hosbach 1997).

It is commonly assumed that longhouses were oriented in the direction of the prevailing wind in order to provide the least wind resistance. A rounded longhouse end provides far less resistance than a high bark-covered side one hundred or more feet long. In summer, this orientation would offer increased ventilation, especially if the ends were removed. In case of a longhouse conflagration, orientation with the prevailing wind could lessen the likelihood of the fire spreading to adjacent structures. However, an examination of fifty-two longhouses in the Mohawk region dating to before A.D. 1650 indicated that only thirty of these were oriented west-northwest (Kuhn et al. 1997).

This suggests that while wind direction may have played a role in longhouse orientation, it was not the only consideration. Space limitations on hilltops, microclimatic effects, and slope are other variables that could affect orientation. Where a slope is present, longhouses would be expected to be oriented downhill to facilitate water runoff (Latta 1985, 43).[10] A sample of more than two hundred longhouses in Ontario revealed little association between wind direction and orientation, suggesting that other factors were more important (Warrick 1984, 27).

As J. V. Wright has wryly observed, "Attempting to reconstruct longhouses by simply looking at dots on an archaeological floor plan has its limitations" (1995, 20). This is especially true regarding height and roof structure, but potential plans have been put forward. Historic accounts describe longhouses as being as tall as they were wide (Wright 1995, 15).

Large internal support posts supported the weight of the structure. Pairs of these vertical posts, along with a horizontal member, formed what J. V. Wright has referred to as a pi frame, after the shape of the Greek letter (1995). The literature on longhouse construction describes two alternative building techniques using this frame (Prezzano 1992, 287; see fig. 39). In the version favored by J. V. Wright, the roof was formed of a separate set of poles attached to this frame. In this design, the exterior side walls would not be weight-bearing. This type of construction was apparently described by Lafitau and Bartram (Prezzano 1992, 287).

Kapches describes a structure in which the external poles are bent over and lashed

---

9. This is the width of a door recorded by Tuck (1971, 59) for a longhouse at Furnace Brook.

10. A McIvor site longhouse is an exception, being built laterally across a slope (J. V. Wright, personal communication).

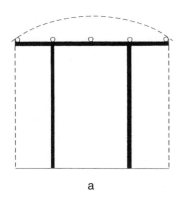

a                                    b

Fig. 39. Two alternative longhouse construction options. The pi-frame is shown in black. J. V. Wright argues for option a (in Wright 1995, 13).

together at the top, reinforced by internal vertical support poles and cross braces (1993, 146–47; see fig. 39b). This type was apparently described by van der Donck for the seventeenth-century Mohawk (Prezzano 1992, 287) and conforms to many people's idea of how longhouses were constructed. However, George Hamell suggests that van der Donck's description of Mohawk longhouse construction may have been generalized from those of the Mahican and Munsee Algonquians with whom he was more familiar (personal communication). Wright persuasively argues that large posts could not be bent over in this fashion and that this design is not feasible (1995).

Structures were covered with bark. Cedar bark appears to have been preferred by the Hurons, though elm, ash, and other barks were used (Heidenreich 1971, 120). J. V. Wright argues that elm bark was well suited to roofing because of its strength and thickness. Also, the inner surface of elm bark that formed the longhouse ceiling is less flammable than that of cedar (Wright 1995, 18). Bark for the structure could have been secured from the timbers used for the frame (Jemison and White 1997).

In addition to removing bark from poles used for building, bark could have been harvested from trees as a way of killing them to prepare new fields (Wright 1995, 19). Basswood fiber could have been secured in the same manner. It was harvested by peeling bark to get at the cambium layer. This fiber was used to tie the bark to the framework as well as to lash cross pieces to the upright posts.

Bark is easiest to remove from trees when the sap is running in May and June (Fenton 1978, 301; Finlayson 1998, 51). In 1724, Lafitau observed sheets of bark being prepared for future use, first by removing the rough outer surface and then by stacking the sheets so that they dried without warping (Lafitau 1977, 20). Huron linguistic evidence suggests that the bark used for the roof was made more pliable by warming with water before being used (Steckley 1987, 30). Beauchamp translates the Onondaga name for Butternut Creek as "bark in the water," suggesting that bark was stored there until needed for repairs (1905, 107). Some antler and stone chisels found on Iroquois sites could have been used in peeling bark, while antler or bone awls could have served to perforate the bark so that it could be tied onto the frame (Ritchie 1953, 5).

Lafitau implies that the bark sheets were placed on the longhouse framework horizontally (1977, 20). The rough outer bark was probably planed or adzed away, promoting water runoff. Horizontal placement would allow the bark sheets to span the vertical members to which they were attached and would counter the tendency of the bark sheets to curl. If the rough outer surface were not removed from the bark sheets, then it would make more sense to orient the bark sheets vertically on the sides and roofs of the longhouses as the texture of the bark would then facilitate water runoff. However, the problem of the bark tending to curl along its vertical axis would remain.[11]

There were smoke holes cut in the roof that could be closed in inclement weather by using long poles (Ritchie and Funk 1973, 299; Wright 1995, 16). They, along with open doors, would have provided the only natural light (Lafitau 1977, 19–22). Champlain states that the smokey interiors caused many individuals to have eye problems (Biggar 1971, 314).

Walls are often represented archaeologically by a row of paired staggered post molds. It is generally assumed that the outer posts formed a second frame that held the bark shingles in place (Prezzano 1992, 287, 290; Snow 1997, 82). Paul

Lennox suggests that poles were laid horizontally between the two rows of upright posts, forming a substantial wall (1984, 16). Alternatively, staggered posts may have served to attach a double layer of bark at least part of the way up the structure, possibly with insulating moss in between the layers (Mohawk 1994, 153; J. V. Wright, personal communication). In Ontario and the Niagara Frontier region of western New York, shallow wall trenches are found associated with the exterior posts (Kapches 1980). These may have allowed bark sheathing to be covered with soil. Wall trenches were not used in the Five Nations Iroquois area.

In 1634, Van den Bogaert observed animals painted on the gables of houses (Gehring and Starna 1988, 8). These are assumed to be representations of matrilineal clan affiliation. Such symbols would have served to inform visiting Iroquois where they might find hospitality with members of their clan (Richter 1992, 21). At a more abstract level, such symbols serve as "social boundary communication" differentiating social groups, especially common in situations where there is involvement in trade beyond the local community (Blanton 1994, 11, 122).

## The Interior

Longhouses were entered through a doorway that could be closed with a moveable sheet of bark or reed mats (Sagard-Théodat 1968, 102). In winter, skins were used for additional protection (Lafitau

---

11. I am indebted to George Hamell for the discussion of the placement of bark sheets.

1977, 19–22). The Huron language distinguished between this outer door and an inner door leading to the living area (Steckley 1987, 23). A visitor would pass through the end storage or "porch" area, containing large bark casks of dried and shelled corn, firewood, and mats (Grant 1907, 314; Lafitau 1977, 21; Prezzano 1992, 284; Snow 1997). At Furnace Brook (Onondaga), Tuck uncovered small post molds two to four feet inside the ends of longhouses, suggesting narrow storage areas (1971, 59).

Entering the second interior doorway, one would be in the living area, with a wide corridor down the center and hearths centrally located about every twenty feet. These were shared by two families, one on either side (Wright 1995, 16; Snow 1995a, 45). Relatively few interior partitions have been identified in New York longhouses. It is possible that a pair of the large pi frames supporting the structure also defined a living compartment (Hosbach 1997).

Commonly, families shared sleeping platforms or berths along each wall. From historic descriptions, we know these were set about a foot above the ground, high enough to avoid the damp ground but low enough to minimize exposure to smoke (Fenton 1978, 303; Snow 1997, 70). Father Joseph Lafitau in 1724 describes them as follows: "These platforms, shut in on all sides except that of the fire, serve them as beds and benches to sit on. Reed mats and fur pelts cover the bark which forms the floor of the berthes" (Lafitau 1977, 20–21). Snow argues that these berths

took up between half and two-thirds of the length of a family's compartment (Snow 1995a, 126; 1997, 70). There would, therefore, have been room at either end of these berths for additional storage of corn, mats, and firewood as well as hides and furs (Lafitau 1977, 19–22).

Two forms of hearths are found in longhouses: deep basin-shaped depressions and shallow areas of ash or fire-reddened subsoil (Tuck 1971, 112; Ritchie and Funk 1973, 264). Snow suggests that the deeper hearths were used for cooking, some serving as roasting pits (1995a, 128–29). The shallow hearths found inside longhouses are diffuse in outline, the location of the fire apparently shifting (Tuck 1971, 112; Snow 1995a, 128). Following Le Jeune's observation in the *Jesuit Relations* of "fires according to the season of the year" (10:251), Snow argues that these shallow hearths functioned in winter primarily for heating (1995a, 129). Champlain noted that in winter Hurons slept on mats near the fire rather than in the berths (quoted in Grant 1959, 314).

In a cross-cultural study of houses, Richard Blanton has observed that domestic structures frequently contain a feature or space that serves to connect residents with supernatural forces (1994, 80). In 1650, Adriaen van der Donck observed carved images within neighboring Algonquian houses that probably functioned in this manner (Kraft 1996, 88). In similar fashion, Krusche argues that carved poles were often placed inside Iroquois longhouses (1986, 25–27). Snow thinks such

posts were present at the Elwood, Otstungo, and Garoga sites (1995a, 100,
124; 1997, 76). Some large post molds at
these sites were filled with cultural debris,
suggesting that the post was removed upon
abandonment of the longhouse. Large interior posts probably had a longer use life
than exterior posts, as their bases would
have stayed drier and hence less subject to
dry rot (Sohrweide 2001, 9). Typically,
posts were left in place.

## Storage

In 1632 Sagard wrote that corn husks were
tied back and the ears hung from a rack
"like tapestry draped the whole length of
the lodge" (Sagard-Théodat 1968, 104).
When dry, the corn was shelled and stored
in large casks at the ends of the longhouse,
or in an unused space. Crops are less likely
to rot if stored above ground than in pits,
and are also more readily accessible (Prezzano 1992, 315–16). One could argue that
longhouses were built as much to house
the "three sisters" as members of the matrilineage or clan segment. After a good harvest, longhouses must have been like huge
horizontal silos, filled with maize, beans,
squash, and other foodstuffs.

At the Mohawk Garoga site, 80 percent of the storage pits at the site were
found inside longhouses, generally under
berths or areas away from the main aisle.
Only a portion of these may have been in
use at any one time. Some cylindrical pits
were over two meters deep and a meter or
so wide (Onion 1964; Snow 1995a, 150).
William Ritchie observed that an adult
would have had difficulty excavating such
deep and relatively narrow pits, and he pos-
tulated that these might have been excavated by children (Onion 1964, 64). Snow
notes that Garoga longhouses lack end
storage compartments, and suggests that
the extensive use of pits inside structures
was a space-saving device on a site where
population was "tightly packed" (1995a,
164). Alternatively, crops stored in pits are
protected from the accidental fires that
were a common concern.

While either crowding or fear of fire
may explain the presence of the storage pits
at Garoga, in general the presence of numerous deep storage pits on some sites, especially Mohawk, and their general
absence on Seneca, Cayuga, and Onondaga sites remains unexplained (Ritchie
1973, 298; Prezzano 1992, 294). If the
village were temporarily abandoned after
the harvest and before the next summer,
crops would have to be concealed and protected in subsurface pits (DeBoer 1988;
Prezzano 1992, 315–16). On the other
hand, if even a few members of each longhouse were in continuous residence, crops
could be stored above ground within the
longhouse. In December of 1634, van den
Bogaert observed Mohawk houses full of
corn while most of the inhabitants were
away hunting deer and bear (Gehring and
Starna 1988, 4). Father Frémin was later to
observe a similar pattern among the Seneca
(Thwaites 1896–1901 54:117; Abler
1970, 33).

In 1616, Champlain observed that the
Huron suspended clothing and provisions
from interior poles to keep them dry and

away from mice (Grant 1907, 314). Smoked fish were also stored in bark casks (Biggar 1971, 3:122–25) or suspended from the rafters (Tooker 1970). Firewood was kept under the berths. In summer, corn husk slippers might be placed under the berths while people slept (Fenton 1978, 303).[12] Occasionally important personal items were buried in small pits in the longhouse, which protected them from fire and theft (Lafitau 1977, 22; Sagard-Théodat 1968, 91–95).

Space above the berth was also used for storage, including wood and bark dishes and household utensils (Lafitau 1977, 19–22; Fenton 1978, 303). Dishes and utensils were constructed from materials at hand. The occasional use of the carapace of the box turtle as a bowl dates back to the Owasco period (Ritchie 1980, 280). Spoons or ladles were described as being as large as a small dish (Sagard-Théodat 1968, 72). These were sometimes cut from deer skulls or formed from turkey breast bones (Ritchie 1953, 9). The Garoga site has yielded fragments of pottery ladles (W. Lenig n.d.). Surviving wooden ladles from the seventeenth century onward often reflect considerable artistic ability (Prisch 1982).

## Household Activities

Longhouses were used for sleeping and many other activities from late fall through early spring. It is assumed that in milder weather many household activities took place outside. Unfortunately, conditions for the preservation of organic material on Iroquois sites are generally poor, so many activities are not reflected archaeologically. More sophisticated archaeological excavation and analysis is needed to refine our picture of where and when various activities were carried out in a village.

Corn required processing before it was eaten. To remove the outer seed coat or hull from corn kernels prior to pounding into flour or making soup, the kernels were boiled in water with wood ashes. The kernels were then placed in a sievelike washing or hulling basket that was then dunked and twirled in water to separate the hulls from the kernels (Parker 1968, 49–50; Waugh 1973, 61–62; see fig. 40). This alkali treatment with wood ashes also serves to enhance the nutritional quality of the maize, increasing the amount of lysine as well as niacin that can be metabolized (Katz et al. 1974). The widespread distribution of this technique among maize-growing cultures in North America argues for its early diffusion (Katz et al. 1974, 772).

Corn was pounded in a wooden mortar with a large wooden pestle (see fig. 41) or was ground between a large flat stone and a smaller one held in the hand.[13] Corn dishes were prepared in a variety of ways. To make corn bread, bark fans were used to

---

12. The Iroquois are the only people in the Northeast known to have worn twined corn-husk slippers in summer.

13. The wooden mortars were hollowed out by burning, the charred wood being scraped away. This was the same method used in making dugout canoes (Beauchamp 1905, 91).

Fig. 40. Washing corn. Painting by Ernie Smith. Courtesy of the Rochester Museum and Science Center, Rochester, N.Y.

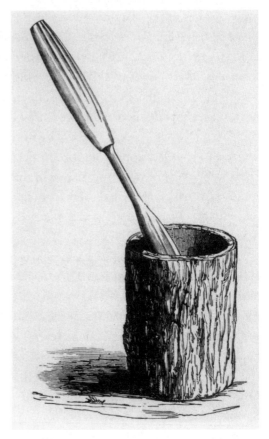

Fig. 41. Corn mortar and pounder (Morgan 1962, 371).

winnow the seed coats from the kernels (Grant 1907, 314). In addition to water, beans, blueberries, dry raspberries or even deer fat might then be added. Loaves were then baked in the coals of a fire (Grant 1907, 314–15).

If corn was to be used for soup, a few handfuls of pounded corn along with the bran were placed with water in a pot and cooked at a hearth. The pot was stirred from time to time and chunks of meat and fish were sometimes added, as were beans and squash (Grant 1907, 315). Squash was also cooked whole in the coals (Thwaites 1896–1901, 10:103; 15:161–62). Most historic accounts of the Iroquois indicate that they ate one primary meal during the day, but that family members could help themselves from a pot near the fire when hungry. Pits containing large quantities of fire-altered rock served to roast large game.

Early European visitors remarked on the fact that food was always shared, and that no one in a longhouse or village went hungry as long as food was available. If a house burned, residents of other houses would assist those who had lost their home and stored food. The Iroquois regularly provided food and lodging to visitors, and thought European colonists rude when they did not return this hospitality.

Van den Bogaert states that in an Oneida chief's house, there were three or four daily meals (Gehring and Starna 1988,

6). In 1634 at the time of his visit, most Oneida had never seen a European, so it is probable that his presence prompted feasting in addition to the usual Iroquois hospitality. He ate bear meat, beaver, venison, and hare cooked with chestnuts, in addition to various corn breads baked with dried blueberries, sunflower seeds, chestnuts, beans, and pumpkins (Gehring and Starna 1988, 6, 12, 21).

The Iroquois were able to start a fire by striking chert against iron pyrites, creating a spark that ignited tinder. Heavily battered chert objects have been traditionally identified as "strike-a-lights," but these may be misidentified. Experimentation suggests that fire starters may look more like a scraper with a damaged edge (Jack Holland, personal communication). Morgan also describes and illustrates the use of a bow drill to create friction for starting fires (1962, 381–82; see fig. 42).

Mats were made of corn husks or rushes, and these were put on the longhouse roofs and floors (Thwaites 1896–1901 42:205; 58:209; 59:129, 133, 155; Monckton 1992, 55). The term for corn husk mat is reconstructible for the proto-Five Nations language, implying antiquity for this item of material culture (Mithun 1984, 279). Mississauga women to the north wove mats with dyed reeds (Sagard-Théodat 1968, 102).

Flat bone mat needles with rounded ends and a center perforation are known from a number of Iroquois sites (Tuck 1971, 76, 89, 158; Wray et al. 1991, 235). Their shape suggests a weaving rather than

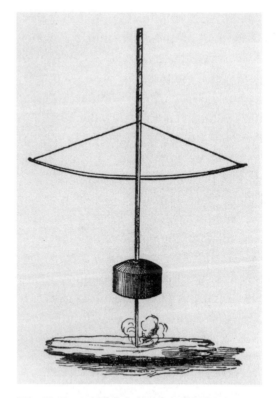

Fig. 42. Bow drill for starting a fire (Morgan 1962, 381).

sewing function (Wray et al. 1991, 235). Forty-six examples were recovered from the Onondaga Barnes site (Tuck 1971, 158). Perforated deer ribs were apparently also used as weaving tools for making mats (Ritchie 1980, 277). At the Hubbert site (Ontario, early fifteenth century), bone awls and bodkins were more common inside longhouses than elsewhere, suggesting that utilitarian tasks were being performed inside (Thomas 1997).

European visitors to longhouses found them to be crowded, dark and smoky, with dogs, mice, and fleas also in residence (Thwaites 1896–1901, 8:95, 105–7;

10:35; Warrick 1996, 12). Archaeological excavation of these structures generally does not yield a great deal of debris, suggesting that the Iroquois, like most people, regularly cleaned their living areas, especially of broken pottery (Schiffer 1987, 59; Prezzano 1992, 329, 368–69). Faithkeepers would go from house to house at the start of the Midwinter ceremony admonishing, "Prepare your houses. Clear away the rubbish" (Morgan 1962, 209). Artifacts found in the interiors of houses tend to be found along walls and in corners. Debris may have accumulated under berths. Ethnoarchaeological studies suggest that often objects are kicked away from heavily used areas (Hayden 1982, 48; Schiffer 1987, 63; Snow 1995a, 127; Prezzano 1992, 321).

If a longhouse were destroyed by fire, material not retrieved afterward would be expected to be where it was last used or discarded, rather than being swept up. Gary Warrick's analysis of burned longhouses revealed more chert cores and stone tool manufacturing debris present than in houses in the same Ontario Iroquoian site that were not burned, suggesting that some stone tool manufacture took place inside longhouses (1984, 94). Susan Prezzano's analysis of debitage and broken points caught along the end walls of the early longhouse at Boland supports Warrick's conclusion (1992, 435). If men were the primary makers of formal stone tools, as is commonly assumed, this is not surprising. Men were most likely in residence in the village during the most in-

clement weather and likely to carry out tool manufacture and repair indoors.

## Ceramics

Potsherds are one of the most commonly recovered artifacts from the excavation of Iroquois village sites (Tuck 1978, 329). More than any other artifact, they symbolize the household and female activity. They are also the most commonly studied Iroquois artifact. The styles of pottery found on sites vary over time and from area to area. The study of this variability and the meaning that can be attached to it has occupied generations of archaeologists.

Since each pot is handmade, no two Iroquois pots are identical. Within a community, however, pottery styles tend to fall into a limited number of broadly defined types. It is possible that Iroquois women worked together while making pottery, and ethnographic studies indicate that individuals who work together in decorating pottery tend to produce a similar product (Braun and Plog 1982, 510).

Based on Sagard's early seventeenth-century description of Huron pottery manufacture, it is assumed that women were the potters in Iroquoian culture (Sagard-Théodat 1968, 109). It is also assumed that ceramic production was relatively unspecialized, with women in each household manufacturing pottery (Warrick 1984, 110; Allen 1992). Clay deposits are relatively common in New York, and in most cases women would not have had to travel far from the village to obtain clay. At the Mohawk village site of Garoga, pits probably dug for clay were found on flat ground below the village (Snow 1995a, 147).

Before being shaped into a vessel, the clay was processed by removing impurities. Crushed rock particles called grit were added to give additional strength to the clay while the vessel was being constructed and to prevent cracking during firing. If the clay were dried before being shaped into a vessel, water was added to achieve the necessary pliability. Water would also have been used during the process of vessel formation to smooth the surface of the vessel or to prevent it from sticking to working surfaces.

Pottery precedes maize horticulture in New York. Pots changed over time from large, thick-walled containers to smaller, thin-walled containers that were more efficient cooking vessels. Thinner walls increase thermal conductivity and thermal shock resistance, producing a more efficient and longer-lasting cooking vessel (Braun 1983; Brumbach 1995, 64).

Like later Iroquoian pottery, most Owasco ceramics appear to have been formed by modeling clay into shape and using a paddle and anvil, rather than adding on coil strips. Perhaps as a consequence of this method of construction, vessel bases are customarily the thickest part of the pot. The base of a broken pot or the base of a large dried gourd could have supported the pot as it was constructed, allowing the pot to be turned as the potter built the pot upwards. For larger vessels, the base could have been set in a depression

in sand lined with fabric, as the eastern Cherokee did (Harrington 1909, 224–25). Before firing, pots must be dried. The Iroquois and other Northeast peoples did not use kilns, so the pottery was fired at a relatively low temperature in an open fire. Since firing of vessels would have created unwanted smoke and posed a fire hazard, firing was probably done outside away from the houses (Kapches 1994a, 94, 101).

Vessels are earth colored, the final color being determined by both the clay and the firing atmosphere. The pots were fired upside down. The soot that gathered inside the pot usually left the interior darker than the exterior (Peter Pratt, personal communication). Pots often have a mottled appearance with dark areas (fire clouds) as a result of drafts or contact with the fuel. The archaeological context from which ceramics were recovered also affects the color we see today. In some cases, different colored potsherds have been fitted together, the different colors resulting from different depositional contexts.[14]

Summer was probably the best time to make pottery (Allen and Zubrow 1989). Clay is more pliable when it is warm, making summer the best time to secure the clay

14. A few early Iroquoian pots were decorated with a band of red or black paint. George Hamell reminded me of a few sherds from the Footer site [Seneca] while J. V. Wright called my attention to black bands of paint about one inch wide on the necks of a few Uren and Middleport vessels in Ontario.

and shape it. Drying pots before firing is most efficiently carried out in the summer under conditions of low humidity. Finally, firing is most successful under conditions of low wind and no precipitation (Allen and Zubrow 1989). Evidence for ceramic production sites is difficult to recover archaeologically, however, and in some cases it may have been overlooked.[15]

We do not know how many pots an Iroquois family had at any time or how long they lasted. A survey of the ethnographic literature suggests four to five pots of varying size per family with a use life of six months to three years (Schiffer 1987, 49; Warrick 1988, 30; Allen 1992).[16] If we assume each family "consumed" three pots per year, then a longhouse with six families would need 18 pots every year, or 180 over a ten-year period. While this is only a rough estimate, it points to the importance of ceramic production.

It is assumed that the primary function of most Owasco and Iroquois ceramic containers was cooking. Dishes for individuals were made of wood or bark. Sometimes carbonized food remains have adhered to the interior of pots. These organic residues can be dated and have the potential for being analyzed to determine the identity of the food. The Iroquois also used pots to brew various teas from plants including hemlock, maple, and sassafras (Morgan 1962, 330). A separate pot may have been used for boiling tea from one for cooking food (Allen 1992). Occasionally pots are found in small pits, generally within longhouses, and it is assumed that they were being used for storage (Funk 1973, 324). A comparative study of such vessels might indicate whether storage was a primary or secondary function.

Owasco pots were generally large, holding between two to twelve gallons (Ritchie 1980, 291). The vessel bases were pointed and the rims were flared and non-collared above a constricted neck (Ritchie 1953, 10). The surface treatment of the body of the pot was formed by pressing a cord-wrapped paddle onto the wet clay, while the top part of the pot was decorated with a cord-wrapped stick design (Ritchie 1953, 10). Cord marking as a decorative technique was used for a longer time on pots than on ceramic pipes, the latter presumably manufactured by men (Boucher 1883; Ritchie 1980, 303–4). Careful study of corded impressions on ceramics can reveal aspects of cord technology, such as the direction of the twist, which appears to be culturally determined (Carr and Maslowski 1995, 321).

In eastern New York, Oak Hill ceramics (c. A.D. 1350–1400) have attributes of both Owasco and Iroquois pottery. Vessels have collars, an Iroquoian trait, with corded designs, an Owasco technique. Incising as a decorative technique on collars

15. See Kapches (1994a) for an Ontario example.

16. Warrick (1988) estimates three years and Allen (1992) two years for the use-life of an Iroquoian pot.

appears earlier in the Genesee region, perhaps as a consequence of contact with Ontario Iroquois populations to the west (Niemczycki 1986, 37; Dodd et al. 1990, 330). While some Iroquois pots are noncollared with a thickened lip, most have collars with incised decoration. Iroquois pot shape shifted from high-collared vessels in the fifteenth century to lower-collared vessels in the sixteenth and early seventeenth centuries. Designs on the surface of the pots consist of straight lines arranged in vertical, horizontal, or oblique patterns. Curvilinear designs are absent, and some designs bear a resemblance to the kind found on basketry or early porcupine-quill work.

During the course of the sixteenth century, pots tend to become more round (Tuck 1978, 329). While there is variability in size, smaller pots with thinner walls become common, a form more resistant to thermal shock and more efficient for cooking corn soup or corn mush (Braun 1983; Chilton 1998, 152). The small size of these pots would have made cooking large game or fish impossible (Latta 1991, 379). Game animals were probably roasted or cooked over the fire. There are some larger vessels that were presumably used for feasting. The Onondaga had separate terms for large and small pots (Waugh 1973, 57).

While the majority of vessels on Iroquois sites are collared, noncollared vessels with a thickened lip are universally distributed, sometimes constituting over 20 percent of an assemblage (Bradley 1987, 121,

Niemczycki 1984, 48). Why this distinction was maintained over the entire Five Nations is not known. Preliminary analysis suggests that noncollared vessels often lack evidence of carbonized food remains, suggesting that they were used for storage or tea brewing. Pots may also have been used as water drums or for water scrying, a form of divination. However, it seems likely that only a few vessels would be needed for these latter purposes.

Patricia Galloway hypothesizes that where menstrual structures are absent, a distinctive ceramic assemblage that served as "menstrual ware" might be present (1997, 57–61). Iroquois women did not retire to separate menstrual structures but rather cooked food for themselves during their menses in small pots (Sagard-Théodat 1968, 67). Small cooking pots have been recovered from a number of Iroquois sites as well as graves of females. They typically hold about 1.5 liters, which may be taken as a typical serving size (Snow 1994b, 107). Regular cooking pots generally hold five times that volume, and Snow has suggested this implies an average family size of five (Snow 1994b, 107).

In a pioneering study of Owasco and Iroquois ceramics, Robert Whallon noted that over time, more clearly defined types and more homogeneous pottery was manufactured, a trend that he related to an increasing emphasis on matrilocality and the growth of matrilineal descent groups (1968, 240). Mima Kapches came to a similar conclusion regarding the development

Fig. 43. Effigy from ceramic vessel, Richmond Mills site (Seneca). The height is about 2.7 cm. Drawing by Gene Mackay; photograph by Jack Williams. Courtesy of the Rochester Museum and Science Center, Rochester, N.Y.

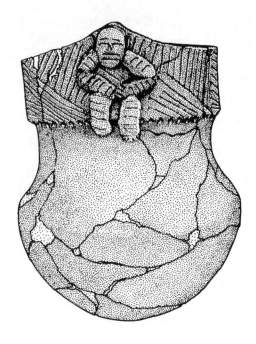

Fig. 44. Ceramic vessel with full-figure effigy under castellation, Adams site (Seneca). The height of the pot to the noncastellated portion of the rim is about 19 cm. From Wray et al. 1987, 88. Courtesy of the Rochester Museum and Science Center, Rochester, N.Y.

of matrilocality from studying changes in the use of space in longhouses (1990).

When archaeologists study ceramics, they typically impose their own analytic categories on the material. While these analytic categories vary depending on the problem and the researcher, they may not correspond with those of the native makers and users of the object. Similarly, researchers make educated guesses as to the cultural significance of the object. Alternative suggestions are always possible. Such is the case with effigy faces.

During the sixteenth century, human face effigies appear on New York ceramics, almost always placed under a castellation (see fig. 43).[17]

While not restricted to Five Nations Iroquois pottery, they appear to be most common on Onondaga and Oneida ceram-

17. J. V. Wright (personal communication) notes their earlier appearance in Ontario on Pickering ceramics, such as those from the Boys and Bennett sites. A vessel with effigy faces was also recovered from a tenth-century ossuary on the North Branch of the Susquehanna River near Forty Fort, Pennsylvania (James Adovasio, personal communication).

ics. Full-figure effigies begin to replace face effigies toward the end of the century (see fig. 44). The limbs of these figures are marked with ladderlike incisions (Bradley 1987, 55; Wonderley n.d.). Similar vertical ladderlike incisions are sometimes found as ceramic decoration under castellations without effigies. Where this decoration appears on St. Lawrence Iroquois pottery on vertical ridges around the rim, it is referred to as the "corn ear" motif.

Anthony Wonderley (n.d.) has suggested that the face effigies and full-figure effigies may represent Cornhusk people, mythical humanlike horticulturalists associated with food crops and impersonated in historic times by men wearing husk face masks pretending to be Husk Face women (Wallace 1972, 54). Husk Face people were led by women, and it was women who made and used the pottery and raised the crops. The corn ear motif found on St. Lawrence Iroquois pottery may have had similar symbolism. More than decoration, these depictions suggest giving thanks and invoking good will and protection (Whitney 1974, 9; Wonderley n.d.).[18]

While cooking pots are typically viewed by us today as humble, everyday objects, to the Iroquois they stood as symbols of family and hospitality (Fenton 1978, 303; Dennis 1993, 87). Ceramics were made from clay, which came from "Mother Earth." Women shaped this clay into culturally prescribed forms. Fire then transformed these clay forms into ceramics, just as it transformed the contents of cooking pots into edible food. Human or corn effigies on these containers may have served as a visual form of thanksgiving for the gift of corn, beans, and squash.

18. Another possibility is that the markings represent tattooing (Tom Abler, personal communication).

# ❖ 5 ❖

# THE VILLAGE

## Development

The term "village" has been used loosely by archaeologists to refer to any large site. Only a small fraction of such sites have been systematically excavated in New York. It is therefore probable that some sites now classified as village sites were actually recurrently occupied camps used for some specific purpose like fishing or chert procurement.

Typical Iroquois villages consisted of longhouses surrounded by palisades. They are frequently located on hilltops or other defensible terrain. It is assumed that after a period of ten or more years a community moved to a new location.

Since few Iroquois village sites in New York have been totally excavated, it is difficult to generalize about their internal structure. Furthermore, changes may have occurred in the structure of a village during its occupation. The village plans that are published are based on the observation and excavation of post molds and other features. These present a static picture of village structure. Yet each village had its own

"life history," undergoing expansion or contraction and episodes of rebuilding as needed.

It was maize, a storable resource, that facilitated village life. Longhouses and stockaded villages, like maize, first appear adjacent to the New York Iroquois. In Ontario, these elements are present at the ninth-century occupations of the Porteous and Miller sites (Kenyon 1968; Stothers 1977; Prezzano 1992, 435–37). Between A.D. 900 and 1000, the Ontario Glen Meyer (southwestern Ontario) and Pickering (south-central Ontario) cultures attest to the spread of longhouses, villages, and maize.

In New York, nucleated villages first appear south of the Five Nations core area in the upper Susquehanna drainage. Boland is an example of such early fortified communities and may be thought of as marking the beginning of settled horticultural village life in New York (Prezzano 1992, iv; 1996, 10). To the west, more than twenty Iroquoian sites have been found in the floodplain of the Allegheny River. While little is known about most of these, the Kinzua site (36Wa52) is both early and stockaded (Dragoo 1976, 77–79).

Between A.D. 1100 and 1200, villages in the Susquehanna drainage shift from the floodplain to more elevated positions, less subject to flooding and more easily defended (Prezzano 1992, 438). Storage pits are larger and deeper. An example is the Bates site (c. A.D. 1190), a fortified hamlet on a terrace of the Chenango River (Ritchie 1973, 225–52). It consisted of a single longhouse that underwent a series of expansions (Ritchie 1973, 232). Presumably females sharing this structure considered themselves to be members of the same kin group. After about A.D. 1300, the upper Susquehanna Valley is largely abandoned until the early eighteenth century (Prezzano 1992, 403).

In both New York and Ontario, there is a trend over time toward larger communities (Ritchie and Funk 1973, 364; Tuck 1978, 328). Some Oak Hill (c. A.D. 1350–1400) phase sites in the Mohawk Valley may have consisted of single structures like the earlier Bates site (Bamann 1993, 23), but villages with multiple structures were generally present across Iroquoia by this time (Warrick 1996, 15).

From the fourteenth through the sixteenth centuries, sites become larger in part through the merging of smaller communities (Tuck 1971, 225; Bamann 1993, 21). Sites are increasingly located on hilltops rather than river valleys, suggesting defense as a major concern (Tuck 1978,

326; Richter 1992, 17; Hasenstab 1996, 22). These villages are presumed to consist of multiple structures, each inhabited by a clan segment or lineage. The shift to nucleated sites on defensible terrain occurs in the fifteenth century in the Mohawk area (Bamann 1993, 29). The sites of Getman and Elwood may be taken as typical, with one hundred to two hundred people living in three to six houses (Snow 1995a, 90).

It is in the sixteenth century that large villages of eight to ten acres appear, perhaps accommodating up to two thousand individuals (Ritchie and Funk 1973, 363; Bamann et al. 1992, 450). They represent the nucleation of smaller communities into a few core villages (Hasenstab 1990, 121–22). These large villages were more compact in layout with longer longhouses (Bamann 1992, 450). The Adams site (Seneca) is a good example, with a population of between eight hundred and one thousand (Wray et al. 1987, 25). While new social opportunities arose as a consequence of these larger communities, the primary motivation for construction of these towns is believed to lie in the desire for increased security (Warrick 1996, 20).

In general, a village of about two thousand people appears to have been the upper size limit for the New York Iroquois. In addition to straining available local resources, large villages increased the potential for conflict between inhabitants. Traditionally, the Iroquois relied on consensus for decision making. In a large village, the chances of factional disputes increase (Fenton

1998, 21). Using evidence from the journal of van den Bogaert, Dean Snow gives an estimate of 3300 residents for the Mohawk town of Tenotoge (1995a, 297), which is identified with the Failing site. If this is accurate, this very large village would have been an exception for the New York Iroquois.

## Location

In addition to considerations of defensibility and access to potable water, several other factors played a role in determining the location of a village and associated fields (White 1963, 4). Iroquois often settled near wetlands and swamps (Funk 1992, 25), which served as habitats for a variety of useful animals and plants. White-tailed deer tend to gather or yard over winter in marshy areas, especially cedar swamps, which provide both food and cover for them (Smith 1987, 60; Hasenstab 1990, 92). New York wetlands serve as stopover points for migratory waterfowl, another important seasonal resource for the Iroquois (Bradley 1987, 13). Beaver, muskrat, fish, and freshwater mollusks provided additional faunal resources (Funk 1992, 32).

A wide variety of plants used by the Iroquois were likewise found in or adjacent to swamps and boggy areas, including blueberry, which is also found in old fields (Monckton 1992, 46). Cedar trees killed by flooding from beaver dams were easily harvested for longhouse or palisade con-

struction.[1] Proximity to wetlands did have disadvantages, such as increased numbers of mosquitos. Village hilltop locations may have helped alleviate that problem, however.

During the height of the fur trade in the seventeenth century, local beaver were heavily hunted, probably causing many beaver dams to fall into disrepair. When drained, the rich organic soil at the bottom of a beaver pond would have been ideal for a farming plot (Cronin 1983, 105–7). Soil and pollen data are needed to establish the likelihood of this practice.

Moving from north to south, New York State consists of three broad physiographic subdivisions: the Lake Erie/Ontario lowlands, the rolling till plains, and the dissected Allegheny Plateau (Hasenstab 1990, 73). More moderate temperatures are found along the Erie and Ontario lake plains, with cooler temperatures on the higher Allegheny Plateau. This causes a reversal in the distribution of some plants, with a few southerly species growing on the Ontario lake plain but not on the more southerly Allegheny Plateau (Bradley 1987, 13). The lake plains also contain the most extensive wetlands.

Despite the advantages of the lake plain, the core areas of all Five Nations fall on the rolling till plains (Hasenstab 1990, 76; see map 3). The key determinant ap-

1. Large numbers of cedars also die competing for sunlight with companion trees, so flooding is not necessary for harvesting large numbers of dead cedars (J. V. Wright, personal communication).

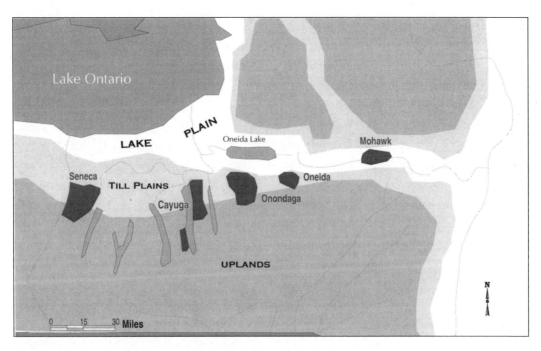

Map 3. Schematic representation of till plains along with the core areas of the Five Nations.

pears to be soil. The till plains west of the Mohawk Valley provide a loamy, lime-rich soil excellent for growing maize, beans, and squash.[2] The growing season on the Allegheny Plateau is shorter. Over time, village sites are increasingly located on the rolling till plains (Hasenstab n.d.). This shift reflects the increased importance of horticulture to the Iroquois as well as their sophistication regarding optimum growing conditions.

The Onondaga escarpment runs east-

west through the heartland of Iroquoia, with sites generally located on it but near the Lake Ontario plain. Between A.D. 1200 and 1400, proto-Cayuga and proto-Onondaga groups moved their villages to the top of the escarpment while apparently maintaining fishing and other special-purpose camps on the lake plain (Robert Hasenstab, personal communication).

In addition to good farmland, the escarpment and rolling till plains provided chert for tools and allowed for cold-air drainage of fields. Because of the movement of cold air down slope, fields located on hilltops or slopes would have experienced more frost-free days than fields located in valley bottoms.

The location of villages on the till

2. Robert Hasenstab (personal communication) notes that beans develop fungus and plant virus when grown in wet areas in acid soils. He hypothesizes that a move into the uplands away from wet areas would have facilitated the adoption and growth of beans.

plains also permitted the exploitation of resources of the two adjacent zones. This exploitation is reflected in small special-purpose sites, especially fishing stations along the lake plain. One such site was visited by Jesuit missionaries in 1655.[3]

Another consideration in determining village location was the availability of suitable building materials. Builders of Iroquoian communities required stands of young forest for house and palisade posts rather than virgin woods (Heidenreich 1971, 113). J. V. Wright argues that eastern white cedar posts would have been ideal for the vertical elements, as white cedar is rot resistant (Wright 1995, 17). Rafters and roof superstructure would need a strong but flexible species such as white elm, maple, or white ash (Snow 1997, 81). Older elm and cedar trees were needed for large sheets of bark. Securing trees for building would have resulted in cleared land for garden plots.

Even though Iroquois sites were located on defensible terrain, the location was often sheltered from the prevailing winds. Bradley notes this for Onondaga sites (1987, 50), and Charles Wray noted this for Seneca sites (Wray, cited in Hasenstab 1996, 20). For example, the Seneca sites of Adams, Cameron, and Culbertson all have hills to the west that block prevailing winds (Hasenstab 1996, 20).

One consequence of the elevated location of most village sites that is seldom mentioned in the literature is the opportunity afforded for surveying the countryside, or what in Geographic Information Systems jargon is referred to as "vantage." As Don Rumrill observed for the Mohawk, "just about every seventeenth-century village site has a view that is absolutely breathtaking" (1985, 1). It is reasonable to assume that twentieth-century archaeologists were not the first to appreciate this.

## Village Structure

Champlain observed that longhouses were spaced at least three to four yards apart to prevent fire from spreading (Biggar 1971, 3, 125). During Father Simon Le Moyne's visit to the principal Onondaga village in 1654, some houses were destroyed by fire (Tuck 1971, 171–72).

While palisades served as the first line of a village's defense, the placement of houses within a palisade may also have been motivated by defensive considerations. Sagard stated that an open space was left between the palisade and Huron longhouses to facilitate defense (Sagard-Théodat 1968, 92). William Finlayson argues that at the Draper site in Ontario, houses were placed so as to create defensible corridors and reduce access to the center of the village (1985, 407; 1998, 20). The excavation plan of the Nodwell site, also in Ontario, exhibits lines of posts link-

---

3. The Jesuits Chaumonot and Dablon visited an Onondaga fishing village at the mouth of Salmon River (Bradley 1987, 114).

Fig. 45. Iroquois village. Illustration by Ivan Kocsis. Courtesy of the London Museum of Archaeology, London, Ontario.

ing longhouses to palisades (Wright 1974, 5; Finlayson 1998, 20). These lines presumably acted as cordons to restrict access to the village.

Regular maintenance may have extended to the areas between longhouses. Such an activity would promote and maintain a sense of community. Pierre Chaumonot, visiting Onondaga in 1654, found the "streets cleaned" (Thwaites 1895–1901, 42:87). Visiting a Mohawk village in 1634, van den Bogaert observed houses "row on row in the manner of streets" (Gehring and Starna 1988, 4). The "streets" referred to by Chaumonot and van den Bogaert were not streets in the sense of a modern city, but rather spaces between longhouses allowing foot traffic. Ethnoarchaeological studies suggest such spaces can also be cleared by the trampling actions of people (see fig. 45).

Major excavations at the Garoga site

(Mohawk) between 1960 and 1964 by William Ritchie and Robert Funk of the New York State Museum revealed portions of at least thirteen longhouses, with two longhouses overlapping the palisade lines on the west (see fig. 46).

These latter two houses must not have been contemporaneous with the palisade. This Garoga site plan was recently produced by Robert Funk in a reanalysis of post mold plots. It provides more detail and more houses than the one previously published (Ritchie and Funk 1973, 314). Houses were clustered on top of a hill with three middle longhouses bisecting the village. Dean Snow suggests that the three groups of longhouses may reflect the three Mohawk clans (1995, 164). Robert Funk suggests that the arrangement of houses appears to have maximized the available space, adding support to the idea mentioned in chapter 4 that the many storage

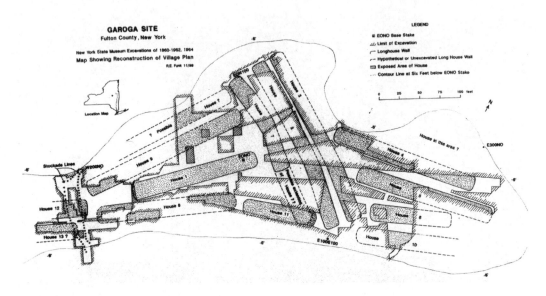

Fig. 46. Village plan of the Garoga site (Mohawk). Courtesy of Robert Funk.

pits inside the Garoga longhouses were a space saving device (1967, 81). The position of the middle longhouses would also have presented barriers to an enemy attempting to move across the village.

In the past, large-scale village excavations often involved bulldozing the plow zone to facilitate recording the location of post molds and pits. This provided data on the structure of these villages but often little information on the distribution of material. If a site is not threatened with immediate destruction, more effort should be expended to record the location of plow-zone materials with respect to village structures.[4] We lack information on which

tasks customarily took place inside or outside longhouses and to what extent longhouses differed from one another in terms of artifact inventory.

Faunal analysis of an early fifteenth-century Iroquoian site near Barrie, Ontario, revealed that fish harvested in large numbers during the spring spawning run were processed outside the longhouses. Conversely, fish that were procured at other times of the year, probably singly or in small numbers, were processed within the longhouse (Thomas 1997). This makes sense for two reasons. Processing large numbers of fish would be messy, an activity best accomplished outdoors. Secondly, harvesting such fish was probably a community activity, so processing the results of such activity would be most appropriate in a public rather than private space.

Small structures, referred to as cabins,

4. There are numerous studies which indicate that plowing does not necessarily obliterate significant artifact patterning (Trubowitz 1978; Engelbrecht 1994, 6–7).

have been identified on both prehistoric and historic Ontario and New York sites (Kapches 1984; Ritchie and Funk 1973, 259–62). The function of these is not clear. In Ontario, the Jesuits refer to small structures used to temporarily house guests or shamans (Thwaites 1895–1901, 10:199; 11:265; 12:237; Kapches 1984; Prezzano 1992, 291). Small Ontario structures could also have been winter homes for Algonquian families. Some Algonquian people are known to have spent the winter with the Huron, and Algonquians often lived in single-family structures. In New York, three small oval structures were recorded on the Kelso site (Onondaga, late fourteenth century) (Ritchie and Funk 1973, 259–62). It is possible that one of these functioned as a sweat lodge (Ritchie and Funk 1973, 259).

Sweat lodges within or immediately adjacent to longhouses have been tentatively identified on Ontario Iroquois sites (MacDonald 1988). Possible sweat baths within longhouses are most often found in the longest houses, which also were most likely the scene of feasting and ritual events (Warrick 1988, 35). Their use by men of different lineages living in a longhouse would have served an integrative function.

Small circular structures adjacent to longhouses but lacking hearths were probably corn cribs. The Onondaga sites of Kelso, Howlett Hill, Furnace Brook, and Atwell have such structures, suggesting that this was a tradition among the Onondaga (Tuck 1971, 31, 85, 157). Lafitau referred to towerlike bark storehouses

among the Seneca and noted that in order to prevent mold, the bark side walls had holes to provide air circulation (1977, 56). Even if Conrad Heidenreich overestimated the reliance of the Huron on maize, his calculation that six families in a longhouse would need to store 324 bushels of dried shelled corn a year is instructive (1971, 195). To do so would require four bins eight feet high and four feet in diameter.

Several historic accounts exist of captured bear cubs being kept in cages, either in pens within longhouses or outside (Sagard-Théodat 1968, 220; Gehring and Starna 1988, 6, 35–36; Prezzano 1992, 293). One possible pen was identified in a longhouse at the Oneida Buyea site by Theodore Whitney (1970, 3), but alternatively it may have been a structure used for storage (Hosbach 1997). In 1634, van den Bogaert tried to buy a penned bear when at a Mohawk village, but the Mohawk would not sell it to him (Gehring and Starna 1988, 9). Champlain observed that bears might be kept for two or three years before being killed for a feast (Grant 1907, 315–17).

In summer, most activities probably occurred outside, including cooking. At a number of sites, deep outside hearths suggest summer cooking (Ritchie 1980, 309; Ritchie and Funk 1973, 168, 169).[5] On the Kelso, Schoff, and Bloody Hill (Onondaga) sites, roasting pits were large enough to have cooked large mammals, in-

5. Kelso, Furnace Brook, and Bloody Hill all have deep outside hearths.

cluding deer, bear, or humans (Ritchie and Funk 1973, 169, 263–64). The last appears to have been the case at Bloody Hill (Tuck 1971, 113). These roasting pits were apparently used once (Ritchie and Funk 1973, 264).

Drying racks may be represented by small scattered post molds on sites. Theodore Whitney suggested this possibility for a cluster of small post molds at the Buyea site (Oneida). In a mid-eighteenth-century visit to the Iroquois, Bartram describes a four-post drying rack for berries (Prezzano 1992, 293–94). Drying racks could have been used for a variety of products, from fish and venison to tobacco.

Historic accounts refer to large war posts erected in towns (Beauchamp 1905, 135–37). These were painted with pictographs to record military campaigns, numbers of prisoners taken, and other information. Iroquois picture writing was also marked on trees in the forest to communicate information about hunting or war parties (Beauchamp 1905, 132–36).

It is possible that some pits found on sites that lack substantial quantities of refuse may have served as latrine pits (Ritchie 1973, 278). Snow identified a possible latrine pit just outside one end of a longhouse on the Mohawk Martin site (1995a, 245), while Marjorie and Peter Pratt suggest a similar function for a pit in a longhouse at the Crego site, an Onondaga fishing village (1998). They conjecture that this pit may have been used by someone who was ill or elderly.

Villages are commonly depicted in books and museum displays as devoid of trees, but there is little information on this subject. Beauchamp suggests that palisaded villages may have had a tree in the center that was notched for climbing in order to see outside the palisade (1905, 159). When the Jesuit father Simon Le Moyne prepared to enter an Onondaga village in 1661, he stated that he could hardly see the village as houses, palisade, and trees were covered with people (Thwaites 1895–1901, 47:75).

## Palisade

Palisades or stockades typically surrounded Iroquois communities, at least on the sides that were vulnerable to attack. On hilltop sites, palisades generally follow natural contours, so that the village area enclosed by the palisade reflects the naturally defensible portion of the site. In a number of cases, then, village size may reflect topography more than population size. Because of this, community population estimates based on site size must be used cautiously.[6]

Excavations have revealed single as well as multiple rows of palisade posts. Three rows are common, with the inner and outer posts probably lashed to the vertical center row (Prezzano 1992, 251). Palisade posts were generally set between 15 cm and 30 cm apart (Prezzano 1992,

---

6. Rowlands (1972, 449) points out a similar phenomenon for Maori hill forts, which often enclosed a larger area than would be dictated by the population size.

249). While the diameter of palisade post molds varies within sites, over time there is an increase in size (Ritchie and Funk 1973, 363; Prezzano 1992, 242). Sixteenth-century post molds tend to be up to a foot or more in diameter (Wray et al. 1987, 13; Ritchie and Funk 1973, 363). Interestingly, some of the largest palisade posts are from the early sixteenth-century Garoga site (Mohawk). These were up to two feet in diameter (Funk 1973, 331–32) and because of their date, it assumed that they were cut without metal axes.

Recovered fragments of wood from posts have been identified and include either white or red cedar, a variety of maple, and eastern hemlock.[7] Of these, cedar was probably preferred as it is the most decay resistant and grows straight. Untreated hard maple and eastern hemlock posts have an average in-ground use life in the Northeast of only around 4.5 years, while eastern white cedar has an average use life of nearly 27 years (Warrick 1988, 37). It is probable that palisades with more than three rows of posts indicate rebuilding.[8]

There may have been considerable variation in palisade height, even around the same community, but it is thought that the majority were somewhere between four and ten meters tall (Prezzano 1992, 248). At the Kelso site (Onondaga, Oak Hill phase), profiles of a line of large post molds indicated that the posts were set in the ground at an oblique angle to buttress the outer wall of the palisade. Extrapolation from the post mold angles yields a point of intersection with the outer posts at twelve feet, suggesting a minimum height for that palisade (Ritchie 1980, 307). Champlain observed that the palisade around the Iroquois village he attacked in 1615 was some thirty feet high, while he estimated a triple palisade around a Huron village at thirty-five feet (Grant 1907, 283, 292).

Bark, branches, and small saplings were woven between the upright palisade posts, creating a wall up to eight or nine feet high (Sagard-Théodat 1968, 91–95; Tuck 1971, 3; Ritchie and Funk 1973, 259; Prezzano 1992, 251). Sagard also mentions large tree trunks placed lengthwise to strengthen the upright posts of Huron palisades. The upright posts were apparently lashed to these horizontal members, which were placed behind the upright posts. Excavation of the palisade at the Indian Fort Road site (Cayuga), revealed a similar arrangement (Jones and Jones 1980). While some post molds might suggest a flimsy two-wall palisade, such posts could

---

7. Prezzano (1992, 237) summarizes Bradley (1987, 215), Ritchie and Funk (1973, 258, 317), and Pratt (1963, 60; 1976, 101).

8. More than three rows of posts would seem unnecessary. I suggest that multiple row palisades, especially those greater than three rows, be considered a possible relative indicator of village duration. This follows a similar line of reasoning to that of Warrick (1988) who suggested that the post mold density of

longhouse walls was such an indicator. If the old palisade was in poor shape, newer walls might be expected to be on the outside, with the older decaying walls on the inside becoming a source of firewood.

have held a formidable horizontal timber wall in place (Pratt and Pratt 1998).

In 1615, Champlain (Grant 1907, 292) mentions galleries associated with the palisade around an Iroquois village. Galleries may have been constructed between a double—or triple-walled palisade to provide a fighting platform, with the outer posts being taller in order to shield men on the galleries (Ritchie 1980, 314). Such an arrangement was suggested for the Mohawk Getman site (Ritchie 1973, 301). Water for putting out fires, stone missiles, and weapons could be stored there (Grant 1907, 292; Sagard-Théodat 1968, 91–92; Tuck 1971, 3; Ritchie 1973, 301; 1980, 314).

At the late fourteenth-century Kelso site, an area of post molds four feet by three feet inside the palisade line may represent a watchtower guarding an entryway (Ritchie and Funk 1973, 257). Sagard mentions both watchtowers and galleries (Sagard-Théodat 1968, 91–95). Outward projections of the wall, or bastions, have been observed on some prehistoric sites, including Boland (Prezzano 1992, 253).

The extensive nature of these defensive works suggests that a great deal of time and energy went into their construction and maintenance. Larger villages required palisades of greater length, but there was an economy of scale operating. Doubling the palisade perimeter increased the village area by a factor of four (Snow 1994b, 52). Thus, in terms of energy expenditure, it was more cost efficient to build a palisade around a large village than palisades around two or three smaller villages whose area totaled that of the large village.

The existence of palisades indicates that hostilities were not confined to battlefields and that villagers were afraid of direct attacks. Cross-culturally, where three or more "barriers" exist to insulate inhabitants of a settlement, war is likely to occur at least once every two years (C. Ember and M. Ember 1996, 7).

There were generally only one or two gateways in a palisade. These were often labyrinthine passageways created by overlapping palisade lines that required people to walk single file. These could be easily closed off. The Huron used such entryways (Sagard-Théodat 1968, 91–95) and examples have been recovered archaeologically from a number of sites. In 1634, van den Bogaert observed a relatively wide main entryway of 3.5 feet into an Oneida village, but a second entryway was only 2 feet across (Gehring and Starna 1988, 12).

In 1851, *Antiquities of the State of New York* by Ephraim Squier illustrated many of the extant earthworks in New York. Most of the earthen enclosures Squier illustrated have since been destroyed, but those in association with village sites are assumed to have had a defensive function, such as those around the large Seneca sites of Adams and Tram. They were formed by piling earth around the base of a palisade, leaving a ditch immediately in front.

In the Midwest, earlier earthen enclosures are viewed as ceremonial in function, leading some to question the automatic assignment of a defensive function to these features around New York Iroquois sites (Neusius et al. 1998).[9] Even if the primary function of earth rings in New York were as support for a palisade, these surviving defensive features probably took on an added dimension of sacredness to later Iroquois. This would explain why early nineteenth-century Iroquois on the Buffalo Creek Reservation chose the early sixteenth-century Buffam Street earthwork in south Buffalo as the place for their cemetery. Interestingly, Henry R. Schoolcraft mapped a mound within this earthwork, suggesting use of this area as sacred space for thousands of years (quoted in White 1961, 60).

In addition to defense, palisades may have had various secondary functions. They could have served as both windbreaks and snow fences (Reid 1975, 7). A palisaded village on a hill must have been an impressive sight, and it is little wonder that Europeans referred to them as castles. Van den Bogaert, in his 1634 visit to an Oneida village, stated, "Above the entrance stood three large wooden images, carved as men, by which three locks fluttered that they had cut from the heads of slain Indians"

(Gehring and Starna 1988, 12). A single scalp was hanging by the secondary entrance. While perhaps not as impressive as the English practice of sticking the heads of criminals on pikes outside the castle or town wall, both practices were clearly designed as a public display. William Bradford wrote that an Algonquian leader's head had been impaled on their fort "for a terror unto others" (cited in Kupperman 2000, 227).

Archaeologists frequently find extensive middens just beyond the palisade. These served as major disposal areas for village refuse (Prezzano 1992, 325; Monckton 1992, 17). In some cases, potsherd mends have been made with one piece having come from inside a longhouse and another piece from a nearby midden, indicating the dumping area for an individual longhouse. Analysis has shown that sometimes a single longhouse used two or more middens, or that two or more longhouses used the same midden (Warrick 1984, 119). Of course these studies also indicate that longhouse residents cleaned their floors of debris.

## The Clearing

Iroquois communities were surrounded by fields and open areas. Open areas were probably expanded by fires as well as by the need for firewood. Historic accounts suggest that clearings around villages could be considerable and that their size increased over time. Descriptions of the Huron coun-

---

9. Tim Abel (personal communication) suggests earthworks have both sacred and defensive dimensions, even if the "defensive" function is against spirit forces. No doubt these enclosures served multiple functions. I speculate that some early Midwestern enclosures may at times have been used for sacred games of lacrosse or its forerunner.

try during the first half of the seventeenth century indicate extensive corn fields, even at some distance from settlements.

When Galinée accompanied La Salle from Lake Ontario to a Seneca village in July of 1669, a distance of some twenty miles, he observed "for the most part beautiful, broad meadows" (Day 1953, 338). In addition, Galinée noted a clearing around a village approximately five-and-a-half miles in circumference (Hamell 1980, 95). In 1671 the Cayuga heartland is described as "consisting of almost uninterrupted plains" (Thwaites 1895–1901, 56:49).

In western New York, a number of early Iroquoian communities are located on the edge of what are described as "oak openings" or plains in the early nineteenth century.[10] An argument can be made that these openings in the forest cover occurred naturally as a result of the underlying limestone of the Onondaga escarpment (Zenkert 1934, 54–55). They could also have been remnants of tall grass prairies that were once more extensive (Wykoff 1988, 89–90). The apparent proximity of early Iroquoian communities to such areas is suggestive, and it is possible that they were maintained and expanded by human agency. Such areas would have supported a large number of deer.

While the ethnic affiliation of populations in the Niagara Frontier region of western New York is uncertain, they are customarily regarded as a branch of the Erie (Engelbrecht 1991). The *Jesuit Relations* of 1656 lists what is probably an Erie name, Gentaguetehronnons (Thwaites 1895–1901, 42:197), which is translated as "people who bear or carry a field" (Steckley 1985, 12). This literal translation makes no sense, but John Steckley suggests a metaphorical interpretation like "these are people always found with such a clearing" (personal communication). If so, then the name may refer either to the tendency of this group to settle near open areas, or to extensive clearing associated with them.[11]

The dichotomy between forest and clearing runs through Iroquois oral tradition and ritual. According to George Hamell, to cross from forest to clearing is to cross a metaphorical threshold from "the other world" to "this world" (1987, 69). The world of the forest is seen as a different physical, spiritual, and social realm. It is one of potential danger, where powerful, humanlike spirits could be encountered. The ritual "Welcome at the Woods' Edge" serves to reaffirm kinship and allow entry into the world of the village.

This dichotomy between forest and clearing is part of the spiritual landscape. In

10. Sites in Western New York near openings include: Allen, Zephyr, Brompton, Country Meadows, Piestrak, Spaulding Lake, Thruway Commerce Park, Tweely-Roth, Brothers of Mercy, and Christiansen (Norbert Bartochowski, personal communication).

11. Roy Wright (1974, 66–68) examines linguistic variants of this name and wonders if it is coincidence that one of the founding members of the mission of La Prairie (de la Magdelaine) was an Erie woman.

some cases it may have been an accurate reflection of physical reality. In most cases, however, former village locations with their cleared but abandoned fields were only a few miles away. The possible abandonment of some fields and the clearing of others would have led to a vegetational mosaic around settlements. Historic accounts suggest that in some cases the forest was miles away, and even then it was not unaffected by human use.

## Community Movement

Iroquoian communities periodically moved their location. Seventeenth-century sources suggest ten to twelve years as the typical duration of a village, but there was considerable variability (Starna et al. 1984, 197). In 1681, a Jesuit missionary found the inhabitants of the principle Onondaga community in the process of moving their crops and possessions some five miles to a new location after having been in their former location nineteen years (Thwaites 1895–1901, 62:55–57). It is generally assumed that small fifteenth-century villages moved less frequently than larger sixteenth—and seventeenth-century ones since they would have been slower to deplete local resources.

Archaeologists have sought various means of measuring the length of time a particular site was occupied. If site size (and presumably population) is held constant, then a rough indication of relative village duration may be achieved through measuring the depth of middens and numbers or density of artifacts. However, these methods are very imprecise.

A more promising approach is to measure the amount of rebuilding by measuring the density of post molds along walls. This density may be expected to vary directly with the length of occupation. Warrick developed an index using wood decay rates and the density of house wall post molds (1988). Using this index, he suggests occupations of between twenty and fifty years for communities of the sixteenth century and earlier, and fifteen-year occupations for seventeenth-century villages (Warrick 1988, 51).

For the large sixteenth—and seventeenth-century Seneca villages, the average distance that the western community moved is 2 miles, while the eastern community moved an average of 3.4 miles (Vandrei 1987, 14). Archaeological evidence suggests the large eastern and western communities moved at different times (Wray et al. 1987, 4–5). This would have provided a defensive advantage, as the Seneca would have been more vulnerable if both communities moved at the same time (Saunders 1986, 211). Also, one might expect that men from one village helped in building the other village, especially if it were a longhouse of their matrilineage or clan.

In most cases, village removal must have been a gradual process, allowing time for new fields to be cleared and new structures to be built before the entire community moved. In the early eighteenth century, Lafitau stated that several years before village removal, men went in winter to prepare new fields, staying in temporary shanties while doing this (1977, 70). Such advance preparation was not always possible. In 1677 Wentworth Greenhalgh visited a newly established Oneida village that lacked adequate corn supplies, forcing these Oneida to go to the Onondaga for corn (Campisi 1978, 481).

When archaeologists look at the distribution of material on a village site, they are not seeing a picture of everyday life. Instead, what they see reflects the culmination of activity on a site, including changes since its abandonment. One would suppose that a village removal would be a time to dispose of worn-out or broken items stored for potential future reuse (Schiffer 1987, 67). In addition to this "clutter refuse," one would expect to find evidence of abandonment-stage refuse (Schiffer 1987, 98). This results when standards of cleanliness are relaxed in anticipation of a move, and refuse is discarded in areas previously not used for that purpose.

It is possible that a few people chose to stay in the old community, perhaps those who were very old (Hamell 1980, 94; Fenton 1998, 59). After the community moved, some older people who died after the move may have been buried in the former village near the bones of their family and friends. This could explain the occasional phenomenon of grave goods of a slightly later period appearing on some sites. Stray European trade beads are sometimes recovered from what otherwise appear to be precontact village sites,

suggesting that they were dropped as offerings.[12]

In 1634, shortly after the Mohawk suffered a major smallpox epidemic, van den Bogaert traveled through the Mohawk country, observing eight villages. Snow suggests that rather than eight separate Mohawk communities being in existence at this time, four communities were relocating from larger to smaller villages as a consequence of the epidemic (1995a, 288).

The reasons archaeologists and ethnohistorians generally suggest for village removal is the exhaustion of resources in the immediate vicinity of the village, particularly soil and firewood. The larger the community, the sooner some of these resources would have been exhausted (Tuck 1971, 213–14). As more and more land was cleared for fields, women would have had to walk farther from the safety of the palisaded village.

Clark Sykes has argued that soils were not the limiting factor in the time a community could remain in one place (1980). Computer modeling of the land needed to support communities of two hundred or fewer individuals suggests that such communities could have remained indefinitely in the same location (Snow 1995a, 28). Charles Vandrei argues that even the large

12. Peter Pratt (personal communication) notes this on the Oneida Vaillancourt [Bigford] site and the Onondaga Pen site. A Staffordshire china spaniel ornament dating to the first quarter of the eighteenth century came off the Pen site, which is believed to date to the end of the seventeenth century.

Seneca villages had sufficient productive soils within a two-kilometer radius (1987, 12). Hasenstab argues that Iroquois farming practices, which included intercropping of maize and beans, would not have exhausted the soil (n.d.). These arguments suggest that factors other than soil exhaustion should be considered in attempting to understand village relocation.

Sagard noted that the Huron went far in their search for dry wood (Sagard-Théodat 1968, 94). Women carried it on their backs using tumplines, except when there was snow on the ground and they could pull sledges loaded with wood (Sagard-Théodat 1968, 91–95). Then they wore snowshoes. Champlain states that women gathered firewood in March and April when they were not busy with other tasks (Grant 1907, 327). Lafitau observed that over time women had to travel increasing distances for firewood (Lafitau 1977, 69, 70). Analysis of wood charcoal on Huron sites indicates that maple was the predominant species used as fuel (Monckton 1992, 87).

Like farming, the gathering of firewood appears to have been carried out by work parties of women (Fenton 1998, 23). Unlike trips to hunting camps or fishing stations, women were probably unaccompanied by men when gathering firewood. This activity took women far from the safety of the village, but if undertaken between late fall and early spring when needs for firewood were greatest, women would have been least likely to have been attacked by enemy raiders. Iroquoians tended not to

wage war during this time, as there was no leaf cover (Trigger 1990b, 53).

Physical deterioration of the wood and bark palisade and longhouses also must have encouraged people to relocate. Even if relatively rot-resistant woods were used in constructing the palisade and longhouses, after ten to twenty years it is likely that maintenance of these structures would be a concern. Harvesting of trees for building the original structures and clearing fields for horticulture would leave nearby trees suitable for rebuilding in short supply. At some point, it was probably easier to move the entire community to a new location than to bring building materials to the old spot (Pratt 1976, 12). A fire that destroyed all or a portion of a village could have served as a catalyst for community relocation (Heidenreich 1971, 215–16).

Other factors may also have played a role in the decision to move the community. Sanitation problems can arise from the accumulation of refuse and human waste (Guldenzopf 1984, 90; Finlayson 1985, 434). Europeans observed that mice were a problem in longhouses, and this nuisance probably increased over time. Insect infestations are more likely to arise in fields where the same crop is grown every year, but shifting farming to a new location could minimize this risk (Starna, Hamell, and Butts 1984).

The depletion of game in the immediate vicinity has been suggested as a reason for village removal, but this seems unlikely. In late fall and winter, the pattern was for hunting parties to leave the village, sometimes traveling considerable distances. The movement of these hunting parties would be little affected by a village move of a few miles. Furthermore, should a village move to a new area lacking the open areas and edge environments favored by deer, it would be a number of years before these environments could be created and deer densities increased (Finlayson 1998, 50).

Human modification of the environment in the vicinity of the village would have contributed to an increase in the number of many of the species hunted. If game were depleted in the immediate area of the village as a result of heavy human predation, recolonization by the same species from surrounding areas is likely, as they would have found the open areas around the village attractive.

In some cases, social reasons may have played a role in the dynamics of village removal. When first constructed, longhouses are assumed to have been the appropriate length for the number of members of the lineage or clan segment occupying them. The village structure can therefore be taken as a reflection of village organization at the time of construction. Demographic changes over a generation could render the original longhouse size obsolete (Snow 1996, 168). Village size could also change, either as a result of the influx of newcomers or the departure of others, for whatever reason. Such changes would result in a lack of fit between the existing village structures and the village population.

The actual motivating factor for the inhabitants of a village to move may have been spiritual. The Iroquois were said to have moved their villages in response to dreams. While early European observers viewed this as irrational, it is likely that such a dream occurred or was acted on when one of the above factors encouraged it. For the Iroquois, spiritual concerns were given primacy, and a dream to move the community provided a culturally appropriate reason to act.

A sense of spiritual pollution may also have prompted village removal. The animate souls of deceased individuals were associated with their bones. In traditional Iroquois thought, ghosts of the dead who had been neglected or offended were a possible cause of illness (Herrick 1995, 67). The souls of individuals buried in the vicinity of the village may have been viewed as causing "ghost sickness" or other problems for the living (Hamell 1988). An Iroquois variant of the Huron Feast of the Dead, called the Ohgi:we:, was performed when village removal was complete. This was to inform the dead of the move (Lafitau 1977, 247; Fenton and Kurath 1951, 143; Fenton 1998, 23). It can also be viewed as a community ritual that includes the dead (Fenton and Kurath 1951, 164).

## Abandoned Villages

An abandoned village and its associated fields would have provided a variety of resources. The *Jesuit Relations* state that house and palisade poles were sometimes moved to new settlements (Thwaites 1895–1901, 62:55–57). That the poles were recycled is also suggested by the Huron phrase translated as "to transport a house somewhere else" (Steckley 1987, 21). This is supported archaeologically by the discovery of refuse-filled post molds, which must have filled with debris after the poles were removed (Ritchie and Funk 1973, 265; Snow 1995a, 314). Aged palisade and house posts not suitable for structural reuse could have been a source of firewood for the inhabitants of the new town, although cedar as firewood would have been extremely hazardous because of its tendency to produce explosive showers of sparks (J. V. Wright, personal communication).

Today, the soil found on an Iroquois site is typically dark and rich in organic content, a result of refuse and charcoal being incorporated into the soil. The rich soil and cleared spaces of the old town could have supported crops or wild plants used by people now in the new town.

Nut trees and berry patches could have expanded into previously cultivated areas. Abandoned fields provide an ideal environment for amaranth, chenopodium, pokeweed, and other useful plants that today are regarded as weeds (Moeller 1996, 64–65). Deer would have found both browse and mast in this environment. One factor in the relatively short relocation distance of Iroquois communities might therefore have been continued access to this patch of resources.

In some cases, reoccupation of the same village area occurred after a brief hiatus. New radiocarbon dating dates from the Roundtop, and Maxon-Derby sites suggest multiple Owasco occupations (Hart 2000, 5). Excavation at the Kelso site, an Oak Hill phase site in the Onondaga area, revealed two partially overlapping stockaded villages, each with Oak Hill material. William Ritchie suggested only a short period between occupations, just long enough for soil fertility and sources of firewood to be replenished (1980, 305). New radiocarbon dates on Kelso material suggest earlier occupations as well (Hart 2000, 15). A similar situation appears to be the case with the Tara site in Ontario, where two early Pickering stage villages overlap (Finlayson 1998, 79, 178, 372).[13]

In other cases, two hundred or more years elapse between occupations. For example, the historic Mohawk regularly built villages on top of fourteenth—and fifteenth-century villages (Rumrill 1985, 37; Snow 1995a, 162). Similarly, the late seventeenth-century Onondaga villages of Weston and Pen are in close proximity to the early fifteenth-century Keough and Bloody Hill sites (Tuck 1971, 188). Presumably the natural advantages the location offered to the first villagers continued to be of importance. Whether the existence of an earlier occupation made the location more attractive for Iroquois centuries later remains unknown. It does seem likely that the later Iroquois would have been aware of the earlier occupation from both surface indications and oral tradition.

13. Pickering is contemporaneous with early Owasco.

Knowing that Iroquois villages were not permanent, archaeologists have sought to trace the successive locations of specific Iroquois communities. In assessing whether a number of village sites formed a sequence, geographic proximity as well as artifact changes are considered. Since ceramics are typically the most common artifact recovered from Iroquois sites, high ceramic similarity between two sites is taken as a likely indication of the movement of a community from one site to the other, especially if the sites are close geographically. During the course of her lifetime, an Iroquois woman typically would have made ceramics while living at two or three village sites. The assumption is that she would continue to make pottery in the same general style, as might her daughters and female relatives, thereby providing the ceramic continuity visible in the archaeological record (Allen 1988).

The actual method by which ceramics are used to temporally order village sites is called seriation. It is based on changing percentages of either ceramic attributes or types. Seriation is more accurate than radiocarbon dating for relatively ordering village sites in a sequence. There is a statistical error associated with radiocarbon dates that is generally greater than the length of time of occupation of most sixteenth—and early seventeenth-century Iroquois village sites (Bamann 1993, 148–49). However, radiocarbon dating does serve to provide estimates of site age in calendar years. Recently, Dean Snow obtained thirty-eight radiocarbon dates on maize kernels for Mohawk sites, serving to clarify dating of the Mohawk sequence. Dates from maize, an annual, are potentially more useful than dates from charred wood, which could be from a tree a hundred or more years old.

While the sequence of village removals in the Seneca and Onondaga areas is well established (Wray and Schoff 1953; Tuck 1971), Snow cautions that the relocation process may not always have been as simple as is commonly assumed (1991, 37). Kin groups in a village are believed to have retained considerable autonomy, and when a village relocated they may have chosen to move to a different community. Such movement could have been facilitated by members of the same clan in the other community (Bamann 1993, 256). If some kin groups moved from one community to another, it would create ceramic similarities between sites that were not a part of the same general village movement, leading to confusion and uncertainty in archaeological interpretation.

In a community where there were crop shortages, individuals or groups may have moved to another community where there was a surplus, a situation that was observed among the Huron (Thwaites 1895–1901, 35:177, 183–5; O'Shea 1989, 65). Moving people rather than harvested crops would have provided a more cost-effective solution to the problem of a temporary unequal distribution of resources.

In the seventeenth century, there is evidence to suggest that names of villages were sometimes transferred from the old town to the new town (Fenton and Tooker 1978,

467; Hamell 1980, 94; Snow 1995a, 304). Though composition of these communities might vary over time, the practice of transferring names emphasized continuity, a practice that characterized Iroquois use of names for people as well.

## Fusion

The presence of large Iroquois communities in the sixteenth century suggests a process of village consolidation or fusion, with smaller communities merging to form larger ones. The reason for these mergers is most likely defense (Tuck 1971, 213). There is safety in numbers, and presumably the increased security outweighed disadvantages resulting from an increased number of individuals exploiting local resources. The Mohawk Otstungo site (c. A.D. 1450–1525) appears to be the product of village fusion (Snow 1995a, 115–38).[14] The quality of the soil around Otstungo for corn horticulture is lower than that of earlier sites, suggesting that defense and not resource maximization lay behind nucleation (Bond 1985).

Extensions of longhouses or palisades observable archaeologically suggest the influx of individuals or groups into a community. Examples of probable village expansion occurs at the Cornish site (Seneca) and Furnace Brook site (Onondaga) (Hayes 1965; 1966; Tuck 1971, 59). A major increase in site size in a village sequence also suggests influx of people or possibly the fusion of two communities.

A few village amalgamations may have been unsuccessful. Economically, the most efficient time for a community to fission would be when it relocated, but factionalism or other considerations may have caused some segments of the community to emigrate before this. Typically, palisade lines some distance apart are interpreted as evidence of village expansion, but some may be examples of village contraction. This may have been the case at the Cameron site (Seneca), where the southern palisade was apparently moved northward in a village contraction (Wray et al. 1991, 190). High mortality rates and low birth rates also may have been factors in shrinking village size.

## Village Life

Within a village, one was a member not just of a nuclear family but of a matrilineage, a clan, and a moiety. One had obligations to one's father's kin as well. Kinship provided one with a place in the community and a series of obligations and benefits as a result. In historic times, kin groups were held liable for the actions of their members and had to pay damages if one of their kinsmen killed or injured someone of a different kin group. Within the village, this served to discourage internal fighting and lessened the possibility of village fission. It is assumed that liability for one's kinsmen is as old as multiclan villages.

14. The communities represented by Fox Lair and Second Woods probably merged to form the community at Otstungo (Bamann 1993, 250).

Among the Seneca and other "upper Iroquois," clans were placed on one of two "sides," or what anthropologists refer to as moieties. As larger communities were formed through the fusion of villages, new organizational divisions were required, and moiety organization may have arisen during this process. In oral tradition, the origin of moieties appears in the theme of people living on opposite sides of a lake or stream (Fenton 1998, 60). Cross-culturally, moieties are found in societies of fewer than nine thousand individuals that are involved in external war (C. Ember and M. Ember 1996, 6).

Cross-cultural studies indicate that when villages exceed five hundred people, new mechanisms are needed to maintain community cohesion (Kosse 1990). Moiety organization and representative councils are ways of achieving this. When the Seneca council met, representatives of each moiety sat opposite one another across the council fire, following a protocol for decision making (Fenton 1998, 27). Today, moiety ceremonial functions include burying one another's dead, playing the bowl game, and occasionally playing lacrosse (Fenton 1998, 27).

Iroquois society is described as egalitarian, that is, without great differentials in wealth or access to resources. The archaeology of Iroquois households and villages bears this out, even after European trade materials become common on sites. Though archaeologists have looked for differential wealth between longhouses, this has not been found (Warrick 1996, 16).

There is little evidence for hoarding. A variety of mechanisms served to distribute goods within an Iroquois village such as gift exchange, sharing, gift giving as part of healing rituals, and burial offerings for kinsmen (Trigger 1990a; Warrick 1996, 16). Generosity was valued, and greedy individuals or those who hoarded possessions left themselves open to accusations of witchcraft (Trigger 1978c, 62).

Village life meant more individuals were available to cooperate in economic activities. We know from both archaeology and historic accounts that Iroquoians and Algonquians participated in deer drives.[15] Deer were driven into the water where they were killed from boats or channeled into a small enclosure by means of a long, high, V-shaped fence (Dennis 1993, 38; Socci 1995, 109). To be effective, either method required many participants. In 1793, white settlers in Cayuga County found the remains of a deer drive in the form of a brush fence stretching from Owasco Lake to Lake Skaneateles (Brinkerhoff 1882). Before the formation of permanent villages, neighboring bands would have had to join forces to carry out an effective deer drive. Villages provided ready human resources for this and other cooperative activities.

Life in a large village would have pro-

---

15. The Little site [c. A.D. 1000–1200] near London, Ontario, is interpreted as a deer drive (Williamson 1986). Beauchamp (1905, 179) notes that the town of Pound Ridge in Westchester County, N.Y., was the site of a deer pound at the foot of a high ridge.

vided social and sexual opportunities not available in small hamlets. For example, in a hamlet like Bates, which had a single longhouse, all young unmarried males and females were probably members of the same clan and therefore would have avoided sexual relations with one another. A multiclan village of two thousand people would have provided individuals with many potential partners. In the seventeenth century, sexual activity between young Iroquois was regarded as normal, and a woman might not enter into a long-term relationship with a man until the birth of a child (Kinietz 1965, 94; Trigger 1990b, 78).

Large villages formed crowded islands of population in an otherwise sparsely settled landscape. This had disadvantages. The Adams and Culbertson sites are large early villages in the Seneca area, dating to the end of the sixteenth century. Examination of skeletal material from these sites suggests that famine, possibly along with epidemic diseases, severely affected these populations (Wray et al. 1987, 239). There is a high frequency of multiple burials at these sites, and there is a high incidence of pathologies that are caused by nutritional deficiencies (Wray et al. 1987, 242). The community at Culbertson is believed to have moved to the Tram site, which is only three-quarters of a mile northeast of Adams, and famine appears to have prevailed during the early years of occupation at Tram as well (Wray et al. 1987, 242; 1991, 390–91).

There is evidence for droughts along the eastern seaboard at the end of the six-

teenth century (Quinn 1979, 577; Stahle et al. 1998), but whether the famine inferred for the Seneca area is related to drought is uncertain. These large sites, each with possibly eight hundred to one thousand individuals, were only 1.5 miles apart, raising the question of whether there were too many people in too small an area, given the probable importance of wild plant foods in the diet. Later contemporaneous sites in the sequence are located at a greater distance from one another, reflecting the typical pattern for the Iroquois.

Problems with both waste disposal and infectious disease are directly related to village size and length of occupation (Guldenzopf 1984, 90). Bigger is not always better! With the development of large villages in the sixteenth century, Iroquoians had to learn to cope with new, more crowded conditions. If conditions were unsanitary, dysentery may have been a problem. It is possible that the high mortality rate observed for infants and children at the Seneca Cameron site is explainable in this light, rather than as a result of the introduction of European diseases (Wray et al. 1991, 392). Tuberculosis, another infectious disease, was common among Iroquoians living in crowded longhouses in winter (Pfeiffer 1980; Trigger and Swagerty 1996, 362).

Emile Durkheim argued that participation in rituals promotes group solidarity, an observation for which there is worldwide support. Healing rituals may have functioned in this manner. Curing societies were composed of individuals from differ-

Fig. 47. Antler maskette from the Steele site (Seneca). About 3.5 cm. in height. Drawing by Gene Mackay; photograph by James Osen. Courtesy of the Rochester Museum and Science Center, Rochester, N.Y.

ent kin groups. Small effigy faces recovered from Iroquois villages may have signaled membership in the False Face medicine society (Beauchamp 1922, 37; see fig. 47).

Iroquois living in villages would have participated in a variety of community-wide events including games of lacrosse, snow snake, and others that often involved gambling. Dancing also would have promoted solidarity in addition to being a way people gave thanks. Morgan viewed dancing of such centrality that he predicted that when the Iroquois stopped dancing, they would cease to be Indian (1962, 263). Condolence rituals organized by moiety also may have become important with the growth of large communities. Sempowski sees change in mortuary behavior in the large early Seneca sites as reflecting rituals designed to integrate individuals into this larger group (1997).

Fear initially brought people together in larger communities. Rituals evolved to keep harmony within these communities.

# IROQUOIS NATIONS

## Historical Perspective

Owasco artifact styles differ from later Iroquois ones. As a consequence, early archaeologists assumed the Owasco culture was unrelated to that of the later Iroquois. The change to Iroquois-style artifacts was thought to reflect a migration of Iroquoian speakers into New York. James B. Griffin cautioned that migration might not be the explanation for this change (1944), a view supported by Richard MacNeish's subsequent study (1952). MacNeish demonstrated ceramic continuity between Owasco and Iroquois culture, the "in situ" hypothesis. Following MacNeish, archaeologists began to point out additional continuities between the Owasco and later Iroquois culture, including the presence of stockaded communities with longhouses. Today, the Owasco culture is seen as part of the continuum of Iroquoian development.

This does not mean, however, that the Owasco culture was characterized by the same social or political institutions as the later Iroquois. Owasco population was scattered in small hamlets rather than clus-tered in a few large villages. While Owasco ceramic style is distributed over a wide area, there is no indication that the makers of this pottery constituted a cohesive social group or shared a common ethnic identity or language (Lounsbury 1978; Ritchie 1980, 300). Projecting a label like "Seneca" back in time to the Owasco is like referring to inhabitants of Europe of A.D. 1000 as Frenchmen or Germans. Neither France, Germany, nor the Seneca, Cayuga, Onondaga, Oneida, and Mohawk existed as recognizable nations that early (Engelbrecht 1999).

The extent to which Owasco culture can be derived from earlier cultures in New York remains a subject of debate. William Divale argues that matrilocal, matrilineal groups are typically intrusive into previously occupied regions, this organization giving them both a defensive and offensive advantage (1984). Dean Snow sees discontinuities in the archaeological record and has used Divale's argument to advance the case for an Iroquois migration into New York at the expense of more thinly settled, hunter-gatherer Algonquian-speaking peoples (1995b, 70–71). Snow cites the sudden appearance of multifamily residence, horticulture, and compact villages in New York as evidence for migration.

Robert Funk and others have questioned Snow's argument that there are discontinuities in the archaeological record suggesting migration (1997, 26). Linguistic reconstructions favor a long occupation of Iroquoian speakers in central New York and northern Pennsylvania with subsequent expansion both north and south (Lounsbury 1978, 336). As William Starna and Funk argue (1994) and even Snow admits (1995c, 7), a choice between in situ development or migration for Iroquois origins is too simple.

Framing the issue of Iroquois origins in this manner stems from a taxonomic mind set, pervasive in archaeology, that attempts to define the Iroquois by a list of traits including language, maize horticulture, longhouses, incised ceramics, and matriliny. These components of Iroquois culture developed at different rates and were shared by many cultures. As Bruce Trigger has suggested, small groups may have been incorporated into Iroquoian populations, bringing new ideas with them (1985, 82). The story of Iroquois origins involves more than a choice between migration and the in situ hypothesis.

## Ethnogenesis

John Moore uses the term "ethnogenesis" to describe the development of cultures that have their origins in several different antecedent groups (1994, 925). The fusion and fission of Iroquoian communities suggested by the archaeological record fits this model. So do the linguistic data. Floyd Lounsbury notes that the development of Iroquoian languages "cannot have been one of a series of simple and permanent bifurcations but must have been one of recurrent separations and fusions" (1978, 336).

The Oak Hill horizon (A.D. 1350–1400) marks the transition between the Owasco and Iroquois culture in eastern New York (D. Lenig 1965; Snow 1995a, 78). The Oak Hill horizon parallels the Uren and Middleport substages in the Ontario Iroquois sequence. Both the Oak Hill horizon and the Uren substage exhibit artifact similarities over a broad area (Wright 1966, 56–59; Snow 1995a, 76). The implications of these similarities in artifact styles in Owasco and early Iroquois cultures are imperfectly understood. It is possible that they reflect a network of alliances among small communities. In small hamlets, mate selection is limited, so individuals often marry someone from another hamlet. This would imply at least temporary alliances between some communities, involving diplomacy, reciprocal feasting, and other activities that moved both people and artifact styles between communities.[1]

In the fifteenth and sixteenth cen-

1. See Williamson and Robertson (1994) for a discussion of Iroquoian peer polity interaction. Although lacrosse leaves no trace in the archaeological record, it might have played a role in intercommunity interactions. The game calls for speed,

turies, there was a transformation in the distribution of Iroquois population across what is now New York State. Instead of small dispersed sites, one sees clusters of sites in areas that in historic times are associated with the Seneca, Cayuga, Onondaga, Oneida, and Mohawk.[2] Areas between these site clusters were abandoned. During this time, ceramic style became more localized, suggesting that women did not move regularly between these areas (Ritchie 1980, 317).

The cause for this shift in the distribution of population appears to have been warfare. Fifteenth—and sixteenth-century communities were generally located in defensible positions and were surrounded by palisades. These Iroquois communities were faced with conflicting alternatives. There is safety in numbers, so larger communities meant greater security. On the other hand, increasingly large communities led to problems of resource availability, sanitation, and social and political integration. While it is believed that small villages could exist indefinitely in some areas, the larger the community, the more frequently it would have had to shift its location.

The solution to the problem of external threats that Iroquois communities achieved secured their later survival. Rather than moving together into a single very large community that would quickly stress local resources, alliances were established between communities that then moved a few miles from one another (Tuck 1971, 214). Such alliances sought to prevent hostilities and perhaps provide for the common use of important resource localities such as swamps, fishing stations, or chert quarries. It is these allied communities that are ancestral to the later Seneca, Cayuga, Onondaga, Oneida, and Mohawk. *

Like earlier mergers between small scattered Owasco and Oak Hill communities, the formation of alliances between larger Iroquois communities may have been facilitated by marriages. With matrilocality, males move from their mother's longhouse to their wife's. In this system, brothers may end up in different longhouses, or even different communities. If males marry into a different community from that of their birth, they still have obligations to their sisters and their sister's children, members of their matrilineage. They would therefore have important ties to their natal community as well as ties to any communities in which their brothers or other kinsmen might be living.

The emergence of Iroquois nations should be thought of as a process rather than a single event. In order for a collective desire for peace to prevail over the desire of individual kin groups for revenge, en-

stamina, and other qualities needed in warriors. Games could have served as a means of testing the strength of a potential enemy or ally. As in Mesoamerica, ball games also had spiritual significance (Trigger 1978b, 803). Rubber was not available for balls in North America, so ball games necessarily had to take a different form.

2. Wayne Lenig (personal communication) cautions that we know relatively little about the distribution of Owasco settlement.

hanced integrative mechanisms were re-quired. Among the historic Iroquois, vil-lage or tribal councils met to settle internal disputes. In 1655, the Jesuit father Pierre Chaumonot referred to an Onon-daga council of thirty elders (Thwaites 1896–1901, 42:93–95; Tuck 1971, 6). In-dividuals in allied villages may have partici-pated in common calendrical ceremonies, medicine societies, and condolence rituals, creating additional bonds.

**Seneca**

The Seneca, who called themselves Notowa'ka:', Great Hill People, were the most populous of the Five Nations Iro-quois. Their historic homeland lay south of Rochester between the Genesee River and Canandaigua Lake. Their hunting territory extended north to Lake Ontario and to the south beyond the western Finger Lakes (Abler and Tooker 1978, 505).

In the legend of Bare Hill, the original Seneca emerge from the top of a large hill (Ge-nun-de-wah-ga) along Canandaigua Lake, where they build a village. The vil-lage is subsequently encircled by a great serpent and becomes overcrowded. People face starvation. The serpent is eventually slain, disgorging the bones of those he has eaten. Their skulls were believed to be rep-resented by fossil stromatolites along the lake shore (Abrams 1976, 6–7; Anderson 1996, 158; see fig. 48).

In a migration tradition recounted by Lewis Henry Morgan, the Iroquois moved into what is now New York State from the north and settled on the Seneca River (1962, 6). Later they split up and settled in their respective homelands becoming dis-tinct nations. An analysis of the Sky Woman myth found two distinct Seneca traditions (Abler 1987). The existence of different traditions suggests that the Seneca arose from more than one group. The archaeological record lends support to this notion (Niemczycki 1984, 14).

Fig. 48. The Legend of Bare Hill. Painting by Ernie Smith. Courtesy of the Rochester Museum and Science Center, Rochester, N.Y.

Between A.D. 1350 and 1450, village sites were located on hilltops and were between one-half and two acres in size (Niemczycki 1984, 92). The rich agricultural land in the Genesee Valley was abandoned by the mid-fifteenth century, presumably in response to warfare (Niemczycki 1986, 41). Palisaded villages were located in the hills to the east of the Genesee.

Both Donald Lenig (1965, 71–72) and Mary Ann Niemczycki (1986; 1995, 44, 49) believe an Ontario Iroquois population entered western New York in the thirteenth century, occupying the Ganshaw site and others in the Oak Orchard Creek drainage, some thirty miles west of the Genesee River. William Wykoff hypothesizes that the onset of drought conditions around A.D. 1280 led to this movement (1988, 16–82). However, the Oak Orchard area would have been a poor choice for farmers fleeing drought, as the sandy soils here dry out quickly (Nancy Herter, personal communication). Christine Dodd et al. argue that ceramic similarities between these sites and those in Ontario have been overstressed, and that this migration hypothesis is not yet clearly demonstrated (1990, 356). Shortly after A.D. 1500, sites such as Alhart (c. A.D. 1440–1510) in the Oak Orchard Creek drainage and surrounding area were abandoned, the inhabitants presumably driven out, destroyed, or absorbed by the Seneca (Niemczycki 1995, 49).

Excavations at the Alhart site revealed that this community met a violent end. Along with evidence of burning, fifteen skulls were found in a pit, fourteen of them male and the fifteenth a probable adolescent male. No identifiable female remains were recovered. These data suggest the destruction of the village by an enemy raid, with the slaughter of males and the capture and incorporation of females into the victorious group (Wray et al. 1987, 248). Distinctive physical anomalies observed on the skeletal material from Alhart are observable on skeletal remains from the Adams site, one of the first large Seneca villages dating nearly a hundred years later, suggesting incorporation of the Alhart females into the Seneca population (Lorraine Saunders, quoted in Niemczycki 1984, 72).

Some sites in the Seneca region such as Richmond Mills and Belcher were tentatively identified in the past as Cayuga on the basis of ceramics (MacNeish 1952, 47, 87). Niemczycki suggests that a population moved from the vicinity of Cayuga Lake into the historic Seneca territory sometime in the mid-fifteenth century, accounting for the similarity in ceramics between these areas (1984, 68; 1995, 45). The reason for this move is unknown. By the sixteenth century, then, populations both from the east and west had moved into what was to become the traditional Seneca homeland. Belcher and Richmond Mills may be said to start the Seneca pattern of two large contemporaneous villages (see fig. 49).

Following Belcher and Richmond Mills, a total of fourteen (seven pairs) of large village sites are known for the period from around A.D. 1560 to 1687. These sites are clustered about twenty miles south

| | SENECA | | CAYUGA |
|---|---|---|---|
| 1700 | Snyder-McClure | White Springs | |
| | | Ganondagan | Great Gully |
| | | Bunce | |
| | Dann | Marsh | Mead Farm |
| 1650 | Power House | Steele | Rogers Farm |
| | | Warren | |
| | | Cornish | |
| | Dutch Hollow | Factory Hollow | Myers Station |
| 1600 | | | Genoa, East Genoa |
| | Furgle | Cameron | |
| | Adams | Tram | Carman |
| | | Culbertson | Locke Fort |
| | | | Parker |
| 1550 | | | Indian Fort Road |
| | Richmond Mills | Belcher | |
| | | | Schempp |
| | | | Phelpps |
| | | MacArthur | |
| 1500 | | Harscher | Colgan |
| | | California Ranch | Nolan, Payne |
| | | Alhart | Fort Hill (?) |
| | | Long Point | Klinko |
| 1450 | | | Clifton Springs |
| | | | |
| | | | Weir |
| 1400 | | | |
| | | | Underwood |
| | | Footer | Mahaney |
| 1350 | | | |

Fig. 49. Chronological placement of Seneca and Cayuga sites mentioned in the text.

of modern Rochester (Saunders and Sempowski 1991, 13; see map 4).

Charles Wray has estimated the population of each of these villages as between eight hundred and one thousand (Saunders 1986, 14). These large villages relocated every fifteen to twenty years, although each at different times (Wray et al. 1987, 4–5; Saunders and Sempowski 1991, 13). At present, they have been arranged in chronological sequence from the late sixteenth century to the late seventeenth century.

The Adams and Culbertson sites, lo-

| | ONONDAGA | ONEIDA | MOHAWK |
|---|---|---|---|
| 1700 | Pen<br>Weston | | |
| | Indian Hill | | Veeder (Caughnawaga) |
| 1650 | Ste. Marie, Indian Castle | | Jackson-Everson |
| | | Marshall    Thurston | Failing    Naylor |
| | Pompey Center | | Briggs Run |
| 1600 | | Cameron | Wagner's Hollow, Martin |
| | | Bach | Rice's Woods, Barker |
| | Dwyer | Diable | Vanderwerken |
| | | | Smith-Pagerie |
| 1550 | | | |
| | Temperance, Atwell | | |
| | | Vaillancourt | |
| | | | Garoga    Cayadutta |
| 1500 | Barnes | | |
| | | Olcott | |
| | Burke | | Otstungo |
| | Christopher | Buyea | Elwood    Getman |
| 1450 | | Nichols Pond | |
| | | | Second Woods, Fox Lair |
| | Bloody Hill<br>Keough | | |
| 1400 | Schoff<br>Kelso<br>Howlett Hill | | |
| 1350 | | | |

Figure 50. Relative chronological placement of Onondaga, Oneida, and Mohawk sites mentioned in the text.

cated one-and-a-half miles apart, were occupied near the end of the sixteenth century (c. A.D. 1580–1595) and were at least partially contemporaneous (Wray et al. 1987, 3, 179; 1991, 386). In 1848, E. G. Squier mapped an earthen enclosure of about ten acres around Adams. Population of this site has been estimated at eight hun-

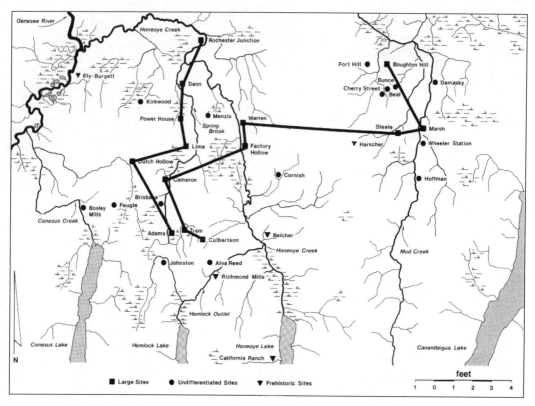

Map 4. Map of Seneca region (c. A.D. 1540–1657). Based on Seneca site sequence map drawn by Charles F. Wray (1973) with current revisions. (After Sempowski and Saunders 2000.)

dred to one thousand (Wray et al. 1987, 9, 240), which is a conservative estimate given the site's large size. Culbertson is less accurately estimated to be between five and eight acres in extent (Wray et al. 1987, 240). Both are significantly larger than earlier sites in the area. Their close proximity suggests peaceful coexistence. There is a small site associated with each of these larger sites, a pattern characteristic of the Seneca for at least a century.

Skeletal studies indicate that Adams and Culbertson males and Culbertson females were genetically similar (Saunders 1986, 197, 254). However, the female

skeletons recovered from the Adams cemeteries differed in a number of respects from other skeletons, suggesting an origin outside of the Seneca area (Wray et al. 1987, 26). Nearly twice as many female as male burials are recorded for Adams (Wray et al. 1987, 20). These "extra" women may have been war captives or refugees (Sempowski et al. 1988, 95). The skeletal data suggest that there was not a single population source from which inhabitants of the two early villages were derived.

Both Adams and Culbertson show affinities with slightly earlier sites in the region (Wray et al. 1987, 252–53). While the ceramics from Adams show some continuities with those from the earlier sites of Richmond Mills, Belcher, California Ranch, and Harscher, they are unusually heterogeneous (Wray et al. 1987, 93; Engelbrecht 1985, 168). These data suggest the consolidation of several local populations, along with the addition of individuals from outside the immediate area (Wray et al. 1987, 239).

To date, three separate cemeteries have been identified with the Adams site (Wray et al. 1987, 11). A common interpretation of multiple cemeteries associated with Iroquois villages is that they represent clan cemeteries. However, the existence of Iroquois clan cemeteries has not been demonstrated (Trigger 1985, 90). An alternative possibility is that these separate cemeteries may reflect earlier, autonomous communities that merged to form the larger community.[3] Wray et al. note an association of different pottery styles with different cemeteries, supporting this interpretation (1987, 97). Also, the number of cemeteries on Seneca sites seems to increase through time (Martha Sempowski, personal communication).

## Cayuga

The Cayuga homeland was on either side of Cayuga Lake and north along the

3. O'Shea (1988, 71) cites Wedel (1936) to the effect that after Pawnee bands coalesced into a single village, members of the respective bands were still buried together.

Seneca River (Niemczycki 1984, 21). Their hunting territory extended north to Lake Ontario and south toward the Susquehanna River (White et al. 1978, 500). The Cayuga called themselves Kayohkno'nq?. The etymology of this is uncertain, but one possibility is "where the boats were taken out" or "People at the Landing" (White et al. 1978, 503; Fenton 1998, 51). In the tradition of the founding of the Iroquois League, the Cayuga chiefs state, "We come from the place where they beach boats" (Woodbury 1992, 220). The late Cayuga chief Jacob Thomas (Hadagehgrentha) said, "When people from the other Five Nations would come here, they would come down Cayuga Lake in canoes" (Doxtater 1998, 48). There is a water route from Cayuga Lake via the Seneca River to both Lake Ontario and Oneida Lake. From Oneida Lake, one can paddle up Wood Creek and, with a portage, be in the Mohawk River (see map 5).

Mary Ann Niemczycki traced ceramic stylistic continuities in the Cayuga territory from the Owasco period in approximately A.D. 1250–1300 to the historically known Cayuga (1984). A dispersed Owasco population developed into two or three Iroquois populations that ultimately formed the Cayuga nation (Niemczycki 1991). Between A.D. 1350 and 1450, sites such as Mahaney, Underwood, and Weir represent a population on the east side of Cayuga Lake (Niemczycki 1991, 29; Robert DeOrio, personal communication; see 49).

Dating between about A.D. 1450 and 1550, the sites of Clifton Springs and

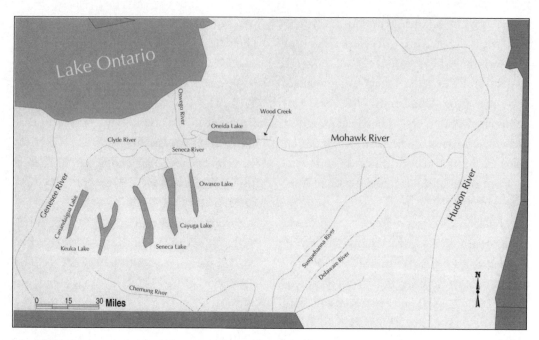

Map 5. Water route with portage from the Mohawk River to the Finger Lakes.

Phelps lie between the Seneca and Cayuga historic heartlands. Niemczycki includes these in her discussion of Seneca development (1984), but it is possible that they relate to the Cayuga (Robert DeOrio, personal communication). Sites on the east side of Cayuga Lake include Nolan, Colgan, and Locke Fort, which may represent one or more communities.

The earliest Iroquois site on the southwest side of Cayuga Lake appears around A.D. 1450 with no known local antecedents, unlike those on the east side (DeOrio 1980, 85). The sites of Klinko, Payne, Schempp, Indian Fort Road, Parker, and Carman may be successive locations of a single community moving in a southerly direction along the southwest side of Cayuga Lake (Niemczycki 1991,

31; Allen 1998). These sites are ceramically similar to sites on the east side of the lake. Niemczycki suggested that the ceramic similarity between sites on the east and southwest sides of Cayuga Lake reflects a high degree of social connectedness (1984, 64). A land route between these sites would be about thirty miles, an unusually distant separation for members of the same group. However, use of canoes would reduce that distance by at least half, giving added meaning to the name "People at the Landing."

The site of Fort Hill in Auburn, New York, is an impressive earthwork still visible in a cemetery. Unfortunately, there is no material available for study. In an early use of dendrochronology, James Macauley reported in 1825 that the earthwork must be older than about A.D. 1555 (DeOrio 1998). Some 175 years later, we are not able to say much more.[4]

Both Carman and Parker on the southwest side of the lake contain traces of European trade materials (Stutzman 1998). Sometime after A.D. 1600, this population apparently joins the eastern Cayuga (Niemczycki 1991, 31). The Genoa Fort site on the east side of the lake dates to around this time, as does the site of East Genoa, just across a ravine (Robert DeOrio, personal communication). The occupation of Myers Station may overlap with one or both of these sites. Many of the known sixteenth—and early seventeenth-century Cayuga sites are on highly defensible locations, suggesting that warfare led to the geographic consolidation of the Cayuga.

## Onondaga

The traditional homeland of the Onondaga, Onotaʔkekaʔ or "People on the Hill," lies between Cazenovia Lake and Onondaga Creek (Blau et al. 1978, 491, 499). Deep Spring near Manlius lay on the trail between Onondaga and Oneida and marked their common boundary (Fenton 1998, 77). Onondaga hunting territory extended north to Lake Ontario and south to nearly the Pennsylvania state line.

4. Both Robert DeOrio and Peter Pratt have suggested to me that Fort Hill may be an Hopewellian ceremonial earthwork, rather than an Iroquois defensive earth ring.

Oral tradition relates that the Onondaga nation formed out of small scattered bands (Fenton 1998, 60). This agrees with the archaeological evidence. Within the vast region that was the historic Onondaga hunting territory were early, small, scattered sites. As James Tuck observed, it is probably not a coincidence that the hunting territory of the later Onondaga nation corresponded with the distribution of these ancestral communities (1971, 216).

Tuck identified a series of sites that represent continuity of occupation in the Onondaga area from Owasco times to the present (1971; see fig. 50).

Owasco sites were generally just north of the Onondaga escarpment on the Ontario lake plain (Bradley 1987, 14), but the late Owasco Chamberlin site (c. A.D. 1290) marks a shift to a hilltop location on the escarpment and the larger settlement size characteristic of the succeeding Oak Hill horizon (Tuck 1978, 491; Bradley 1987, 14, 21). Snow dates Oak Hill to A.D. 1350 or 1400 (1995a, 78). The larger settlements appear to have been the product of community fusion. From the fact that Chamberlin and later Oak Hill sites like Furnace Brook, Howlett Hill, and Kelso were palisaded, we can infer defense as a major reason for these changes (Bradley 1987, 22).

During the Chance phase (A.D. 1400–1525), most sites were in the uplands and heavily fortified. At the beginning of the fifteenth century, a small community relocated a distance of nearly ten miles to within two miles of a large community, the latter having been formed by the fusion of two communities.[5] Tuck inferred that this move marked the existence of an alliance between these two communities for mutual defense, and symbolically marked the beginnings of the Onondaga nation (1971, 215; 1978, 327).

Sites in the Onondaga area increased in size during the late fifteenth and early sixteenth centuries and then stabilized during most of the sixteenth century, with the larger sites being four to five acres and the smaller sites two to three acres (Bradley 1987, 35, 49–50). Based on the presence of northern Iroquoian traits on Onondaga sites, Bradley argued for the assimilation of a group of Iroquoians from Jefferson County, New York, by the Onondaga sometime between A.D. 1525 and 1555 (1987, 85–87).[6]

5. Tuck (1971, 212–15) hypothesized that the community at the Schoff site moved ten miles to the one at Burke, which is near the Christopher site. Tuck further hypothesizes that this latter community was formed by the fusion of the smaller communities of Bloody Hill and Keough. Bradley (1987, 28) suggests there may be intermediate occupations between Schoff and Burke, and that the settlement dynamics of this period need to be further clarified.

6. Peter Pratt (personal communication) suggests that these people might also have come from St. Lawrence County or even Southeastern Ontario or southwestern Quebec. While it is traditional to refer to Iroquoian populations in Jefferson County as St. Lawrence Iroquoians along with populations to the northeast along the St. Lawrence River, it is my opinion that this terminology obscures the fact that numerous separate populations existed in the six

By the early seventeenth century, there appears to be a shift in the settlement pattern from a larger and a smaller village to a single large village (Onontaque) surrounded by smaller hamlets (Bradley 1987, 116). Once northern New York (Jefferson County) was abandoned, Onondaga fishing sites began to expand northward (Bradley 1987, 118).

## Oneida

The Oneida call themselves Oneyote?aka, "People of the Standing Stone," after a large boulder that tradition states was always found near the main Oneida settlement (Campisi 1978, 489). Their homeland was located in the uplands southeast of Oneida Lake where at least thirty-five village sites have been identified (Whitney 1970, 1; Pratt 1976, 9). Most of these are in Madison County, with a few nearby in Oneida County (Starna 1988, 10). In the seventeenth century, their hunting territory ranged from near the Pennsylvania state line to the St. Lawrence (Starna 1988, 10).

It used to be thought that there were no Owasco sites in the traditional Oneida territory that could have provided the nucleus for the later Oneida. However, work by Theodore Whitney at the Jamba site (middle Owasco) and Peter and Marjorie Pratt at the Airport site (late Owasco) now

hundred kilometers between the eastern end of Lake Ontario and the area east of Quebec City (Engelbrecht 1995).

suggest the possibility of at least a partial in situ development for the Oneida as well (see map 2).[7] In a metaphorical sense, this agrees with the tradition that the Oneida sprang from the ground.[8]

Just to the west of the Oneida homeland there are poorly known sites near the village of Cazenovia, dating to around A.D. 1300. These may be transitional between the Owasco and later Oneida (Weiskotten 1988, 12–13). H. R. Schoolcraft recorded a tradition that the Oneida have their origin in two men who separated from the Onondaga (Beauchamp 1922, 154). If the Cazenovia sites are proto-Oneida, then their close geographical association with proto-Onondaga sites of the period adds support for this tradition, as does ceramic data (MacNeish 1952; Whitney 1970; Engelbrecht 1974a; 1974b; 1978, 149). The Nichols Pond site remains the earliest identified Iroquois village site in the traditional Oneida homeland (Pratt 1976).

Linguistically, Oneida is very similar to

Mohawk (Lounsbury 1978, 335–36), and Chance phase ceramics from both the Mohawk and Oneida areas are quite similar (Pratt 1976, 148; Snow 1995a, 91). David Cusick's 1825 account has the first Iroquois family establishing themselves along the Mohawk River, followed by the next who become the Oneida, implying a close Mohawk-Oneida connection (Beauchamp 1892, 12). In historic times, both Oneida and Mohawk had the same three clans: Wolf, Bear, and Turtle. Some of these similarities may be due to the movement of people between the Oneida and Mohawk areas in the first half of the seventeenth century.

In addition to the traditions that the Oneida emerged from the ground, or separated from either the Onondaga or Mohawk, there is a tradition that some Oneida were descended from Chief "Thick-Neck" and his people who lived slightly to the south (Hammond 1872, 751). These multiple traditions support the ethnogenesis model of diverse ancestry for the Oneida.

The number of contemporaneous Oneida villages changed over time. The Olcott and Vaillancourt sites (only 1.3 kilometers apart) are larger than other fifteenth—and early sixteenth-century Oneida sites, suggesting a coalescence of two or more villages to form a single community (Pratt 1976, 151; see fig. 50). Vaillancourt approaches ten acres in size (Hayes and Wonderly 1998). The first Oneida sites containing European material, Bach and Diable, may be partially contemporaneous, reflecting the gradual

7. Dr. Richard Hosbach called my attention to the Airport and Jamba sites, and both Dr. Hosbach and Wayne Lenig helped clarify current dating of Oneida sites for me.

8. Tony Wonderley, Oneida Nation Historian, called my attention to this and other Oneida traditions. "The great enemy of the race of the turtle being destroyed [the evil twin], they came up out of the ground in human form, and for some time multiplied in peace and spread extensively over the surface. The Oneidas so long as they were in a pagan state, used to show the precise spot of ground, where they said their ancestors came up" (James Dean, "Mythology of the Iroquois," New York State Library, Albany, document 13805).

movement of population from an old to a new village (Pratt 1991, 41). By the early seventeenth century, multiple contemporaneous Oneida villages probably existed (Starna 1988, 17; Snow 1995a, 297).

## Mohawk

Mohawk call themselves Kanyuʔkeha:ka, which is generally translated as "People of the Flint" (Fenton and Tooker 1978, 478). Quartz crystals, known locally as Herkimer diamonds, are found on a number of Mohawk sites and are traditionally viewed as spiritually charged substances associated with winter power and ice. This power causes animal hibernation and bird migration (Hewitt 1903, 139). Following J. N. B. Hewitt, Snow suggests that the Mohawk name refers to quartz rather than flint (1995a, 212).

The Mohawk core area was the middle Mohawk Valley, in what is now Montgomery County. Their hunting territory extended north into the Adirondacks and south along the east branch of the Susquehanna (Fenton and Tooker 1978, 466). Recent research by Dean Snow has done much to clarify Mohawk archaeology as well as changes in Mohawk population over time.

Snow argues for population growth from the Owasco to Iroquois periods on the basis of an increasing number of sites (1995a, 52, 79). Some thirty-three Owasco sites are known for the Mohawk drainage and eighteen sites for the much shorter Oak Hill phase, the latter defined

by Donald Lenig (1965). While one would expect population growth during this period, Wayne Lenig cautions that many of these sites are poorly known and may only have been occupied seasonally (n.d.).[9]

During the fifteenth and early sixteenth centuries, communities of between one hundred and two hundred people merged to form a smaller number of better protected communities of six hundred to eight hundred inhabitants (Snow 1995a, 46, 85, 91; see fig. 50). Some of these communities apparently exchanged locations near productive farmland for more defensible locations (Snow 1995a, 137, 164). The Otstungo site is an example of the latter; it is located on a high promontory with a population estimated at 630. Snow suggests the clustering of Mohawk population during the late fifteenth and early sixteenth centuries marks the emergence of the Mohawk as a nation (1995a, 91; 1996, 168).

As part of this clustering, Snow suggests people from the Schoharie Creek drainage moved to the middle Mohawk Valley around A.D. 1450 (1995a, 91). Recently, a site in the Schoharie Valley, Vanderwerken, has been dated to the last quarter of the sixteenth century (Cassedy et al. 1996). Assuming the inhabitants were Mohawk, this

9. Wayne Lenig (n.d.) cautions that little is known of eleven of these and that they might not be Owasco. They are: Jackson Flats (Cnj 54); NYSM #1215 (Cnj 21); Diefendorf (Cnj 75); Little Nose Flats #2 (Cnj 53); Youngdon West (Fda 58?); Randle Flats (Fda 31); NYSM #1134 (Fda 37); Lower Bluebank alias Ripley (Fda 24); King (Fda 52); Empire Lock (Fda 49); and Karker #2 (NYSM 1885).

suggests either that the Schoharie Valley was not totally abandoned in the fifteenth century or that it continued to be seasonally exploited by people from the Mohawk Valley twenty-five kilometers downstream to the north. Alternatively, Wayne Lenig suggests the possibility that the inhabitants of the Schoharie Valley at this time were Algonquian speakers rather than Mohawk (personal communication).[10]

During the sixteenth century, there appear to be three separate sequences of village movement in the Mohawk Valley. In this view, Otstungo is a representative of the western community, Garoga of the central community, and Cayadutta of the eastern community (W. Lenig n.d.). Mohawk oral tradition as recorded by the Rev. Megapolensis in the 1640s speaks of three clan territories. The relationship, if any, between this tradition and the western, central, and eastern communities remains unclear.

By the late sixteenth and early seventeenth centuries, there was an increase in the population of the Mohawk Valley, apparently as a result of immigration (Snow 1991, 38; 1995a, 199). Snow suggests a possible additional influx of population from the Schoharie Valley (1995a, 199). In addition, ceramics from the Mohawk sites of Wagner's Hollow and Barker show

10. Wayne Lenig (personal communication) notes that we are accustomed to thinking of the Schoharie Valley as inhabited by Mohawk people because the Mohawk controlled the area in the eighteenth century. This assumption may not be warranted.

strong similarity with ceramics from northern New York (Engelbrecht 1995, 49–51). This may reflect an earlier movement of some of these northern Iroquoians to the Mohawk region (Snow 1995a, 171; Engelbrecht 1995, 49).

Around A.D. 1600, Snow and William Starna estimate Mohawk population to have been between 8,110 and 10,570 (1989). This is a generous estimate. However, it should be noted that the location of villages at this time along the rich floodplain of the Mohawk River allowed for highly productive farming as well as fishing. It also allowed for control of the river route to the Dutch trading post established in 1614.

**Spatial Dynamics**

In general, contemporaneous villages in the same tribal area are separated from one another by between five and ten miles (Engelbrecht 1980, 113). The two large Seneca communities both moved in a generally northward direction, while the relocation of the two Onondaga communities described an irregular circle. Following Allen (1988), sociopolitical connections between these contemporaneous communities can be inferred not only from their close proximity but from the fact that they move together in the same general direction.

From spacing between contemporaneous communities, one can infer that a catchment of between 2.5 and 5 miles around a village was desirable. These are

slightly greater distances than those between sequential locations of the same
community, which are on the order of 1.5
to 3.5 miles. The logistics of establishing a
new village from a base in the old village,
plus a desire for proximity to older cleared
areas may have encouraged short village relocations.

It is unlikely that horticultural requirements were the major variable in understanding spacing between either contemporaneous or sequential Iroquoian
communities. Calculation of maize requirements for a village of five hundred by
both Stephen Monckton (1992, 87) and
Conrad Heidenreich (1971) suggests that
fields would not need to be located more
than six hundred meters or so from the village. These studies assume the abandonment of old fields and so may overestimate
the amount of land needed. Exceptions
could occur if the immediate vicinity lacked
suitable farmland or if a strategy of widely
scattered garden plots in both well and
poorly drained areas were followed.

The need for firewood for both cooking and heating, and young trees for building repairs or village expansion likely
required the exploitation of wide areas
around settlements. The open areas and
scrub vegetation around villages would
have provided less firewood than a mature
forest, which typically would have been at
some distance from a village (Monckton
1992, 90). A scenario where materials
(other than cedar) from the previously occupied village were used as a source of firewood would be congruent with the

generally shorter distance between successive locations of a community versus the
greater distance between contemporaneous communities.

By the late sixteenth century, population was clustered in core areas (see map
1). To the west, Erie sites were located
some fifty-eight miles from the Seneca, and
Iroquoian sites in Jefferson County, New
York, were located some sixty miles north
of the Onondaga (Engelbrecht 1978,
142).

The Iroquois had long lived in an environment with open areas and secondary
growth created by fires and abandoned
fields. Trigger has observed that open areas
produced by abandoned fields would have
gradually increased over time, providing an
increasingly favorable habitat for deer
(1985, 98).

However, as population clustered in a
smaller number of large communities, the
mosaic of fields, grassland, and brushy
growth around small, scattered villages was
abandoned. If new, large villages were established in areas lacking such a vegetative
mosaic, there would have been an imbalance between population and available
local resources, especially if fear of raids
limited the exploitation of abandoned
areas. These buffer zones would have provided refuge for deer and other animals
(Hickerson 1965).

**External Warfare**

Beyond the world of the village and the nation lay a world of real and potential ene-

mies. Among the Huron, when a chief fell ill, his relatives might accuse an enemy chief of causing the illness through witchcraft, and demand military revenge (Trigger 1990b, 102). Revenge for real or imagined injury and the need for warriors to prove themselves provided the basis for ongoing hostilities. Added to motives of revenge and prestige was the desire for war captives for either adoption or sacrifice. As Robert Hall points out, it was widely believed in North America that a sacrificed captive could act as a servant for a deceased kinsmen (1997, 32). It was also believed that the spirit of a deceased individual could not rest until someone had been adopted as a replacement.

Economic explanations for hostilities between Iroquois nations in the fifteenth and early sixteenth centuries have been advanced but remain controversial. Ritchie suggested that game may not have increased as rapidly as the human population (1980, 281). Richard Gramly further refined this argument, suggesting that hostilities between groups in the Northeast arose over competition for deer hides (1977). As mentioned in chapter 1, it took at least six deer hides to produce a man's clothing, and eight to produce a woman's, not counting moccasins. If these clothes were replaced once every two years, a couple would need an average of seven deer hides a year. Though children would need fewer hides, a village of one thousand people would still need approximately seven thousand deer hides a year, not an inconsiderable number.

In a study of the faunal evidence, Mary Socci found that deer comprise between 91 and 98 percent of the faunal remains from Owasco and early Iroquois sites (1995). Sites dating between A.D. 1400 and A.D. 1666 have fewer, between 62 and 88 percent (Socci 1995, 223).[11] This downward shift could be interpreted as support for Gramly's hypothesis. However, Socci suggests that the downward shift is the result not of a decreased availability of deer but rather of an increase in the amount of time that men spent in warfare (1995, 225–27). Further complicating this argument is that fact that if deer were processed at camps, their faunal remains would be absent from village assemblages.

I suggest that the clustering of Iroquois population in the fifteenth and early sixteenth centuries as a result of warfare diminished the number of deer in the vicinity of the new, large villages. If so, this scarcity would have been an effect, rather than a cause, of warfare. Moreover, it would have encouraged the establishment of hunting camps far from villages, a pattern documented in the historic literature.

In the mid-seventeenth century, European observers remarked on the abundance of deer in Iroquois territory (Thwaites 1896–1901, 56:49–51). It is

11. From A.D. 1070+60 to A.D. 1420+80: Roundtop, Sackett, Cabin, Furnace Brook, Nahrwold No. 1 and Bloody Hill. It should be noted that faunal and floral data from many sites excavated in the past was gathered without the use of flotation. Comparing these samples with those from sites in which flotation was used must be done with caution.

commonly assumed that this was the case earlier as well, but the ratio between humans and deer may have changed. A century or more of community relocations in the core areas of Iroquois nations would have created a vegetational mosaic favorable for deer. Furthermore, by this time the Iroquois had suffered depopulation as a result of diseases introduced by the Europeans. Smaller human populations would have required fewer deer hides for clothing. Also, European clothing and textiles were being acquired through trade, lessening the need for hides.

## Ethnicity

The emerging Iroquois nations were not closed entities, with individuals and groups neither entering nor leaving. Many researchers have commented on overlapping ceramic styles between regions, or the presence of nonlocal ceramics (MacNeish 1952; Engelbrecht 1978; Latta 1991). A comparison of ceramics between areas using both ceramic attributes and ceramic types suggests regular contacts between areas (Engelbrecht 1978). Linguists also see recurrent contacts between the Five Nations (Lounsbury 1978; Chafe and Foster 1981).

Both ceramics and chert characteristic of St. Lawrence Iroquoians appear on Onondaga, Oneida, and Mohawk sites during the sixteenth century, hinting at the possible absorption of some St. Lawrence Iroquoians into the eastern Iroquois nations (Kuhn et al. 1993, 85). If these three Iroquois nations shared a common enemy among some of the St. Lawrence Iroquoian populations, they may have been allies. Such a relationship could have laid the groundwork for the formation of the famous League of the Haudenosaunee, or Iroquois, to be discussed in the next chapter.

Attempts by archaeologists to project ethnicity onto the archaeological record are at best problematic (Starna and Funk 1994; Hodder 1979). Ronald Cohen notes that "ethnic group formation is a continuing and often innovative cultural process of boundary maintenance and reconstruction" (1978, 397). Nonetheless, the clustering of sites during the fifteenth and sixteenth centuries in areas historically associated with Iroquois nations suggests the emergence of larger political units with which individuals probably began to identify. In addition to being members of lineages, clans, and communities, individuals were coming to identify with new, larger polities. They were becoming Seneca, Cayuga, Onondaga, Oneida, or Mohawk.

# ❖ 7 ❖

# THE LEAGUE OF THE HAUDENOSAUNEE

## Origin of the League

Haudenosaunee is translated as "People of the Longhouse" or "The Whole House." The League was described by the metaphor of the longhouse, with the Seneca and Mohawk being the keepers of the western and eastern doors, respectively, and the Onondaga as the central fire keepers. If the presence of only two longhouse doors was dictated by defensive concerns, as argued in chapter 4, then the title of "doorkeeper" takes on a military dimension which is frequently overlooked.

Meetings of the League were generally held at Onondaga, which was centrally located. Five nations originally formed the League of the Haudenosaunee. Using kinship as a model for intertribal association (Wolf 1982, 167), the Mohawk, Onondaga, and Seneca composed one moiety, or side; they referred to the Oneida and Cayuga as "you, our children," and were in turn addressed as "our fathers' kinsmen"

(Woodbury 1992, xxix).[1] The use of moieties or sides in confederacy ritual was apparently extended from its use by an individual nation in its rituals (Fenton 1998, 27).

In 1851, Lewis Henry Morgan published *League of the Ho-de-no-sau-nee or Iroquois*. His classic description is often taken as a blueprint for how the League functioned, but like any viable political institution the League changed over time. The institution described by Morgan in the mid-nineteenth century cannot be taken as a model for what existed under different conditions two centuries earlier. Arising initially to insure peace between member nations, the roots of the League extend to the period before European contact.

The previous chapter discussed the for-

1. These moieties are often incorrectly referred to as Elder Brothers and Younger Brothers (Fenton 1998, 27–28). Groups within the same moiety are "younger brothers;" literally "they are younger brothers to themselves" (Woodbury 1992, xxix).

mation of alliances between communities that led to the emergence of the historically known Iroquois nations. A similar process of alliance building between nations ultimately led to the formation of the League (Trigger 1976, 163; Tuck 1978, 327). It is probable that individual nations concluded alliances with one another before the final league structure was achieved (Trigger 1978a, 344; Engelbrecht 1985). Initially, these may have amounted to agreements not to fight one another and to activate mechanisms to suppress feuding. Such agreements would be adaptive responses to a political environment in which hostilities between groups were the norm. That fighting between Iroquoians was common before the formation of the League is supported both by oral tradition and the ubiquity of palisaded villages.

Oral tradition places the formation of the League before the arrival of Europeans. Conflicting traditions surrounding the date of the formation of the League may refer to different early alliances (Engelbrecht 1985). Some may even refer to earlier alliances between communities that led to tribal formation. One widely cited tradition is that recorded by Pyrlaeus, an eighteenth-century Moravian missionary, who recorded that the League was formed for mutual defense a generation before the coming of Europeans (Fenton 1998, 53).

It is probable that the Onondaga, Oneida, and Mohawk concluded an early alliance. From both an archaeological and linguistic perspective there are many similarities between the Onondaga, Oneida,

and Mohawk on the one hand and the Cayuga and Seneca on the other (Engelbrecht 1978; Lounsbury 1978, 336; Chafe and Foster 1981; Niemczycki 1984). Alternatively, for the first half of the seventeenth century, the Europeans lumped the Iroquois into two groups: the Mohawk and the Upper Iroquois (Tom Abler, personal communication).

As Fenton and others have noted, the formation of the League was a process rather than an event. This view is also embedded in oral traditions (Fenton 1998, 95).[2] A man of vision, referred to by modern Haudenosaunee as the Peacemaker, traveled with Hiawatha, spreading a message of peace to the different Iroquois nations (see fig. 51).[3]

The Mohawks were said to be the first nation to accept the Peacemaker's message, followed by the Oneida. Those joining the League and foregoing fighting with other members become *ongwe hon:we,* people accepting the "Great Law of Equity" or peace (Fenton 1998, 79).

Tradition states that the Seneca were the last to join the League. When they did join, there was both an eastern and a western Seneca group (Parker 1922, 273; Abler and Tooker 1978, 505; Saunders 1986, 13). It has been suggested that the names of the last two Seneca chiefs on the roll call of chiefs were added after the original

2. Fenton (1998, 67) notes that Horatio Hale perceived this in the nineteenth century in his *Iroquois Book of Rites,* published in 1883.

3. The traditional name of the Peacemaker is Deganawi:dah.

Fig. 51. Formation of the League. Painting by Ernie Smith. Courtesy of the Rochester Museum and Science Center, Rochester, N.Y.

council of the League. This, coupled with the fact that the Seneca have the fewest League chiefs (eight), though they are the most populous of the Five Nations (Abler and Tooker 1978, 505), may also reflect their status as late joiners. The pattern of two large contemporaneous villages that characterized the Seneca in the early historic period did not exist until the middle of the sixteenth century (Richmond Mills and Belcher), suggesting that the Seneca joined the League after this settlement pattern had been established.

Cross-culturally, warfare is frequent in a context in which there is "a lack of shared institutions for resolving disputes or common values emphasizing nonviolence" (Keeley 1996, 127). The shared institution of the League and the teachings of the Peacemaker that emphasized nonviolence

provided the means for the Iroquois to resolve differences and achieve peace with one another. Iroquois speakers followed a strict protocol. Speakers advanced well-thought-out, eloquent arguments in council. They were never interrupted. Listeners would take time to reflect on a proposal before responding. There was an emphasis on remembering points earlier speakers had made, and often strings of wampum were used to stand for these points (Thwaites 1896–1901, 38: 261; Fenton 1998, 249, 254–55).

Archaeologists cannot dig up the League, but there are patterns in the archaeological record that reflect behavior surrounding its establishment. The remainder of this chapter looks at these patterns, which includes movement of various nonlocal items across the landscape and the disappearance or relocation of populations. Crucial to this discussion is the dating of sites across Iroquoia. While the relative sequence of sites in the respective Iroquois nations is reasonably well established (see figs. 49 and 50), more work is needed to correlate the regional sequences with one another.

## Marine Shell

While there is little evidence of long-distance exchange during Owasco and Oak Hill times, marine shell and other nonlocal items were appearing on Iroquois sites by the late fifteenth century (Bradley 1987, 21, 25, 34; Snow 1984, 255, 257). The initial appearance of marine shell on Iroquois sites appears unrelated to the development of the European fur trade. Among the Mohawk, half a century elapses between the first appearance of marine shell and the first appearance of European manufactured materials (Kuhn and Funk 1994, 82). The earliest marine shell on a Mohawk site is at Elwood (c. A.D. 1450–1500), while in the Seneca region it is at Alhart (c. A.D. 1440–1510).[4] Marine shell also occurs on Onondaga and Oneida sites before European trade material (Bradley 1987, 92, 221 n. 9).

The presence of marine shell on Iroquois sites steadily increases until the end of the sixteenth century. On the Dwyer site (Onondaga, c. A.D. 1575–1600), a few shell beads have straight bore holes, suggesting that they were drilled with a metal tool. Most shell beads from this time have biconical perforations as the ones on earlier sites do, indicating that they were drilled from both sides (Bradley 1987, 217 n. 27). Unmodified and partially modified marine shell is found on Iroquois sites of the mid-sixteenth century, suggesting local manufacture of some marine shell beads (Bradley 1987, 96). On the Seneca Cameron site, thirty-six shell discs were recovered, which were identified as disc bead "blanks." These

suggest systematic shell bead production (Wray et al. 1991, 351). Such blanks disappear from the record on later sites (Martha Sempowski, personal communication).

As mentioned in chapter 3, shell was viewed as having spiritual significance. The presence of marine shell on inland Iroquois sites of the sixteenth century reflects the existence at this time of a long-distance exchange network. In the seventeenth century, friendly relations between groups were maintained by the exchange of shell beads (Hall 1997, 58). Rather than being a by-product of economic transactions, the presence of nonlocal marine shell on sites reflects the existence of nonhostile relationships or alliances between groups (Dennis 1993, 132, 175).

A number of researchers have suggested that shell may be taken as a material symbol of the Condolence Ritual, which was incorporated into the functioning of the League (Bradley 1987, 179; Kuhn and Funk 1994, 77; Snow 1995a, 154). In this ritual, strings of shell are used by each moiety or side to comfort the other at the deaths of their chiefs. Oral tradition states that the Condolence Ritual initially made use of freshwater shell. Hiawatha collected shells from a lake bed that was miraculously exposed. These became a symbol of "the Good Message and the Power and the Peace and the Great Law" (Woodbury 1992, 329–30).

Over time, discoidal marine shell beads were gradually replaced by tubular shell beads in the form of wampum. Strings of wampum were used during the installation

---

4. Hamell 1977; Bamann 1993, 108–12; Kuhn and Funk 1994, 79. Charles F. Wray thought the radiocarbon dates for Alhart were too early, preferring to date it to the mid-sixteenth century (Martha Sempowski, personal communication). Wayne Lenig (personal communication) sees the introduction of marine shell as an early sixteenth-century phenomenon, rather than a late fifteenth-century one.

of new chiefs in the positions left vacant by those who had died (Fenton 1998, 81). The spiritually charged nature of shell underscores its importance in these rituals (Fenton 1998, 125).

## Pipes

Cynthia Weber examined pipes throughout Iroquoia and concluded that there are pan-Iroquoian pipe styles (1971, 56). It is not clear when this pattern emerged, but it may have occurred first among the eastern Iroquois and then later among the Seneca and Cayuga.[5] As artifacts typically associated with males, one can infer male travel over a wide area, with pipes used in gift exchange (Kuhn 1985). What was exchanged was not just the object but also the spiritual power inherent in that object (Kuhn 1986, 17).

In addition to pipes for personal use, numerous historic references point to the use of pipes on diplomatic occasions. Perhaps it is in this context that we see increased pipe use (Sempowski 1997). A recent analysis of the clay composition of Mohawk and Seneca ceramics revealed five pipe fragments from late sixteenth—and early seventeenth-century Seneca sites that were probably made in the Mohawk Valley (Kuhn and Sempowski 2001).[6]

Stone pipe bowls that used a separate stem occur as a minority type on many sites (see figs. 52 and 53). Such pipes may have been used in the fashion of historically known calumets from the Midwest. These were often used for welcoming visitors or for affirming alliances (Paper 1992, 163; Hall 1997, 121). The existence of the Iroquois League and the associated diplomacy such an organization required would have called for the frequent public use of pipes.

## European Goods

After A.D. 1525, small quantities of European trade goods began to flow through existing exchange networks. European materials were represented mostly by small iron adzes, iron spikes, and large rolled copper tubes made from kettle fragments (Snow 1995a, 28–30). Early European material has been found on the Seneca site of Richmond Mills (Martha Sempowski, personal communication), the Phelps site in the eastern Seneca region (Niemczycki 1984, 37), the Cayuga site of Locke Fort (Mandzy 1994, 140), and the Onondaga sites of Temperance House and Atwell (Bradley 1987, 69).

Some European trade material recov-

---

5. The dating of this phenomenon is not clear. From the perspective of the Mohawk region, Wayne Lenig (personal communication) sees the widespread establishment of native pipe styles by the second half of the fifteenth century. From the perspective of the Seneca region, Martha Sempowski does not see this phenomenon until the early seventeenth century.

However, as Wayne Lenig points out, the sample of sixteenth-century Seneca pipes is smaller.

6. One pipe fragment is from Dutch Hollow; three pipe fragments are from Factory Hollow. One pipe fragment, also believed to have originated in the Mohawk Valley, came from the earlier Cameron site (Sempowski and Saunders n.d.).

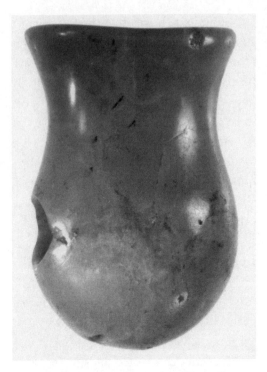

Fig. 52. Large vasiform pipe bowl from the Dutch Hollow site (Seneca). Maximum height: 7.6 cm. Courtesy of the Rochester Museum and Science Center, Rochester, N.Y.

Fig. 53. Vasiform stone pipe bowl from the Huntoon site (Seneca, c. 1720–1750). The maximum height is approximately 6 cm. Courtesy of the Rochester Museum and Science Center, Rochester, N.Y.

ered from sixteenth—and seventeenth-century sites is useful for providing chronological ordering of village sites. For example, after A.D. 1580, glass beads increased in frequency on Iroquois sites (Bradley 1987, 158). The style of these trade beads changed over time. It is now thought that substantial quantities of manufactured European goods did not reach the Seneca until the end, rather than the middle, of the sixteenth century (Wray et al. 1991, 4–5, 386–87).

European activities along the East Coast and the presence of European trade material on Iroquois sites has led to the designation "protohistoric" for sixteenth-century Iroquois sites. Initially, however, the European presence along the coast appeared to have little impact on Iroquois life. By the end of the century, this began to change, though it was at least another generation or two before most New York Iroquois came face to face with Europeans (Kuhn and Funk 1994, 77). The Mohawk, being the most eastern of the Five Nations, were the first to be directly affected by European activities along the Atlantic coast (Fenton and Tooker 1978, 467).

Beginning in the early seventeenth century, the similarity in the amount and kinds of European trade material on all sites of the Five Nations is striking (Bradley 1987, 104, 221–22 n. 14; Wray et al. 1987, 252). From this, one can infer regular contact and exchange between these nations. The maintenance of peaceful relations between the Five Nations Iroquois would have served to redistribute materials among member nations, explaining the presence of these goods among communities that had less direct access to them. The distribution of these goods would have operated to strengthen ties between members of the League (Trigger 1985, 161).

According to George Hamell, Native Americans equated native copper and quartz crystals with European metal and glass beads, viewing them as another form of these supernaturally charged substances (1983). While Europeans may have thought these items of little economic value, native peoples wished to acquire them because they were similar to existing symbolically charged substances (Hamell 1987; Bradley 1987, 110; Dennis 1993, 174). Additionally, their association with strange newcomers probably seen as possessing supernatural powers would have initially enhanced their value (Trigger 1985, 155–56).

Today, we view seventeenth-century "stabilized" or oxidized metal in museum display cases, and to most visitors these objects are dull and uninteresting. But when new, polished metal, crystals, and glass reflect the light of the sun or fire. To traditional Iroquois, all objects possessed animate power or orenda, but these reflective substances must have been seen as possessing orenda in abundance.

What the Iroquois were initially seeking was European metal, not European manufactured objects (Bradley 1987, 170–71). The metal happened to come in the form of copper kettles and iron axes, but these were then transformed into objects that fit the Iroquois universe. The similarity of many metal forms to traditional ones is an argument for native manufacture (Bradley 1987, 74–75). Tubular copper beads resemble tubular bird bone beads, while copper disc pendants resemble stone, shell, or bone ones, the latter made from modified epiphyseal caps (Bradley 1987, 75, 171–72). Brass cones resemble modified deer phalanges.[7] Small brass hawk bells on the Seneca Adams and Tram sites were left intact, and may have been equated with bone and brass tinkling cones.

Evidence that the Iroquois are working European metal during the last half of the sixteenth century comes from the presence of metal scrap on sites of this period (Bradley 1987, 74; Wray et al. 1987, 48; Prezzano 1992, 177). At first the same techniques were used as in working native copper: cold hammering, heating, and abrasion (Bradley 1987, 74). Later additional techniques were added. At the Seneca Cameron site, some pieces of brass

7. In burials from Cameron and Tram, brass cones consistently occur in sets of three (Wray et al. 1991, 249–50).

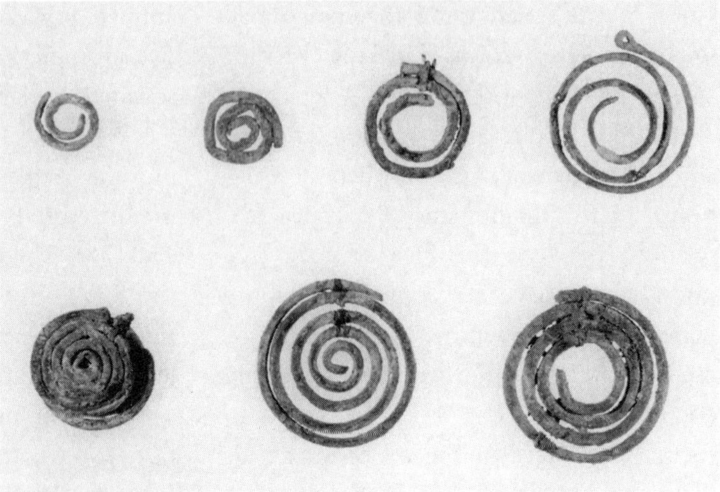

Fig. 54. Brass spirals, Adams site (Seneca). Diameter of lower right is: 4.2 cm. From Wray et al. 1987, 60. Courtesy of the Rochester Museum and Science Center, Rochester, N.Y.

kettle scrap have lines indicating scoring with a sharp object. It is thought that the brass was folded back and forth along such scoring to break it (Wray et al. 1991, 253). This was no longer necessary when iron scissors became available to the Iroquois during the second quarter of the seventeenth century (Bradley 1987, 132). Some fragments from European kettles exhibit secondary use wear as knives or scrapers (J. V. Wright, personal communication; Thibaudeau 2002).

Some native-made metal objects, like brass spirals, have a wide distribution in the Northeast during the last half of the sixteenth century (see fig. 54). These spirals may have symbolized the tail of the mythical underwater panther, a source of supernatural power and healing (Bradley and Childs 1991, 16; Hamell 1998). These spirals also illustrate the creative use of European materials by native peoples to produce a new form, the product of the interaction of two cultures (Snow 1994a, 3).

On a number of sites with early European trade material, the quantity of shell is greater than on earlier sites, suggesting that European goods enhanced rather than replaced ritual use of native materials (Bradley 1987, 95–96, 221 n. 10). At the Seneca Tram site, 1,608 marine shell beads were recovered. All of these were from mortuary contexts (Wray et al. 1991, 146). There is, however, an even more dramatic increase in the quantity of European material than in local material (Bradley 1987, 97). Occasionally, both metal and shell were added as inlays to objects of native manufacture, especially pipes (see fig. 21). These inlays were probably seen as further enhancing the spiritual power of the object.

As the acquisition of European goods became more important to native groups, alliances that started out as "nonaggression agreements" became increasingly important in securing access to these goods (Trigger and Swagerty 1996, 387). This must have been the case with the League of the Haudenosaunee. Assuming nations were not in direct competition with one another, trade increased the frequency of friendly intergroup contacts. Both trade and diplomacy became avenues for males to acquire prestige in addition to warfare (Campisi 1978, 482). Men demonstrated their abilities by wearing and giving away quantities of trade goods, especially beads (Cannon 1991, 145–47).

**The Exchange Network**

The Iroquois were strategically located near the headwaters of major drainages in the Northeast, including the St. Lawrence, the Mohawk/Hudson, the Delaware, and the Susquehanna (Bradley 1987, 111; Hasenstab 1990, 73). By the early seventeenth century, the Mohawk controlled the canoe route through Lake Champlain and the Richelieu River into Canada (Snow 1995a, 197). The Allegheny River in southwestern New York feeds into the Ohio and ultimately the Mississippi. Iroquois connections with the Ohio area are traceable to the last quarter of the sixteenth century (Drooker 1997, 334).

Population clusters in the fifteenth and sixteenth centuries formed nodal points in an indigenous exchange network. Because of the wide geographic area this network covered, it cannot be assumed that all material traded to the Iroquois came by the same route. Along with marine shell, Onondaga sites of the late fifteenth century have yielded native copper from Lake Superior; nonlocal lithics, some of which may have

come from the east; and an incised walrus ivory dagger (Bradley 1987, 38, 42, 65, 213–14 n. 45). The Gulf of St. Lawrence is the closest place with walrus populations (J. V. Wright, personal communication). An Oneota-style redstone disk pipe was recovered from the Seneca Richmond Mills site (Drooker 1997, 46, 334).

It has been suggested that early European trade material reached the Iroquois via the St. Lawrence. The Basques and other Europeans were fishing before 1550 in the Grand Banks (Turgeon 1990; Cassedy et al. 1996, 32). Basque traders used high-purity copper kettles, and fragments of these have been identified on late sixteenth-century Iroquois sites, most frequently in central New York (Fitzgerald et al. 1993; Cassedy et al. 1996, 31). Peter Bakker has argued that the word *Iroquois* is derived from Basque and means "killer people," implying that the Iroquois had to fight for access to trade along the St. Lawrence (1990).

James Bradley has made a case for both European material and marine shell reaching central New York via the Susquehanna River from the mid-Atlantic coast, noting similarities in European material on both Onondaga and Susquehannock sites (1987, 90). While the amount of early European material moving up the Susquehanna River is currently debated, most feel that sixteenth-century marine shell reached the New York Iroquois via this route (Snow 1995a, 154; Bradley 1987, 67, 89; Sempowski 1994, 51). Marginella shells found on Onondaga sites occur only as far north as North Carolina (Bradley 1987, 90). Additionally, the presence of *Busycon laeostomum* on Ontario Iroquois sites argues for a Chesapeake Bay source via the Susqehanna River, as this species occurs only between southern New Jersey and Virginia (Pendergast 1989, 102).

By the late sixteenth century, regular trade between the French and Algonquins was occurring at Tadoussac along the St. Lawrence, and in 1600 a trading post was established there (Trigger and Swagerty 1996, 354, 382). European goods on Mohawk sites from this time most likely came from this source, either through trading or raiding (D. Lenig 1977).

Toward the close of the sixteenth century, less marine shell is found on Mohawk sites, followed in the early seventeenth century by a similar falloff on the Seneca sites of Dutch Hollow, Factory Hollow, Warren, and Lima (Sempowski 1989, 86–87; 1994, 52; Kuhn and Funk 1994, 80–82). It is possible that this difference is more apparent than real, the result of both dating discrepancies and noncomparable samples (Wayne Lenig, Martha Sempowski, personal communications). It may also indicate that these two nations were involved in slightly different exchange networks, which is not surprising given their different locations.

Ontario Iroquoian sites do not exhibit a comparable decrease in shell material. Rather, shell is scarce in Ontario until about A.D. 1590, after which it is present in significant quantities throughout the first half of the seventeenth century (Pender-

gast 1989, 102). Ontario groups may have been getting their southern marine shell via little-known groups south and west of the Iroquois such as the Massawomeck, who were in turn getting it from Chesapeake Bay suppliers (Pendergast 1991a, 70; 1992, 8).

Using the analogy of a modern power grid, symbolically charged substances could move through alternate networks provided connections were kept in good order and maintained by reciprocal exchange. If a blockage occurred, alternate sources were sought. Failure to "stay connected" was reflected in a decline of spiritually powerful materials, which reflected an inability to maintain the necessary alliances resulting in exchange.

Snow suggests that Mohawk sites between 1580 and 1614 lack the quantity of European material found on Seneca sites or Iroquoian sites in southern Ontario (1995a, 232). Algonquian groups north of the Mohawk may have hindered Mohawk access to the French on the St. Lawrence, so Mohawk and Oneida raiding along the St. Lawrence may have been directed at gaining access to European materials (Trigger and Swagerty 1996, 387). It is at this time that Mohawk-made pipes appear on Seneca sites, along with small quantities of Normanskill chert, available near the Mohawk.

Like the difference in marine shell, it is possible that the difference in relative quantities of European trade material on Seneca and Mohawk sites of the early seventeenth century are more apparent than real. Much of our information on Seneca material culture of this period comes from graves, while Mohawk data is generally from village excavations. Because of the Iroquois practice of including marine shell, glass beads, and metal as burial offerings, the greater quantity of these materials in collections from Seneca sites may reflect the nature of these collections, rather than the relative quantity of European material on Seneca and Mohawk sites.

The establishment in 1614 of Fort Nassau, a Dutch trading post near what is now Albany, provided the Mohawk with a more convenient source of material than Tadoussac (Snow 1996, 171). In 1617, Fort Nassau was destroyed by floods, but in 1624 Fort Orange was established. These Dutch posts became an important additional source for European goods found on Mohawk sites as well as on sites of the other Iroquois nations (Snow 1996, 173).

Life was not always made better by European technology. As European metal became abundant in the seventeenth century, copper-alloy kettles began to replace ceramic containers for cooking. While superior to native ceramics in terms of durability, cooking food in such vessels can result in hemolytic anemia (Saunders 1996, 35). Children are at greatest risk, and this anemia can result in a pitting of the upper walls of the eye sockets, a condition known as cribra orbitalia. Evidence of cribra orbitalia is typically interpreted as a sign of either iron or vitamin C deficiency. In the case of seventeenth-century Iroquoian populations, cribra orbitalia may also signal copper toxicity (Saunders 1996, 40).

We know that furs, textiles, European clothing, and other perishable items circulated through the exchange networks of the sixteenth and early seventeenth centuries, but these are rarely preserved in the archaeological record. As a consequence of increased travel, ideas also probably spread, but documenting this is difficult. It has been suggested that the distinction between peace chiefs and war chiefs may be southern in origin. Also, the fact that both the Creek and Iroquois confederacies had fifty chiefs is striking and suggests contact or diffusion, although the timing is uncertain (Trigger 1978b, 803; 1985, 63).

**Travel**

Overland travel in a climax forest with underbrush and deadfalls can be very slow going (Miller 1994, 49). For an organization like the League to operate effectively, clear trails between areas were needed. "Keeping the road clear between us" was a diplomatic phrase, but it was vital. Contrary to popular thinking, not all communication before modern technology occurred in slow motion. According to Lewis Henry Morgan, information could be transmitted a hundred miles a day with a trained runner (1962, 441). The success of the confederacy was in part a result of its organized runners (Nabokov 1981, 18).

Iroquois people have a tradition of hospitality. This tradition facilitated the movement of diplomats, traders, warriors, and runners. Many of the same clans were found among the different Iroquois na-

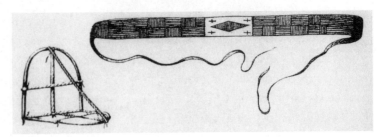

Fig. 55. Burden strap and frame from the Onondaga Reservation (Beauchamp 1905, plate 27).

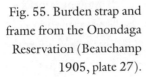

tions, so traveling Iroquois would seek hospitality with members of their clan. As mentioned in chapter 4, van den Bogaert observed what were probably clan emblems painted on the exterior of longhouses (Gehring and Starna 1988, 8).

To trade for marine shell and European items, men spent more time hunting beaver and other fur-bearing animals. During this same period, both warfare and diplomacy also took men away from the village. These male absences from their wives potentially had a negative effect on Iroquois fertility. The prolonged absence of males probably also served to strengthen the matrilocal extended family (Trigger 1978c, 62).

In historic times, women also traveled between Iroquois nations. In 1634, van den Bogaert encountered three women, probably Oneida, who had traveled for six days to reach Mohawk villages to sell salmon and tobacco (Gehring and Starna 1988, 6). When Pierre Chaumonot and René Ménard traveled from Onondaga to Oneida in 1656, their provisions were carried by women (Thwaites 1896–1901, 44: 31).

Goods were typically placed in a burden frame that was attached to a burden strap (tumpline) passed across the forehead (Beauchamp 1905, 163–67; see fig. 55).

In winter, travelers wore snowshoes (see fig. 56). Morgan was told by the Seneca that they could travel fifty miles a day with snowshoes (1962, 377).

During the sixteenth century, there is a trend of increasing ceramic similarity between areas (Ritchie 1980, 317; Engelbrecht 1971; 1972). Since women are assumed to have been the potters, this trend could be interpreted as reflecting an increased movement of women between nations, perhaps as female traders or porters. The trend of increasing ceramic similarity extends to Iroquoian sites in the Niagara Frontier region of western New York, outside the traditional homeland of the League (Engelbrecht 1971; 1972). Because of this, increased ceramic similarity between nations cannot be taken as a direct reflection of the League but rather as increased travel between nations.

Travelers were provisioned with parched corn meal. The corn was first roasted and then pounded (Grant 1907, 315–16). While small amounts could be eaten without additional preparation, it was considered dangerous to do so because

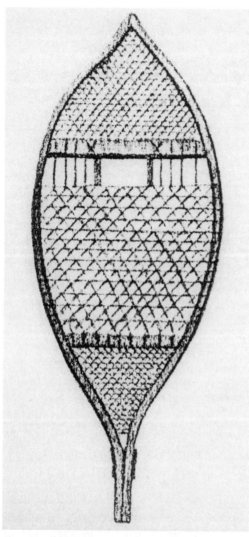

Fig. 56. Onondaga snowshoe (Beauchamp 1905, plate 1).

needing to hunt or gather. This gave the Iroquois a tactical advantage over northern Algonquian groups lacking maize (Scheele 1950, 82; Otterbein 1964, 60).

Ceramic vessels are fragile and large vessels are heavy, so most scholars have discounted the possibility that they were carried between nations. It is possible, however, that small pots were carried for cooking parched corn, and Martha Latta cites historic evidence that small ceramic pots were placed in canoes (1991). Stray finds of ceramic pots in the St. Lawrence and Lake Champlain by divers support this evidence (P. J. Wright 1980; Lewis 1994, 25; Abel and Fuerst 1999).[8]

Birch bark canoes, presumably manufactured in Canada, became common among the New York Iroquois in the eighteenth century. Iroquois elm bark canoes have suffered in comparison with birch bark canoes, but some elm bark canoes reached greater size. These canoes were made from the bark of a single large tree, probably white elm, which was turned inside out. The rough outer layer of bark was removed from the inside of the canoe.

8. The number of ceramic vessels—more than thirty-nine— and the long time-span represented by the vessel styles (Point Peninsula through Iroquois) at the underwater locus of the Red Horse Lake Portage site (Phillip Wright 1980) are more suggestive of offerings, perhaps to "Underwater World Grandfathers," than of multiple canoe accidents, although Phillip Wright does not view this as a ceremonial deposit. The Iroquois cast both tobacco and wampum beads into waterfalls and deep places as offerings (Snyderman 1961, 590).

parched corn greatly expands when hydrated (Waugh 1916, 88). Ideally, travelers cooked parched corn with water in a pot, though water might be added to it in a small wooden cup or bowl (Waugh 1916, 88). Because parched corn was lightweight and therefore easily portable, it allowed war parties to cover great distances without

Fig. 57. An Iroquois elm bark canoe (Lahontan I, opposite 80).

Birch bark canoes made use of smaller pieces of bark stitched and glued together (Kalm 1966, 363–65; Charlevoix 1966, 293). Elm bark is thicker and tougher (Fenton and Dodge 1949, 192). Elm bark canoes carrying as many as thirty men were observed in the late seventeenth century (see fig. 57).[9] Quantities of both men and goods could have been moved in these large canoes over the network of rivers and lakes adjacent to the New York Iroquois.

As illustrated in map 5, there is a water route up the Mohawk, with a portage ("the Carrying Place") to Wood Creek that flows into Oneida Lake. From there one can take the Oneida River to the Oswego River and paddle along the south side of Lake Ontario, or go up the Seneca River to Seneca and Cayuga Lakes (Morgan 1962, 369). There is oral tradition that supports the idea that this water route was used in the

story that the Peacemaker left the Mohawk country in a canoe to visit the Cayuga (Fenton 1998, 92). Describing his canoe as white suggests it was made of birch bark. In 1765 the Rev. Samuel Kirkland traveled in the opposite direction in a bark canoe from Seneca Lake to the Mohawk River. The bark canoe was made by the Seneca and carried four adults and four children (Fenton and Dodge 1949, 201–2).

## Disappearing Populations

The formation of the five Iroquois nations resulted in five population clusters. Coincident with this process and with the formation of alliances between Iroquois nations, we see the disappearance of Iroquoian populations in areas peripheral to the Five Nations.

For example, the Upper Allegheny Valley in southwestern New York and northwest Pennsylvania and the adjacent Lake Erie plain contain a series of Iroquoian sites variously termed part of the Upper Ohio Valley Iroquoian tradition, Allegheny Valley Erie, Allegheny Valley Iroquoian, or Chautauqua phase. Research carried out by Marian White and Jack Schock of SUNY-Buffalo in the late 1960s and early 1970s

9. Lahontan (1970, 81, 138) observed an Iroquois elm bark canoe with thirty men paddling side by side. Charlevoix (1966, 293) noted that elm bark canoes were the largest. A model of an elm bark canoe collected in the early nineteenth century and preserved in the Peabody Museum in Salem, Massachusetts, was decorated with diagonal red stripes, as were the paddles and accompanying fish spear (Fenton and Dodge 1949; Fenton 1978, 309).

and Donald Dragoo and Stanley Lantz of the Carnegie Museum of Natural History has revealed Iroquoian occupation starting in the tenth century and terminating around A.D. 1525. The reason or reasons for the abandonment of this area and the fate of this population remains obscure.[10]

Iroquoian populations at the eastern end of Lake Ontario in northern New York are represented by at least fifty-five sites (Engelbrecht, Sidler, and Walko 1990; Engelbrecht 1995). During the course of the sixteenth century, there was a gradual population decline in this region followed by abandonment. This parallels the fate of other Iroquoian populations in the St. Lawrence Valley (Pendergast and Trigger 1972; Pendergast 1991b).

Ceramic comparisons suggest the incorporation of some of these Iroquoians into the eastern Iroquois nations (Bradley 1987, 85; Kuhn, Funk, and Pendergast 1993; Snow 1995a, 216; Engelbrecht 1995). Traditions recalling a northern origin for the Iroquois may relate to this influx (Bradley 1987, 87). Ceramic evidence also suggests that Iroquoian populations along the St. Lawrence were incorporated into the Huron confederacy during this same period (Wright 1979, 71–75; Pendergast

1985; Jamieson 1990, 82; Ramsden 1990; M. Pratt 1991, 44). The evolution of the Huron and Iroquois confederacies during the time that Iroquoian populations in the St. Lawrence and northern New York were disappearing suggests that the latter populations were unable to maintain an independent existence in competition with larger confederacies (Engelbrecht 1995).

Another example of "disappearing Iroquoians" is really an example of relocation. During the fifteenth century, scattered hamlets identified as Susquehannock were located in southern New York and northern Pennsylvania along the north branch of the Susquehanna River, to the south of the emerging Cayuga, Onondaga, and Oneida. During the sixteenth century, the Susquehannock relocated. Janet Brashler suggests that the Susquehannock first moved to the south branch of the Potomac River in West Virginia during the early sixteenth century, and later moved to the lower Susquehanna Valley (1987, 27–28). Barry Kent dates the Susquehannock settlement at the Schultz site in Lancaster County, Pennsylvania, to around A.D. 1575 (1984, 332), although Martha Sempowski thinks this date may be too early based on the kind and quantity of glass beads present (1994, 61). In Pennsylvania, the Susquehannock apparently occupied a single palisaded village (Bradley 1987, 98; Kent 1984, 16–18, 304–6, 324–25).

It is possible that the Susquehannock moved to be in a more advantageous geographical position to secure marine shell and European trade goods. Additionally,

10. There has been a lack of systematic deep testing on the floodplain of the Allegheny River, so it is possible that some later sites have been undetected. The Kinzua Dam has now flooded portions of the Allegheny Valley. Stanley Lantz sees the development of the Lake Plain Iroquois as separate from that of the Allegheny Iroquois (Engelbrecht and Sullivan 1996, 19).

they may have moved to get away from the Iroquois confederacy. Historical records indicate that the Susquehannock were fighting with the Iroquois in the early seventeenth century (Bradley 1987, 98; Trigger and Swagerty 1996, 388). Sempowski sees a break in trade between the Seneca and the Susquehannock around A.D. 1609–1615 (1994, 60).

The suppression of blood feuds between League members served to channel aggression outside the League. This need not imply the mobilization of large armies representing all confederacy nations. Fenton suggests that war parties were still primarily a village affair, though sometimes they coordinated with those of neighboring nations (1998, 245). Ultimately, the formation of confederacies in the Northeast enlarged the geographic scale over which intergroup conflicts occurred.

It may have been the failure to maintain strong alliances that forced some Iroquoian populations to relocate or join stronger, larger groups. If alliances can be measured by the amount of nonlocal materials preserved on sites, then this proposition can be tested archaeologically, provided accurate cross-dating of sites in different areas is achieved. One would expect that the most recent sites in areas that were abandoned would contain less nonlocal material than contemporary sites in areas that remained occupied.[11]

The sixteenth century saw broadened horizons for native peoples of the Northeast. Spiritually charged material, individuals, and ideas moved over great distances. Peaceful exchange between nations implies the existence of alliances. The increasing influx of European materials into this system increased exchange and possibly conflict between native groups. The evolution of large confederacies, such as the League of the Haudenosaunee, may be seen as an adaptive response to these conditions and the culmination of a long process of alliance building between villages and nations. It was also a triumph of native diplomacy and vision over narrow local interests.

11. I suspect that this was the case with the abandonment of northern New York. The site sequence in this area needs to be carefully correlated with those in surrounding areas in order to test this.

## ◄ 8 ►

## CONTACT

### Strangers on the World's Rim

By the time Europeans entered Iroquoia, the Iroquois had long been aware that strangers had appeared on the eastern world's rim and that they were the source of powerful new materials. Both the inland location of the New York Iroquois and the existing system of native alliances with which the various European powers became involved delayed the European exploration of Iroquoia. Almost a century elapsed between the first appearance of European trade goods on Iroquois sites and written accounts of contact with the New York Iroquois.

The degree to which the sixteenth-century European presence along the Atlantic coast and lower St. Lawrence affected the New York Iroquois remains an interesting question for research. There are no eyewitness descriptions by Europeans of New York Iroquois culture devoid of European material. In 1634 three Dutchman, including Harmen Meyndertsz van den Bogaert, visited the Mohawk and Oneida.

Van den Bogaert was the first to leave a written account of these Iroquois. His journal provides important details, including the abundance of metal tools in these nations. The presence of European metal reminds us that his account is a description of groups affected by the presence of Europeans in North America.[1]

The Iroquois must have viewed these newcomers as possessing powerful orenda (spiritual energy), potentially capable of both good and evil. The Iroquois would therefore have placed them in the same category as sorcerers or shamans. Early seven-

1. See Gehring and Starna (1988) for a scholarly treatment of the journal of Harmen Meyndertsz van den Bogaert. There have been numerous attempts to match the villages van den Bogaert visited with sites in the archaeological record; see Snow (1995a, 280) and Snow, Gehring, and Starna (1996, xxii) for a listing of possible Mohawk sites. Pratt (1976, 134) suggests that the Oneida village of Onneyuttenhage is probably the Thurston site. The assemblage is appropriate for that time, and a snuff box with the date of 1634 was recovered from there, indicating that the site was occupied after that date.

teenth-century French missionaries among the Huron, "the black robes," were clearly viewed in this light.

Van den Bogaert was repeatedly asked to fire his gun. From the Iroquois perspective, orenda can reside in an object, and clearly guns had power. By extension, Europeans had great orenda, reflected not just in guns, but in shiny metal implements and glass beads (Scheele 1950, 12).

In one Mohawk village, van den Bogaert was offered a mountain lion skin as a cover (Gehring and Starna 1988, 7). Because of the panther's prominence in myth and material representation, we may assume that these panther skin robes were highly prized and probably viewed as particularly appropriate for a European. The inference that van den Bogaert was regarded as having special powers is reinforced by the fact that the next day at a different settlement he was asked to cure a sick man (Gehring and Starna 1988, 8).

Skeletal evidence indicates that a few nonnative individuals were incorporated into Iroquois society by the turn of the seventeenth century, long before historic records document this. At the Seneca Tram site (c. A.D. 1595–1605) a skeleton identified by Lorraine Saunders as that of a black woman was found buried in a cemetery (Wray et al. 1991, 28–32). She had been infected with yaws in childhood, a disease found in tropical environments. In her grave, eight chunks of chert were found in a line before her face and chest (Wray et al. 1991, 431).

Iroquoians painted themselves black on the death of relatives or friends or when at war (Sagard-Théodat 1968, 209; Fenton 1978, 303). Black mineral pigment was derived from graphite or coal (Wray 1973, 26). Did the Iroquois transfer the "power" of this state to this black woman? New England Algonquians were frightened of the first African they saw, viewing him as supernatural (Kupperman 2000, 122–23). Was this black woman a refugee from the short-lived Spanish Jesuit mission in Virginia, 1570–1572? Did she travel up the Susquehanna River along with individuals carrying marine shell? Archaeology does not provide the answer to these questions, but her burial in a Seneca cemetery does suggest her adoption into Seneca society.

At the Seneca Dutch Hollow site (c.1605–1620), analysis of the skeletal remains from the associated cemetery revealed a white male and three females who showed an admixture of Native American and Caucasian physical traits (Lorraine Saunders, personal communication).[2] Again, this discovery raises many questions. What was the nationality of the man and how did he get there? Was he the father of the three younger females? Was his

2. The Caucasian male comes from Burial 48 (Ritchie 1954, 8–9), being the lower of two flexed males (one directly above the other). The grave also contained rich burial offerings, which Lorraine Saunders feels are primarily associated with the uppermost male, who was Native American. A projectile point was found among the ribs of the Caucasian male.

nal foreign policy. Ef-Iroquois nations to maintain al-

# CONTACT 147

"whiteness" taken as a symbol of orenda, as was the whiteness of rare albino animals?[3] Regardless of whether their differing pigmentation was initially taken as a sign of a heightened spiritual state, both the black female and the white male were the first examples we have of many nonnative people incorporated by the Iroquois during the course of the seventeenth century.

This study has drawn on the written record of early contacts between Europeans and Iroquoians to supplement the archaeological record. This must be done cautiously. The written record is one seen through European eyes and filtered through European ideas and experience. These early written records, like snowshoe tracks seen long after they were made, do not always give us a clear picture.[4] Nonetheless, some general patterns emerge.

## National Agendas

Neither Europeans nor Iroquois should be thought of in monolithic terms. The different geographic location of the Five Nations influenced the nature of their contact and experiences both with European powers and neighboring native societies. The fact that the Five Nations were members of a

3. According to Sahagun, Moctezuma's emissaries viewed the white-skinned, fair-haired Spanish conquistadors as deities (N. Saunders 1988, 240).

4. "Snowshoe tracks" is the metaphor the Huron used to describe writing, or marking paper with a pen (Sagard-Théodat 1968, 73).

league did not preclude each nation from having an independent foreign policy. Efforts by Iroquois nations to maintain alliances with competing European powers provide the background for understanding Iroquois warfare and diplomacy during the seventeenth century.

The French along the St. Lawrence River became allies of the Huron, and it is in the role of an ally that Champlain and some of his men accompanied Huron warriors in an attack on an Iroquois village in 1615.

There has been a great deal of controversy over the location of this battle, and some still think it occurred against an Oneida village (Pratt 1976, viii–ix). Since the early furors over the identity of the site of the battle, Peter Pratt has clearly determined that the attack was not against the Oneida but against the Onondaga and that it took place at Onondaga Lake (Pratt 1976, 1977)—indeed, at the present site of Carousel Mall (Peter Pratt, personal communication).

From the reaction of the Iroquois to musket fire, this must have been their first exposure to European firearms (Grant 1907, 291). Judged by native standards, the Huron were the victors in this encounter, for they had frightened the Iroquois. Champlain, however, wounded and viewing it from a European perspective, judged it a failure, for the Huron had acquired neither wealth nor territory.

In 1614 the Dutch founded Fort Nassau on Castle Island just south of Albany.

Fort Orange, constructed ten years later, became the nucleus for Albany (Snow 1995a, 239). The Dutch were primarily interested in commerce rather than converting the Iroquois, changing their customs, or acquiring their land (Thwaites 1896–1901, 43:287, 291; Dennis 1993, 141; Fenton 1998, 252).

There is a major increase in the quantity of trade beads on early seventeenth-century Iroquois sites. These constitute a polychrome bead horizon that correlates with Dutch trading activity (Kenyon and Fitzgerald 1986). These beads are found in abundance on the Seneca sites of Dutch Hollow (c.1605–1620) and Factory Hollow (c.1610–1625), the Onondaga Pompey Center site, the Oneida Cameron site, and the Mohawk sites of Martin, Rice's Woods, and Wagner's Hollow (Kenyon and Fitzgerald 1986; W. Lenig 1996; Sempowski and Saunders n.d.). While Dutch Hollow and Factory Hollow had a variety of polychrome beads, the later Seneca sites of Warren and Cornish show a diminution in the variety of beads recovered (Sempowski and Nohe 1998, W. Lenig 1996). These later beads were also cheaper to manufacture.[5]

Fort Orange provided the Mohawk with a closer source of European goods than the French on the St. Lawrence. While

early Dutch traders apparently traded regularly with the Iroquois, starting in 1624 the West India Company developed a close trading relationship with the Mahican, causing the Mohawk to turn to the French in Canada (Lenig 1996). In 1628, following a four-year war between the Mohawk and Mahican, the Mahican abandoned their lands on the west side of the Hudson near Fort Orange. While an increase in Dutch goods on Five Nations Iroquois sites might be expected after that date, there are indications in the historical record that the Dutch-Iroquois trade did not go smoothly (W. Lenig 1999). The archaeological evidence appears to support a decline in Dutch goods on Seneca sites (Martha Sempowski, personal communication).

The visit of van den Bogaert to the Mohawk and Oneida in 1634 was prompted by a decline in the number of beaver pelts the Iroquois were bringing to Albany. Dean Snow has suggested that the timing of van den Bogaert's visit shortly after a major smallpox epidemic points to the epidemic as a major cause of the disruption in trade, rather than increased trade with the French (1995a, 36). Snow estimates a mortality rate of 63 percent during that epidemic (1995a, 281).

That the Onondaga and Oneida continued to trade with the French is supported by van den Bogaert's journal (Gehring and Starna 1988, 12, 19). The ability of the Onondaga to deal directly with the French provided them with an alternative source of European goods besides the Dutch (Bradley 1987, 182) and

---

5. Trade beads on Ontario Iroquoian sites (Neutral and Huron) differ from those on contemporaneous Iroquois sites in New York, suggesting a primarily French source for beads in Canada (Kenyon and Fitzgerald 1986; Wray et al. 1991, 410).

enabled them to play off French interests against those of the Dutch and later the English (Blau et al. 1978, 492). This was to become the Iroquois strategy for much of the seventeenth century.

Following the defeat and dispersal of the Huron confederacy by the Iroquois confederacy in 1649–1650, the French began missionary activity among the New York Iroquois, beginning with the Onondaga in 1654. Many of their former Hurons converts were now living among the Iroquois, and the Jesuits attempted to duplicate their Huron missions, giving them similar names such as Ste. Marie among the Onondaga and St. Michel among the Seneca. In fact, many of the Huron living with the Seneca had come from the Tahontaenrat village of Scanonaenrat, where the former St. Michel had been located. The *Jesuit Relations* contain a description of these missions during the late 1650s and 1660s.[6] The missions were

abandoned with a renewal of French-Iroquois hostilities during the latter part of the seventeenth century.

In 1664, the English gained control of the New Netherlands. Unlike the Dutch, they had an interest in acquiring Iroquois land (Dennis 1993, 141). In 1677, Wentworth Greenhalgh and a companion rode on horseback through the Five Nations seeking to advance English interests. They left a brief written record of their impressions of Iroquois villages as well as the number of Iroquois warriors (Fenton 1998, 303).

**Craftsmanship**

Seventeenth-century Iroquois sites provide evidence of sophisticated native craftsmanship using newly introduced materials. Early in the seventeenth century, copper and brass kettles were reworked into awls, triangular projectile points, rolled conical points, knife blades, needles, and saws (Pratt 1976, 213; Bradley 1987, 133–35, 173; Wray et al. 1991, 244; see fig. 58).

On the Seneca Cameron site, the awls were sharpened triangular pieces of sheet brass, one of which was found still set in a wooden handle (Wray et al. 1991,

---

6. The Jesuit Father Simon Le Moyne briefly visited the principal Onondaga village in August 1654, and the next year Fathers Dablon and Chaumonot built a bark chapel there (Thwaites 1896–1901, 42:125; Tuck 1971, 171–72). In 1656, they constructed what they hoped would be a permanent mission, Sainte Marie de Gannentaha, located along Onondaga Lake (Thwaites 1896–1901, 42:61–97, 215; 43:133–35,161; 44:185–87). The mission was abandoned two years later in 1658.

French Jesuits maintained missions among the Mohawk from 1655 to 1658. Among the Cayuga, French missionary activity was sporadic between 1656 and 1668. The French Jesuit missionary Jacques Bruyas established the mission of St. Francois Xavier among the Oneida in 1667 (Thwaites

1896–1901, 51:121, 221). In 1656, another French Jesuit, Father Pierre Joseph Marie Chaumonot, established the mission of St. Michel among the Seneca (Thwaites 1896–1901, 44:21; Abrams 1976, 14; Abler and Tooker 1978, 505). This village burned in 1670 and was rebuilt (Thwaites 1896–1901, 55:79; 57:190–91; Abler and Tooker 1978, 505–6).

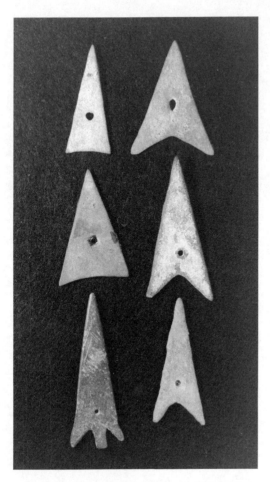

Fig. 58. Six copper points from the Briggs Run site (Mohawk). From Snow 1995a, 252. Photo courtesy of Dean Snow.

244–45). Traces on the wooden handle suggest it was covered with an animal skin (Wray et al. 1991, 330). The copper triangular points are similar in form to the triangular Madison points of stone, while the conical copper points imitate conical antler points. Some experimentation with projectile point form can be seen in the presence of a few stemmed, pentagonal, and other shapes (Bradley 1987, 173; Wray et al. 1991, 255).

Along with European copper and brass, wrought iron appears with increasing frequency on sites of the seventeenth century. Wrought iron can be worked much the same way as copper and initially the same sort of modification of the original iron artifact occurred (Bradley 1987, 76; Wray et al. 1991, 327). On the Oneida Diable site and the Seneca Tram and Cameron sites, round iron awls were found hafted in bone handles (Pratt 1976, 212; Wray et al. 1991, 57, 122; see fig. 59). It is likely that the bone handles were made locally. There is an increase in abrading stones (whetstones) on sites with iron tools, suggesting a direct relationship (Wray et al. n.d.).[7]

While seventeenth-century Iroquois used metal for utilitarian tasks, the shininess of metal axes and knives plus the mysterious nature of their origin would have made these objects desirable regardless of any functional superiority (N. Saunders 1998, 239). Ritual items were also made out of European metal. Brass rattles, effigy figures, pipes, and pipe liners have been recovered from the early seventeenth-century sites of Dutch Hollow, Factory Hollow, and Fugle (Sempowski and Saunders n.d.). A brass rattle was also found on the Mead Farm site (Cayuga, mid-seventeenth century) (Mandzy 1994,

7. In 1815, a large tree was cut down on the Onondaga Indian Castle site. Near the center of the tree was a large chain, surrounded by 178 annual rings, indicating a placement date of 1637 (Tuck 1971, 187). Bradley (1987, 205) estimates this site to have been occupied between 1655 and 1663.

Fig. 59. Iron awl with bone handle, Tram site (Seneca). Length of handle is 7.1 cm. From Wray et al. 1991, 122. Courtesy Rochester Museum and Science Center.

145). Cut pieces of kettles consisting of three rivet holes from the rim have been found on some sites. They resemble the punctate effigy faces sometimes found under the rims of ceramic vessels and may have carried similar cultural meaning.

The presence of French Jesuits in Iroquois settlements of the mid-seventeenth century is reflected archaeologically in the appearance of metal rings, medallions, and crucifixes. Jesuit religious use of these metal objects as well as rosary beads probably reinforced the Iroquois view of glass beads and metal objects as spiritually charged substances.

Ethnologists have suggested that splint basketry was introduced to Native Americans by European colonists and that they partially replaced bark containers (Fenton 1940, 219; Brasser 1975, 87; Campisi 1978, 481). However, the basic technique of plaiting with wooden splints has a documented time depth in the Northeast of over twelve millennia (Soffer et al. 1998, 62). While no splint baskets from precontact sites are known, archaeology has discovered examples of splint basketry in Iroquoia from early in the seventeenth century. Splint baskets have been recovered from both the Warren site (Seneca c. 1625–1640) and the Steele site (Seneca c. 1640–1655) (Wray et al. 1991, 5). Kathryn Bardwell argues that the tech-

nique of making splints is different from the European method and is indigenous (1986). Black ash logs are pounded to loosen the annual growth rings, or grains. These are then cut to make splints. Contrary to what is generally thought, metal knives are not required for this process. Iroquois archaeological sites typically contain notched chert flakes, which could have been used to trim the splints. The argument for an indigenous splint basketry technology also receives linguistic support from the Seneca term for black ash, which translates as "people pound the wood" (Chafe 1967, 67).[8]

In the 1640s, the Iroquois started using guns on a regular basis, and shortly thereafter they learned how to make simple repairs to them and to mold lead bullets (Snow 1996, 174). Around the same time,

8. James Adovasio called my attention to a plaited basketry fragment from Meadowcroft Rockshelter made of cut strips of birch-like bark and probably dating between eleven thousand and thirteen thousand years ago (Soffer et al. 1998:62). In an unpublished paper, Norbert Bartochowski suggested that notched flakes could be used for trimming splints. I am indebted to Blair Rudes for the Chafe reference.

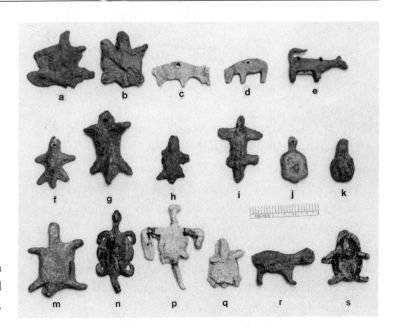

Fig. 60. Lead effigies from
Mohawk sites (Rumrill
1988, 20).

molded lead and pewter effigies appear on sites (Bradley 1987, 152–53; Rumrill 1988, 24; Martha Sempowski, personal communication). The manufacture of these effigies would appear to have been derived from molding shot. Lead turtle effigies are the most common, but there is also lead inlay on a slate pipe bowl from the Mohawk Rumrill-Naylor site (c. A.D. 1632–1646) (Rumrill 1988, 19). No doubt various pewter and lead items like spoons and porringers were treated as raw material to be transformed into these objects (see fig. 60).

While salt was important in the diet of Native Americans in the south and Mississippi Valley before the arrival of Europeans, the Iroquois and other Northeastern peoples began to use salt regularly only after contact (Waugh 1973, 150–54; Fenton

Fig. 61. Corn husk salt
bottle (Morgan 1962,
382).

1978, 298). Mineral salts are found in fish and freshly killed animals, so if these are eaten regularly no additional salt is required. A diet high in plant foods without salt can lead to various health problems, including reduced fertility (I. Brown 1980, 3). Iroquois corn husk salt containers illustrate the adaptation of an indigenous technology to a new use (see fig. 61). They worked well, as the husks absorbed atmospheric moisture, keeping the salt dry.

## Combs

In the hands of Iroquois craftsmen, metal tools enhanced the working of wood, antler, bone, and other traditional materials. For example, wood pipes were made by the Iroquois in the early decades of the 1600s (Neal Trubowitz, personal communication). The influence of metal tools is particularly evident in the evolution of antler combs. Simple bone or antler combs with three teeth have been found on Owasco sites (Ritchie 1980, 290). The handle was sometimes decorated with geometric designs. These objects are believed to have been used as hair ornaments.

The trend during the first half of the seventeenth century was for a broader comb with an increased number of finer teeth. Additionally, geometric designs on the handle tended to be replaced by finely carved human or animal figures (Wray et al. 1987, 36; 1991, 45; Richter 1992, 80–81; Snow 1995a, 271). These seventeenth-century combs are the product of the interaction of Native American and European

Fig. 62. Bird effigy antler comb, Warren site (Seneca). The height is about 7.5 cm. Drawing by Gene Mackay, photograph by Jack Williams. Courtesy of the Rochester Museum and Science Center, Rochester, N.Y.

cultures. The inspiration for the increased number of finer teeth is European, and was facilitated by metal knives.[9] The inspiration for the effigy figures is Native American (see fig. 62).

In Iroquois oral tradition, combs are instruments of transformation. In Onondaga cosmology, a woman-being

9. The trend toward more teeth is well represented by the appearance of antler "cootie" or "double combs" on the Seneca Cameron and Dutch Hollow sites and the Oneida Cameron site (Wray et al. 1991, 217; Pratt 1976, 220).

combs the hair of a man-being and becomes pregnant (Hewitt 1903, 143). The
Peacemaker and Hiawatha comb snakes
out of Thadada:ho?'s hair and rub his de-
formed body with wampum beads (see fig.
51). Their actions transform Thadoda:ho?
from an evil cannibal sorcerer into a right-
thinking leader (Richter 1992, 39). Finally,
William Beauchamp relates a story of an
old woman who meets a stranger. She is instructed to comb her hair, and as she does
so, she becomes younger (1922, 43).

Seventeenth-century antler combs
were more than just a new medium for rep-
resentational art using metal carving tools.
Combs, when used, worn, or carried, assisted individuals in transforming into a desired state or communicating with the
spirit world. The animal and human effigies depicted could be spirit guardians or
shamans, similar to those depicted on pipes
(Hamell 1998, 276). Early Europeans
were no doubt also viewed as in some manner connected to the supernatural, so it is
not surprising to see Dutchmen depicted
(see fig. 63).

Wentworth Greenhalgh's visit to the
Iroquois in 1677 may have been the first
time some western Iroquois saw a horse
and rider. Combs from the Dann site
(Seneca) and Great Gully site (Cayuga) de-
pict a rider on horseback, and are generally
thought to commemorate this event (see
fig. 64). These combs probably carry a
deeper meaning. The first appearance of
men on horseback, whether in ancient
Greece or highland Mexico, has been seen
as a manifestation of something other-

Fig. 63. Antler comb with an effigy of a
European, Ganondagan site (Seneca). The
height is about 9.9 cm. Drawing by Gene
Mackay, photograph by Jack Williams. New
York State Museum Collections. Courtesy of
the Rochester Museum and Science Center,
Rochester, N.Y.

worldly. At the very least, Greenhalgh must
have been viewed as a powerful shaman,
and perhaps the wearer of the comb sought
to emulate his perceived spiritual power.

Both native-made combs and native-

Fig. 64. Antler effigy comb, Great Gully site (Cayuga). The height is about 4.2 cm. Drawing by Gene Mackay, photograph by Jack Williams. Courtesy of the Rochester Museum and Science Center, Rochester, N.Y.

Fig. 65. Antler effigy comb fragment depicting two men in a canoe, White Springs site (Seneca, c. 1688–1710). The height is about 3.5 cm. Drawing by Gene Mackay. Courtesy of the Rochester Museum and Science Center, Rochester, N.Y.

made pipes continued to be manufactured and used long after European equivalents were available (see figs. 53 and 65). Smoking pipes of European manufacture appear on Mohawk sites as early as 1624, and are used along with pipes of native manufacture for most of the century (Snow 1995a, 35).[10] While European effigy pipes of "Good Queen Bess" and Sir Walter Raleigh were probably inspired by native effigy pipes, the continued manufacture of native-made pipes and combs suggests that European alternatives did not meet the spiritual needs of the Iroquois.

10. Pipes generally referred to as *kaolin* are more properly described as made from ball clay, a more inclusive category (Snow 1994b, 90).

**Wampum**

The quantity of marine shell increased dramatically on Seneca sites after 1640 (Martha Sempowski, personal communication). At this time the Iroquois were securing much of their shell from the Dutch at Albany. The Dutch obtained shell either from Long Island or from Curaçao in the Caribbean. A variety of shell ornaments have been found on Iroquois sites of the mid-seventeenth century, including drilled shell pendants in the shape of birds, claws, canine teeth, and crescents (Tuck 1971, 177, 184; Pratt 1976, 142). Their standardized shape suggests that they were of nonlocal manufacture (Martha Sempowski, personal communication).

During the first half of the seventeenth century, discoidal shell beads began to be replaced by short, tubular wampum beads (Bradley 1987, 172–79). These tubular shell beads are similar in form to hollow bird bone beads used earlier (Kuhn and Funk 1994, 82). While copying this traditional bead form, these small tubular beads were mass-produced using metal tools (Peña 1990; Kuhn and Funk 1994, 82). The Dutch were directly involved in wampum manufacture, introducing standardized production techniques in the 1640s (Richter 1992, 85; Peña 1990). The beads have smaller, straighter drill holes of uniform size, unlike the earlier pre-contact handmade beads (Ceci 1989, 72). It is these beads that were used in strings, bands, and the familiar wampum belts that became an important symbol of Iroquois diplomacy in the eighteenth century.

Purple wampum, made from the dark spot on the quahog shell, did not appear on Iroquois sites until the early seventeenth century. The earliest archaeological example of a belt containing purple wampum was recovered from the Seneca Fugle site (c. 1605–1625) (Ceci 1989, 72; Wray et al. n.d.). This was after dark blue glass beads made their appearance in Iroquoia, prompting Hamell to hypothesize that the popularity of these dark glass beads stimulated a demand for dark marine shell beads (1992, 460).

In addition to the Dutch as a source of mid-seventeenth-century wampum, the Mohawk were also receiving it from the Mahican, who in turn were receiving it

from native peoples on Long Island (Brasser 1978b, 203; Sempowski 1989, 91). After the Mohawk victory over the Mahican in 1628, the Narragansett became an important supplier of wampum to the Mohawk (Salisbury 1996, 407). The Mohawk in turn distributed both wampum and European manufactured goods to League members in exchange for furs (Salisbury 1996, 407).

The existence of the confederacy helps explain the movement of wampum between Iroquois nations. After forty years of relative scarcity of shell on Seneca sites, mid-seventeenth-century Seneca sites have been found to contain vast quantities of wampum beads (Sempowski 1989, 87). Estimates of numbers of beads on the Seneca Power House site approach a quarter million (Ceci 1989, 72). Over half the graves associated with this site contained shell beads, some holding several thousand (Sempowski 1989, 87).

The Dutch encouraged the use of shell for commercial purposes. They exchanged European goods with coastal Algonquians for shell beads, *wampumpeag* (Richter 1992, 85). The Dutch then used these shell beads to trade with the Iroquois for furs (Richter 1992, 85), with wampum acting as "the magnet which drew the beaver out of the interior forests" (Weeden 1884, 15). Shell beads facilitated trade the same way that cowrie shells did in West Africa with the Portuguese and later the Dutch (Bradley 1987, 179–80). The dramatic increase in wampum on Iroquois sites during the first half of the seventeenth century coincided with the growth of the fur trade.

Seventeenth-century wampum represents a blending of European and Native American ideas, and it is a product of the interaction of these two cultures (Bradley 1987, 180). In the New Netherlands (c. 1628–1664) and to a lesser extent in New England, it was legal tender (Ceci 1989, 63; Peña 1990). For the Iroquois, wampum had a more complex value. Its ritual associations as a life-enhancing and life-restoring substance gave it added value, both in diplomacy and in exchanges (Bradley 1987, 179).

## Disease

When native populations came into sustained contact with Europeans, they generally suffered high mortality rates, as they lacked effective immunity to many diseases of European origin.[11] Several European childhood diseases proved especially virulent among the genetically homogenous native populations (Black 1992; Snow 1994b, 99). Henry Dobyns (1983) and others have argued that diseases introduced from Europe spread far inland, decimating Native American populations long before they came into direct contact with Europeans. Multiple interments at the Seneca Adams site have been interpreted as

evidence of such an early pandemic (Dobyns 1983, 313–27). More likely, European-derived illness occurred more frequently in the Southeast than in the Northeast, at least in the sixteenth century (Trigger and Swagerty 1996, 366).

Before the devastating epidemics of the first half of the seventeenth century, the population of the Five Nations is believed to have been around twenty thousand (Fenton 1998, 21). A major aim of the Mohawk Valley project instituted by Dean Snow and William Starna was to investigate demographic changes in the Mohawk Valley. Their research indicates that the Mohawk population steadily increased through the sixteenth and early seventeenth centuries. While some of this increase may have been the result of the movement of native peoples into the Mohawk Valley, there is no good evidence of epidemics affecting Mohawk population until 1633–1634 (Snow and Lamphear 1988; Snow and Starna 1989; Snow 1991, 38; Snow 1996).

In a village with everyone sick, people did not receive proper care and routine subsistence tasks were disrupted, leading to hunger. Mortality rates are often highest for the youngest and oldest members of a population during an epidemic. Removal of the older generation through disease resulted in the loss of knowledge and leadership. Matrilineages that appointed senior men to one of the fifty hereditary titles in the confederacy may have lacked eligible candidates, thus weakening the organization (Fenton 1998, 22). The ineffective-

---

11. During the winter of 1535, Cartier recorded the outbreak of disease in the village of Stadacona on the St. Lawrence (Cook 1993, 76–78). This disease could have been of European origin.

ness of traditional curing practices against these new plagues stressed traditional ideological systems (Starna 1988, 18). The Iroquois world was out of balance.

Snow infers that Mohawk population decreased in 1634 from 7740 to 2830, a mortality rate of 63 percent (1995a, 281). In the ensuing decade, population continued to decline as survivors moved from four large communities to three small ones (Snow 1995a, 46). By the early 1640s, the population of the Five Nations was halved by disease (Richter 1992, 59). Severe as these losses from disease were, they do not appear to have been as bad as among some coastal populations, where up to 90 percent of some communities succumbed. The reasons for such differential mortality rates remain to be explored.

**Warfare**

In a 1615 attack on an Iroquois village by the Huron and French, Champlain urged the Huron to continue fighting, but they declined, pointing out that many of their men had been wounded (Grant 1907, 294). This fits the pattern for warfare in nonstate societies. If conflicts are frequent, even low casualty rates in individual battles can become substantial over a period of years. Starting with one hundred warriors, a 5 percent loss in each of four battles per

year would reduce the ranks of warriors to just thirty-six in only five years (Keeley 1996, 91–92). No wonder pre-state societies sought to minimize fatalities on the battlefield! Of the Iroquois view of war casualties, Lafitau wrote, "They feel very much the loss of a single person because of their small number" (1977, 141).

From Champlain, we know that Huron war parties were accompanied by a shaman (Grant 1907, 159–60). Though parallel in some ways to the role of chaplain in a European army, traditionally shamans were also healers, able to remove arrows and apply poultices to wounds. Lafitau found the ability of Northeastern Native Americans to treat wounds "the masterpiece of their medical science" (1977, 204). In general, we may assume that the treatment wounded seventeenth-century Iroquois warriors received on the battlefield compares favorably even to nineteenth-century "civilized" treatment, which favored bleeding the wounded, amputations, and the use of tight, unsterilized bandages (Keeley 1996, 95–97).

The arrival of Europeans changed the conduct of Iroquois warfare. Traditionally, warriors would meet face to face and exchange insults before shooting arrows at one another or engaging in hand-to-hand combat using war clubs (see fig. 66).

These encounters rarely resulted in

Fig. 66. Wooden war club (Beauchamp 1905, plate 7).

large numbers of casualties. Male skeletal remains from late sixteenth—and early seventeenth-century Seneca sites exhibit relatively little evidence of physical trauma that is attributable to combat (Sempowski and Saunders, in press). Chiefs wore large plumes and warriors wore slat armor and carried leather or bark shields (Grant 1907, 164, 282; see fig. 67). Van den Bogaert describes the armor as made "from thin reeds and cords woven together so that no arrow or axe could penetrate to cause serious injury" (Gehring and Starna 1988, 9).

Projectile points manufactured from European metal were able to penetrate this armor, as were the metal axes and tomahawks that began to replace the ball-headed war club (Fenton 1998, 11). Indirect evidence of the use of metal hatchets or tomahawks is present at the Seneca Power House site (c. A.D. 1640–1655) where a middle-aged female exhibited hatchet marks on her skull (Sublett and Wray 1970, 18). These innovations and the subsequent use of muskets were to precipitate a change in Iroquois military tactics.

Seventeenth-century muskets were not overwhelmingly superior to native bows and arrows. Arrows were more accurate than seventeenth-century muskets and the rate of fire was more rapid. The effective range of both muskets and bows was roughly comparable. The advantage muskets had was that they propelled musket balls with such force that slat armor and leather shields proved ineffective against them. Further, musket balls could not be

Fig. 67. Huron warrior wearing slat armor. From Johan de Laet, *L'histoire du Nouveau Monde*, 1640. See Trigger (1976, 1: 71) for an earlier version of this illustration accompanying Champlain's voyages of 1619.

dodged in the manner that arrows could (Abler 1989; Keeley 1996, 51–53).

By the 1640s the Mohawk and other Iroquois were receiving a steady supply of guns from the Dutch at Albany. Formal battles between large numbers of warriors wearing slat armor were no longer fought (Abler 1992, 159). Instead, small war parties shooting muskets from behind trees replaced massed warriors. These changes minimized the risk of fatalities. To suffer casualties would be to negate a major reason for war, the capture of prisoners to replace the dead (Richter 1992, 38).

A skeleton (probably male) from the Seneca Marsh site (c. A.D. 1650–1670) bears mute testimony to the fact that musket balls sometimes found their mark. A musket ball in the mid-shaft of the tibia remained there until the individual died some time later (Sublett and Wray 1970, 18).

Intensified intergroup conflict was increasingly part of the Iroquois world. George Hunt argued that the exhaustion of the supply of beaver within Iroquois territory and their need for more to trade was the primary factor in understanding seventeenth-century Iroquois wars of conquest (1940). Jose Brandão casts serious doubt on this hypothesis, arguing instead that a major reason for warfare was the capture of individuals (1997). Daniel Richter argues that the devastating epidemics of the 1630s and 1640s increased the frequency of "mourning wars," where warriors sought captives for the replacement of individuals who had died (1992, 32–38). Following their acquisition of guns, it appears the Iroquois used their new-found armaments to increase both the supply of beaver and individuals (Salisbury 1996, 409).

In 1638 the Wenro, an Iroquoian group, left their homeland, which is presumed to have been in Niagara and Orleans Counties to the west of the Seneca (White 1978, 407). This area is prime beaver habitat, and the departure of the Wenro was probably related to Seneca efforts to expand their hunting territory westward

(Abler and Tooker 1978, 506). In the 1640s, the Mohawk were regularly attacking Huron traders on the St. Lawrence (Trigger 1985, 262–63). Ultimately the Huron were dispersed by the Seneca and Mohawk during the winter of 1648–49 (Thwaites 1896–1901, 34:123). The Petun, neighbors of the Huron, were attacked and dispersed by the Iroquois shortly thereafter. The Neutral and Erie confederacies fell to the Iroquois in the 1650s. In all these conflicts, the Iroquois had the advantage of more guns.

In September 1666, more than a thousand French troops under Alexander de Prouville, Marquis de Tracy, burned Mohawk villages, destroying many "magnificently ornamented" longhouses as well as the year's harvest (Richter 1992, 104). This was the catalyst for the Mohawk to move their villages to the north side of the Mohawk River, where they had not been since the Mahican attack in 1626, forty years earlier (Snow 1995a, 40). A forty-year hiatus in occupation would have allowed new-growth forests to become established on the north bank, providing building materials for new villages as well as more readily accessible sources of firewood. Mohawk villages were again burned by the French in 1693, serving as a catalyst for the Mohawk to move their villages back across the river to the south side (Snow 1995a, 429, 449).

French expansionist policy prompted a series of attacks against the Iroquois in the late seventeenth century (Brandão 1997, 117). The Seneca were attacked by the

French under De Nonville in 1687. In 1696 a French expedition led by Louis de Buade de Frontenac attacked the Onondaga and Oneida. The principal Onondaga town was destroyed. Both the Weston and the Pen sites have been suggested as candidates for the Onondaga village destroyed at the time.[12] During the latter half of the seventeenth century, only the Cayuga nation escaped French attack.

## Adoption

Cross-culturally, matrilineages are more likely to adopt members than patrilineages. The matrilineal Iroquois provide a striking example of large-scale adoption of both individuals and groups. This practice helped the Iroquois partially replace their population in the face of major losses, though the composition of that population changed markedly during the course of the seventeenth century.

In addition to the nonnative individuals mentioned at the beginning of this

chapter, a male and female with cranial deformations were recovered from the Seneca cemetery associated with the site of Boughton Hill or Ganondagan (c.1670–1687) (Sublett and Wray 1970, 23). While cranial deformation was not practiced at this time among peoples of the Northeast, it was among some Southeastern groups, hence the designation "Flatheads" in English documents (Tom Abler, personal communication). Among the Cherokee, there was a group whose name translates as "big foreheads projecting out" (Witthoft 1949, 40). Perhaps a Seneca social dance which tells of a young man's love for a woman with bumps on her forehead relates to such a Cherokee woman adopted by the Iroquois (Witthoft 1949, 40). In any event, the adoption of diverse people introduced new genes and new ideas to the seventeenth-century Iroquois (Abler 1992, 163).

Women urged young men to bring them prisoners to console them for the loss of kinsmen. Captives, like meat, were tied using a burden strap and led back to the village. John Witthoft (1953, 13) viewed this strap "as the symbol of possession and control of a corpse" (see fig. 55). These prisoners were then made to run the gauntlet between rows of hostile villagers who struck them with clubs or thorns. This allowed villagers who had not directly participated in the war to vent their hatred and aggression against the enemy (Scheele 1950, 86). After running the gauntlet, the prisoner was ritually adopted, to be either sacrificed or incorporated into the group.

---

12. Tuck (1971, 172, 188–89) felt that the Pen site was the major village destroyed by Frontenac, an assessment with which Peter Pratt concurs. Pratt (personal communication) points out that the Pen site appears to have been burned, and a three-walled stockade on the Pen site matches the description given by Frontenac's recorder. However, after ten seasons of excavation on the Weston site, Gregory Sohrweide (1997) has concluded that this was the village burned by Frontenac. Both Sohrweide and Pratt believe the Weston site to be earlier than the Pen site, so accurate dating of material from both sites may resolve this issue.

Those captives destined to be tortured and killed were "the dead in waiting" (Tremblay 1998, 74, citing Viau 1997). Ritually adopted by families who had recently lost a member, they became a focus for revenge. Finger bones found on the Mohawk Garoga site are interpreted as reflecting the torture of prisoners by the amputation of fingers, a practice documented in the historic literature and possibly extended back to Owasco times (Snow 1995a, 160; Peter Pratt, personal communication).[13] Ultimately, these individuals were ritually sacrificed.

Assimilative adoption involved the incorporation of a prisoner into a new group, with loss of former identity.[14] This individual generally took the place of a deceased person and was expected to behave in a manner similar to the deceased. Failure to do so could result in death (Campisi 1978, 482). All individuals adopted into the Five Nations were expected to take part in group ceremonies and reciprocal ritual obligations, in short, to act like Iroquois (Richter 1992, 72). Appropriate behavior resulted in the survival of these "New Iroquois."

Others who were neither killed nor adopted became slaves or "children of nothingness" (Starna and Watkins 1991; Viau 1997; Tremblay 1998, 73). They were social "nonpersons" who might be used in future prisoner exchange or put to work carrying heavy burdens or performing other menial chores (Starna and Watkins 1991, 51). The threat of death hung over them, a fact of which they were reminded by the sacrifice of other captives. However, children of females in this category appear to have become Iroquois.

The French Jesuit missionaries among the Five Nations in the late 1650s estimated that in some Iroquois villages the majority of inhabitants were not of Iroquois origin (Richter 1992, 65–66). In 1656 it was said that the Onondaga had people from seven different nations living in their principal village, while the Seneca had individuals from eleven nations (Thwaites 1896–1901, 43:265).[15] Non-Mohawk refugees were said to outnumber the Mohawk (Thwaites 1896–1901, 45:205–9), and in 1668 two-thirds of the Oneida population consisted of Hurons and Algonquins (Thwaites 1896–1901, 51:123; Campisi 1978, 482).[16]

Hurons joined all the Iroquois nations

13. A standard explanation for the amputation of fingers is that it prevents an individual from drawing a bow string. There is also a possible magical interpretation. To "shoot" someone by pointing a finger is a widespread shamanic concept (Hamell 1983, 14), so amputating a captive's fingers may have afforded the captors protection against magical revenge.

14. Lynch (1985) distinguishes between assimilative and associative adoption.

15. These included Algonquians, Hurons, Petuns, Neutrals, Mascoutens (Fire Nation), various St. Lawrence Iroquoians, Susquehannocks, and Erie (Bradley 1987, 119; Pratt 1976, 42).

16. In addition to Hurons, the Mohawk were taking in New England Algonquians (Snow 1995a, 361).

in what Lynch terms "associative" adoptions (1985, 88). In these cases, their new identity as Iroquois existed along with their old identity as Hurons. Associative adoption may explain the appearance of new burial practices among the Iroquois. An ossuary was discovered at the small Bunce site, which may be a burial site for the Tahontaenrat, a Huron group who settled among the Seneca in their own village called Gandougarae (Martha Sempowski, personal communication). Among the Cayuga, the mission of St. René has been identified with the Rogers Farm site, where a multiple burial is reminiscent of a small Huron or Neutral style ossuary (Mandzy 1990, 18).[17] In 1657, Hurons living with the French in Canada moved to the Mohawk country, some probably eventually settling at the Jackson-Everson site (Thwaites 1896–1901, 43:187; Snow 1995a, 361). The majority of ceramics from this site, which dates from after 1666, are decorated in Huron fashion (Kuhn 1994a, 33). By this period most other Iroquois communities were replacing native ceramics with metal kettles.

## Houses

European technology did not just enhance Iroquois manufacture of splint baskets and hair combs. It was also incorporated selectively into the construction of Iroquois houses.[18] In 1634, van den Bogaert observed interior longhouse doors made of split planks with iron hinges, reflecting European influence (Gehring and Starna 1988, 4, 31 n. 20). Some six or seven years later, the Jesuits found the Neutral fastening their doors against them, implying European-style doors (Thwaites 1896–1901, 21:219; Abler 1970, 30). Such a change may have been motivated by a desire for greater security. In 1646, a Huron war party found the doors to the houses in a Seneca village closed, so they broke into a house through the side wall (Thwaites 1896–1901, 29:253).

While some very large post mold diameters have been observed on sixteenth-century Iroquois sites, large diameters on both longhouse and palisade post molds are more frequent during the early seventeenth century. This trend was possibly influenced by the introduction of metal axes (Ritchie 1980, 285; Dodd 1984, 272; Prezzano 1992, 242, 260). In the Seneca site sequence stone celts or axes disappear early, before many metal axes appear archaeologically (Martha Sempowski, personal communication). Presumably, metal axes were as carefully saved as were stone axes (Lafitau 1977, 71). During the second half of the seventeenth century, the use of work horses by the eastern Iroquois made using larger diameter trees easier. In 1659 and again in 1689, the Mohawk are on

17. One burial at Rogers farm contained eight individuals (Mandzy 1990, 18).

18. Kurt Jordan (n.d.) suggests that eighteenth-century Iroquois houses may be thought of as a hybrid artifact form.

record asking authorities at Albany and Schenectady for horses to assist in dragging logs for palisade construction (Snow 1995a, 362, 426).

Following the epidemic of 1634, longhouses decreased in length. This trend continued through the century, as the Iroquois lost population to disease, warfare, and out-migration (Guldenzopf 1984, 83). Lineages and clan segments responded to these losses by adopting captives and taking in refugees. As a consequence, Snow (1995a, 304, 362) argues that residents of longhouses increasingly formed *ad hoc* social units. For example, at Caughnawaga [Mohawk] longhouses are of standardized lengths, suggesting that houses defined the social units, rather than the opposite (Snow 1995a, 363, 430; se fig. 68). The form remained, but the composition changed (Snow 1995a, 363). Perhaps the probable defensive advantage inhabitants of a longhouse enjoyed was a consideration in retaining the traditional form.

By the mid-eighteenth century and the establishment of a relatively peaceful political landscape within Iroquoia, many Onondaga were living in two family houses. These were the equivalent of the traditional longhouse compartment with a central fireplace (Snow 1997, 72). In the 1750s, Cayuga villages still contained multiple-family houses with three or four fireplaces (White et al. 1978, 501). Moravian missionaries visiting a Seneca village at mid-century were told by a chief that his house was the largest in town, serving as "the meeting place for the Council as well as their fortress" (Beauchamp 1916, 74). A small number of multifamily longhouses probably existed throughout Iroquoia in the eighteenth century, especially outside the Mohawk Valley (Jordan 1997b). In addition to their defensive advantage and political function, these larger structures would have provided spaces for periodic rituals which could not have been held outdoors or in single family dwellings (Witthoft 1961, 71).

When Sir William Johnson began supplying the New York Mohawk with boards in the 1750s they ceased covering their homes with bark, although journals from the Sullivan-Clinton campaign of 1779, some twenty years later, indicate that Seneca houses still had bark roofs (Guldenzopf 1984, 87; Jordan n.d.). Other traditional features of Seneca houses mentioned in these journals include end storage compartments, smoke holes, and berths on either side of a fireplace in the center (Jordan n.d.).

## Settlement

Kurt Jordan (n. d.) points out that there was considerable variability regarding the presence or absence of palisades around Iroquois villages during the latter half of the seventeenth century. When present, they appear to have been rectangular, often with corner projections or bastions which facilitated the use of guns to defend the

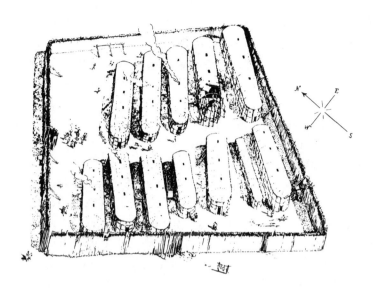

Fig. 68. Reconstruction of the settlement at the Veeder site, commonly known as Caughnawaga (Mohawk, 1679–1693). Courtesy of the Fort Plain Museum.

wall (Snow 1996, 177; Prezzano 1992, 252–53; see fig. 68).[19]

When Frontenac attacked Mohawk villages during the winter of 1692–1693, the palisades had gates (O'Callaghan 1853–1887, 9:550). Gone were the open entryways which could be closed off, observed in Oneida and Huron palisades during the first half of the seventeenth century (Gehring and Starna 1988, 12; Sagard-Théodat 1968, 91–95; Abler 1970, 28).

While smaller communities become the rule after A.D. 1646 in the Mohawk Valley (Snow 1995a, 370), some large Iroquois communities persisted to the west. Ganondagan, a major Seneca village burned in advance of the French attack in

1687, is estimated to have covered 9.1 acres (Huey 1994, 12). The Onondaga Weston site was nine acres (Sohrweide 1997). Villages of such size could have held anywhere from fifteen hundred to two thousand inhabitants.[20]

From 1668 until 1687, when they were attacked by the Marquis de Nonville, the Seneca are described as having two large and two small villages (Abler and Tooker 1978, 505). René de Galinée stated that Ganondagan was surrounded by a rectangular palisade in 1669, but in 1677 Greenhalgh said that it was not palisaded (O'Callaghan 1849–1851, 1:12). Galinée may have visited the Marsh site (Hamell 1980, 95–96), which may have then been called Ganondagan, that name

19. Sites with rectangular fortifications include Caughnawaga, [Mohawk] 1679–1693 (Snow 1995a, 432); the Pen Site 1682–1696, [Onondaga] (Tuck 1971, 188); as well as the palisade described by Galinee for the Seneca in 1669 (Hamell 1980, 95).

20. Using Snow's (1995a, 44) formula of one person per 20 m² of site size, Kurt Jordan (n.d.) calculates that Ganondagan could have housed 1843 people.

later being transferred to the town Greenhalgh visited. Alternatively, the palisade could have been dismantled. The destruction of the Seneca villages in 1687 is usually taken as the end of the Seneca pattern of two large contemporaneous villages, but this pattern continued for at least one other set of sites—Snyder-McClure and White Springs (Wray 1973, 8; Jordan 1997a).

By 1677, three Cayuga communities were located within a mile of one another and two to three miles from Cayuga Lake. At that time they were not palisaded (O'-Callaghan 1849–1851, 1:12). The lack of palisades around these villages may reflect the fact that the Susquehannock had recently been defeated, although the close proximity of the three villages to one another can be interpreted as reflecting defensive concerns.

Relatively peaceful relations between the Iroquois and the French, British, and their various Native American allies afer the start of the eighteenth century allowed the development of a dispersed pattern of settlement across Iroquoia (White et al. 1978, 501; Jordan n.d.). Freed from considerations of defense, factions within a community were free to move. Areas not occupied since the twelfth or thirteenth century were again settled, in some cases perhaps by distant descendants of the earlier inhabitants.

By 1720, the pattern of Seneca settlement was becoming increasingly varied, with one or two larger settlements and many dispersed small villages and hamlets (Jordan 1998; n.d.). Some are located near Seneca and Canandaigua Lakes (Saunders

and Sempowski 1991, 14; Abler and Tooker 1978, 507). Burials were made close to small cabins, rather than in separate cemeteries outside palisades as in the past (Martha Sempowski, personal communication; Jordan n.d.).

Around 1740, some Seneca settled along the Genesee River and become known as the Western Seneca or Chenussios (Abler and Tooker 1978, 507; Jordan n.d.). In the 1750s other Seneca settled at Kanadesaga ncar the mouth of the Seneca River, some seventy-five miles east of Seneca settlement on the Genesee (Jordan n.d.).

After 1736, the Cayuga were located on both sides of Cayuga Lake, although the principal village was on the east side. In 1753, the Tutelo and Saponi were adopted by the Cayuga and in 1771 their principal village was located three miles south of Cayuga Lake (White et al. 1978, 501).

John Bartram found that by 1743, the Onondaga were living in homes scattered for two or three miles along both sides of Onondaga Creek. The council house at this time measured approximately 80 feet by 17 feet and was covered with bark (Bartram 1973, 58). James Tuck identifies the Valley Oaks section of Syracuse as this area of eighteenth-century Onondaga occupation (1971, 193).

Two Oneida villages coexisted in the eighteenth century, the larger one being located near Oneida Creek (Pratt 1976, 144; Campisi 1978, 481). After the Tuscarora Wars of 1711–1713, the Tuscarora moved north and settled on Oneida land (Campisi 1978, 481). Their incorporation into the League in 1722 under Oneida sponsorship is a continuation of the traditional Iroquois process of alliance building and incorporation.

There were two major Mohawk towns in the eighteenth century, Canajoharie and Thienderego (Tionondorage) separated by thirty miles (Snow and Guldenzopf 1998, 34). As the easternmost of the Five Nations, the Mohawk homeland was most vulnerable to encroachment from colonial settlement. Germans from the Palatinate began settling in the Mohawk and Schoharie Valleys on recently ceded land, along with Dutch Irish, Scottish, and English settlers (Snow and Guldenzopf 1998, 34; Fenton 1998, 13). Kurt Jordan has argued that for the Mohawks, the shift to a dispersed single-family settlement served as an adaptive response to this encroachment, and this type of settlement was encouraged by Sir William Johnson (1997b). Small Mohawk households near their fields helped lay claim to land that was increasingly being sought by colonists.

Nucleated villages so characterize our thinking of the traditional Iroquois that there is a tendency to see the dispersed patterns of the eighteenth century as a form of cultural disintegration. While dispersed settlement was probably precipitated by factionalism and necessarily resulted in changes in traditional community organization, clan membership would have continued to link households to one another. The more dispersed pattern of Iroquois settlement in the eighteenth century was both healthier and more economically effi-cient, as the Iroquois gave up crowded village conditions for hamlets located in the midst of fields and newly planted orchards. Fewer people in an area meant firewood and other local resources were not used up as quickly as before. In the absence of endemic warfare in the eighteenth century, the Iroquois achieved a new balance between themselves and the land.[21]

## Exodus

The increasingly dispersed nature of local settlement in the late seventeenth and the eighteenth centuries is but a microcosm of changes occurring on a regional scale (Jordan n.d.). Factionalism, in part between Catholic and non-Catholic Mohawks, led many Catholic converts to move to Canada in the 1670s and 1680s (Fenton and Tooker 1978, 473). Many Catholic Hurons who had been settled among the Mohawk since 1657 also moved north. By the end of the century there were more Mohawks in Canada than in the Mohawk Valley (Fenton and Tooker 1978, 473). In the eighteenth century, these Canadian Mohawks were to play an important role in illicit trade between Montreal and Albany (Fenton and Tooker 1978, 469).

When the Cayugas were at war with the Susquehannock during the 1660s and

21. Kurt Jordan (n.d.) argues that clan membership was a centripetal force that kept some Iroquois households near one another when purely economic considerations would have favored spatially dispersed nuclear families.

early 1670s, thousands of Cayuga founded small villages along the north shore of Lake Ontario to escape the Susquehannock threat (Thwaites 1896–1901, 47:71; 48:77–79; White et al. 1978, 501). Some Seneca and Oneida may have resettled along the north shore as well, and these villages served both as a base for winter hunting and as a stopover point for traders (Konrad 1981, 1987). This northern extension of Iroquois territory was abandoned by 1688, in part in response to threats from the French, but the Iroquois were to expand to other areas.

The defeat of the Erie, Neutral, and Huron left large areas to the west of the Seneca unpopulated, and the Seneca established small settlements in these areas, particularly at Niagara (Abler and Tooker 1978, 505). Later, many Seneca found employment moving goods at the portage around Niagara Falls (Abler and Logan 1988, 12). By the beginning of the eighteenth century, Seneca occupation had spread along the Chemung and upper Allegheny Rivers (Abrams 1976, 20; Abler and Tooker 1978, 507). In Pennsylvania, multiethnic communities containing Seneca, Susquehannock, and other Iroquoians were established at Conestoga, Logstown, and Shamokin while similar such communities in Ohio came to be known as Mingos (Hunter 1978, 591–92; Kent 1984). These communities were close to fur-bearing animals as well as to the English traders who were moving into Pennsylvania and the Ohio country.

In the early sixteenth century, there was a St. Lawrence Iroquoian populaton near what is now Ogdensburg, New York. Some of these people probably joined the Onondaga later in the century. It may therefore not be a coincidence that in the mid-eighteenth century some Onondaga were living in the same place in a settlement called Oswegatchie (Blau et al. 1978, 494–95). By 1762, some Oneida, Mohawk, and others were living on the Susquehanna River at Oquaga (Campisi 1978, 481).

## Nonhuman Newcomers

"Every species and every society represent a column of pilgrims not only traveling in space, but also in time" (Rousseau 1966, 98). The arrival of Europeans in North America, with their associated plants, animals, and pathogens, set in motion an ecological revolution that is still unfolding (Crosby 1972, Cronin 1983).

In 1613, Champlain observed that natives in Canada were beginning to cultivate peas (Grant 1907, 249). The establishment of Jesuit missions in New York in the 1650s allowed the Iroquois to observe Europeans cultivating European crops as well as pigs and chickens (Bradley 1987, 120). This also served as a mechanism for diffusing these same plants and animals to the Iroquois.

A milder West Indies species of tobacco, *Nicotiana tabacum,* was eventually grown alongside the stronger *Nicotiana rustica,* which was still used for ceremonies (Snow 1994b, 90). Watermelon spread rapidly through the Northeast in the seventeenth century, in part because cultivation requirements were the same as for squash (Blake 1981). The spread of apple trees appears to have been accomplished as a result of trade (Keener and Kuhns 1997, 332). By the mid-eighteenth century, European honey bees had settled in Iroquoia (Waugh 1973, 143). Orchards of peach, pear, and apple trees were noted growing near Seneca and Cayuga towns by members of the Sullivan-Clinton army in 1779 (Fenton 1998, 23).

In 1645, Kiotsaeton, a Mohawk, addressed Governor Montmagny and an assembly at Three Rivers as follows: "Our country is well stocked with fish, with venison, and with game; it is everywhere full of deer, of elk, of beaver. Give up those stinking hogs that run about among your houses, that eat nothing but filth; and come and eat good meat with us" (Thwaites 1896–1901, 27:261). Yet there is evidence that within a generation both pig and cattle were being kept on the Mohawk Jackson-Everson site (Anderson 1986, 122; Socci 1995, 133). Pigs were kept in pens, probably much the way bears were (Socci 1995, 112), and like bears, pigs are omnivores. De Nonville observed pigs and fowl on the site of Ganondagan in 1687. Attitudes had changed since the Mohawk orator chided the French in 1645. At Onondaga in 1755, bear cubs were still being kept, though at that time in a small "log house" (Tuck 1971, 4). Eventually, pork replaced bear meat as a ceremonial food (Hamell 1980, 98).

Faunal analysis of material from Joseph Brant's house in the Mohawk valley indicates that deer were still the most important source of meat in the 1760s and 1770s, but many domestic animals were also important. In descending order of frequency, they are pigs, cows, horses, chickens, and sheep or goats (Socci 1995, 219–20).

## Political Defeat and Spiritual Revival

Over a millennium, eastern North America saw the evolution of polities of increasing geographic scale, from hunter-gatherer bands to native confederacies. For most of the colonial period, the Iroquois Confederacy dealt effectively with Europeans and their colonies in North America. However, as the Euro-American population on the Eastern seaboard grew and the area became an increasingly important part of worldwide economic and political interests, conditions for the Iroquois changed. A huge new confederacy composed of thirteen British colonies arose in eastern North America. Once independent of Britain, the new United States forever altered the North American political landscape—and the Iroquois position within it.

Following the American victory over the British in the Revolution, the Iroquois lost their lands in New York, except for some scattered reservations. With the loss of their land, a return to the traditional Iroquois economy was impossible. Old alliances were shattered. The Iroquois were no longer in a position to influence the course of events as they had in the past.

Many Iroquois went to Canada, splitting the Confederacy. The Iroquois world was again out of balance. In the words of Anthony Wallace (1972), Iroquois communities became "slums in the wilderness," plagued by alcohol, violence, and fear of witches.

A new spiritual order was needed to restore balance and harmony in the lives of individuals and communities. This need was met in the form of a Seneca prophet, Handsome Lake. The series of visions he communicated drew on ancient traditions and resulted in a code of conduct, the *Gaiwiio,* or "good word," which is preached to his followers to this day. Poor in land and material wealth by European standards, followers of the *Gaiwiio* were rich in spirit.

# 9

# THE PRESENT

## Population and Cultural Identity

According to the 1990 census, 62,651 individuals identified themselves as Native Americans in New York State. This constitutes around 0.3 percent of the state's population (Garbarino and Sasso 1994, 461). However, the genetic contribution of Native Americans to the population of New York is probably much greater than this figure suggests. Many individuals have one or more grandparent or a more distant ancestor who was Native American, but they do not identify themselves as such. In the past, individuals often faced social and economic discrimination if they were identified as Indian, so they often downplayed this part of their heritage. Governmental assimilationist policies also discouraged maintenance of a separate Native American identity.

Despite past governmental efforts at assimilation, many individuals today identify themselves as Iroquois. Many live off the reservation. While some fall into the category of "American Indians of Multiple Ancestry," what is significant is their cultural identification as Iroquois. To Richard Hill, a contemporary Iroquois, "identity is internal" (1997).

It is on the reservations or Iroquois territories that Iroquois cultural identity and ethnic pride is most apparent. Reserves in Canada and reservations in the United States form cultural islands in a multicultural society (see map 6).

The Oneida in Wisconsin are one of the largest Indian nations in the United States (Campisi and Hauptman 1988, 183).

The U.S. Supreme Court has upheld the sovereign power of native governments in a number of recent cases (Washburn 1996, 402, 408). On July 9, 1998, the New York State Court of Appeals ruled that Indian businesses can sell gasoline and cigarettes on reservation land without collecting state excise and sales taxes. This recognizes Indian sovereignty and saved hundreds of jobs at Indian-run businesses.

The Iroquois have endured in the face of disease, warfare, discrimination, and de-

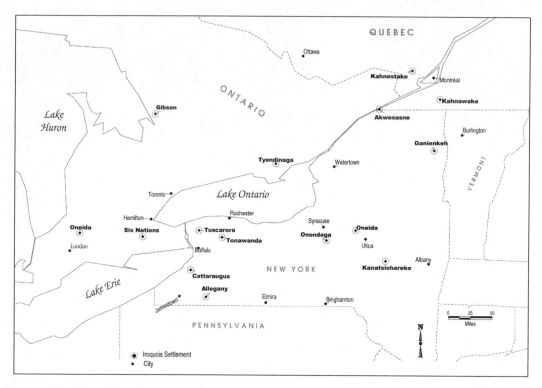

Map. 6. Modern Iroquois settlement.

struction of their economy through the seizure of their land. While many problems exist for Iroquois today, both on and off the reservation, they are a people with a future as well as a past.

## Continuities

In the past, when forced assimilation was the U.S. government's policy, young Iroquois sent to boarding schools were punished for using their native language, so many never spoke it and did not pass it on to their children. Today, there is a new interest in preserving Iroquois languages and teaching them to the young. Young Iro-

quois are taught to take pride in their heritage.

Religious structures called longhouses dot Iroquois country in the United States and Canada and are used by followers of the teachings of Handsome Lake. Cooking and living activities no longer take place in these longhouses, and wood stoves have replaced hearths. However, many of the ceremonies practiced in the longhouses of old are still observed.

The Onondaga longhouses at Six Nations Reserve in Canada and on the Onondaga Reservation in New York State each have a single side door. When asked about this, the Onondaga reply, "It's always been this way" (Shimony 1961, 66). Indeed, one can trace this tradition back to the single side door at the 334-foot-long Howlett Hill site (late fourteenth century). Nonresidents of these early long longhouses probably entered by the side door to attend meetings and ceremonies.[1]

False face masks, or "faces," still make their appearance at ceremonies. To Iroquois, they are charged with power as living beings and demand proper treatment. Some masks are carved and sold as art objects, but that practice is disappearing, as many traditional Iroquois feel that it is not proper. Iroquois concerned with maintaining their cultural and spiritual heritage have demanded the return of both masks and wampum belts from cultural institutions, and many institutions have complied. The Heye Foundation (now part of the National Museum of the American Indian), the New York State Museum, and the Royal Ontario Museum have all returned wampum belts to the Iroquois (Snow 1994b, 216–17; Art Einhorn, personal communication). Wampum still plays an important role in defining Iroquois political, cultural, and spiritual identity (Ceci 1988, 63).

Oral narratives are still recited in ceremonies held between the first frost in fall and the last frost in spring, while the earth

is sleeping (Fenton 1998, 3–4). At Six Nations, individuals are buried with their heads to the west, oriented in the direction of the land of the dead (Shimony 1961, 243). Individuals still draw comfort in the Condolence Ceremony, now sometimes conducted privately (Deer 1998). In this, the "clear minded" condole the grieving by symbolically clearing their eyes, ears, and throats, so that they can once again see, hear, and speak clearly. In May 2000, about one thousand people witnessed a Mohawk Nation Condolence ceremony at Akwesasne. As in the past, participation in a common ritual helped ease tensions among factions and promote pride in being Mohawk.

Many Iroquois living off the reservation know their clan affiliation, and traditionalists still believe that clan exogamy is important. They are uncomfortable with a member of the Seneca Wolf Clan marrying a Mohawk of the Wolf Clan (Abrams 1976, 6). Some observances are unique to a clan or individual. According to Tom Porter of the Mohawk Bear Clan, clan members do not kill bears (Socci 1995, 88), and I have heard of a Turtle Clan member who stopped his car on the shoulder of a highway to carry a turtle across.

The tradition of mutual aid continues, with groups helping with modern house construction on the reservation (Blau et al. 1978, 498). In 1998 the Oneida Nation announced that because of the success of their Turning Stone Casino, they did not need the annual Tribal Priority Allocation to which they were entitled from the fed-

---

1. Mima Kapches (1994b) expanded on the implications of this, including the single Onondaga side door, in an unpublished paper that she presented at the Northeastern Anthropological Association meetings.

eral government. Extending the ancient practice of mutual aid to the confederacy level, they directed the federal government to share their funds with the Seneca and Mohawk Nations and to establish an Urban Indian Service Center in upstate New York.

Many traditional Native Americans believed that words and songs could "tap the power in the universe" (Washburn 1996, 450). Modern Iroquois singers, writers, and scholars have drawn on the power of both song and the word to make significant contributions to modern American society. Oneida singer Joanne Shenandoah was nominated for a Grammy. Modern pow-wows, while not purely Iroquoian, are often well attended and illustrate the continued vitality of Native American dance.

Iroquois artists and craftsmen using both traditional and contemporary media are also making contributions. Seneca artist Carson Waterman's images are now found on Zippo lighters sold worldwide. Potters like Peter Jones have stimulated a renewed interest in Iroquois ceramics, as witnessed by a recent exhibition, "The Death and Rebirth of Iroquois Pottery" at the Seneca-Iroquois National Museum in Salamanca, New York. Mohawk baskets and corn husk dolls are in high demand, and contemporary painters and sculptors often command high prices for their work (see fig. 69).

Iroquois silver work follows the ancient tradition of valuing light, white, and bright materials.

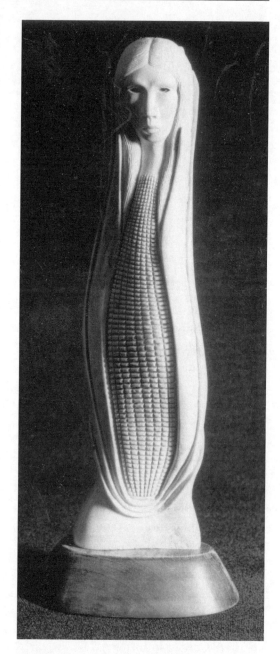

Fig. 69. Corn Spirit by Stan Hill, Mohawk. Moose Antler. Courtesy of the Iroquois Indian Museum.

Modern Iroquois in the high steel industry have helped build this country. In many respects, the role of the modern Iroquois iron worker mirrors that of the traditional warrior (Freilich 1963; Einhorn 1999). Groups of men regularly leave the reservation together for extended periods, returning now with cash rather than captives. These "warriors of the sky" display courage and gain personal prestige through their work on bridges and skyscrapers. After the tragedy of September 11, some fifty Mohawk structural iron workers signed up to help clear the World Trade Center site (Taliman 2002, 19). Women provide communal continuity, set the ceremonial calendar, and choose the male chiefs, as well as raising their chilren and keeping their household going.

Traveling between reservations, teams of young men play box lacrosse, the reservation version of lacrosse. The Cherokee call lacrosse "The Little Brother of War," and similar attributes of speed, skill, and bravery are needed for box lacrosse. Before the game, players pass around sacred tobacco, which is then burned while a traditional prayer is offered to the spirit forces and ancestors for protection and strength (Seabrook 1998).

## The Modern Landscape

Today, vehicles speed along the New York State Thruway, the major east-west transportation artery of the state, following the general route of the major trail linking Iro-

quois nations.[2] Indeed, the existence of a central east-west trail between what is now Albany and Buffalo was a determining factor in the location of modern cities along this route (Morgan 1962, 430). Paralleling this route for much of the way is the New York State Barge Canal, following much of what was the old Erie Canal. The eastern portion of the original Erie Canal generally followed the old east-west canoe route.

A grid of roads, railroads, power lines, gas lines, water lines, and sewer lines now cuts across the land, and fences everywhere mark the boundaries of private property. Streams and springs that once existed have vanished or been channelled as land has been drained, bulldozed, filled in, and paved over. Suburban sprawl extends farther and farther from urban centers. There are old trees, but there are no old growth forests in New York. Widespread deforestation in eastern North America contributes to increased erosion, flooding, and probably global warming.

Even land on Iroquois teritories in New York has not escaped twentieth-century "improvements." A portion of the Kahnawake Reservation was destroyed by the construction of the St. Lawrence Seaway (Wilson 1959, 145). One-third of the Allegany Reservation was flooded by the Kinzua Dam in 1965, even though less destructive alternatives were feasible (Abrams

---

2. See Morgan (1962) for a map showing the major trails in 1720. Route 5 follows the Iroquois trail more closely.

1976, 100; Bilharz 1998). Whole communities were flooded along with the best farmland. The New York State Power Authority took a portion of the Tuscarora Reservation near Lewiston for a major hydroelectric project.[3] The Southern Tier Expressway now slices through the Allegany Reservation, while the New York State Thruway cuts through Cattaraugus (Abler and Tooker 1978, 515).

Once, huge flocks of passenger pigeons darkened the skies. Now these birds are extinct. Other indigenous species, both plant and animal, are threatened either by loss of habitat or nonhuman invaders. The American chestnut is endangered. Purple loosestrife is choking out indigenous plants. Rats and cockroaches, both introduced species, have found niches in American cities. In Lakes Erie and Ontario, lake trout are now at risk. New York health officials warn pregnant women not to eat fish from Lake Ontario because of toxic pollutants. Mohawk mothers at Akwesasne have stopped eating fish from the St. Lawrence so as not to pass on PCBs either in the womb or through breast milk (Cook 1997, 58–59). Recent drilling at Akwesasne struck toxic waste, contaminating well water for many homes on the reservation (Johansen 1999, 7).

Yet some animal species native to the Eastern Woodlands have flourished. Abandoned farms and abundant open areas have created a large deer population, creating problems for outlying suburbanites. Every fall, thousands of modern non-Indian residents of New York take to fields and woods on the first day of deer-hunting season. It is a pattern derived from Native Americans and for many the hunt still resembles a sacred ritual. Technology changes; seasonal rhythms persist.

Despite the changed landscape, Iroquois heritage is evident in the many place names that were adopted in modified version by Euro-American settlers. *Schenectady*, "beyond the pines" originally referred to Albany, while *Ticonderoga* can be translated as "junction of two waterways." Other Iroquois names include *Owego*, meaning "where the valley widens"; *Owasco Lake*, "lake at the floating bridge"; *Tioga Point*, "at the forks"; *Tonawanda*, "swift water"; and *Skaneateles Lake*, "long lake." *Canajoharie, Chautauqua, Chittenango, Onondaga, Saratoga*, and *Schoharie* are also derived from Iroquois names, as is *Ohio*, "beautiful river," the original Iroquois name for the Allegheny which flows into the Ohio.[4]

## Site Destruction and Preservation

In changing the face of the land, modern civilization has destroyed Iroquois villages, camps, and cemeteries. With their destruction, a portion of the past is destroyed. The

3. Edmund Wilson (1959, 137–47) details the high-handed tactics of the Power Authority in this matter.

4. See Lounsbury (1960, 25–26, 49) and Morgan (1962, 415–36, 465–73) for their discussions.

typical location of Owasco and Iroquois village sites is on high, well-drained land, which often constitutes prime real estate for building, unless it has already been altered by gravel mining. Dredging of the Mohawk Barge Canal destroyed the Mohawk village of Dekanohage along the south bank of the Mohawk River (Snow 1995a, 449). Construction of the New York State Thruway in the 1950s destroyed the Mohawk Failing site (c. 1626–1635) (Snow 1995a, 289, 294). Those sites in rural areas that have not been obliterated are often subjected to increasingly deep plowing, which breaks up material and destroys shallow post molds and other features.

Both professional archaeologists and Native Americans are in agreement on the need for protecting archaeological sites from needless destruction. Fortunately, since the 1960s the state and federal governments have passed legislation intended to minimize this destruction. As a consequence, there has been a tremendous growth in what is termed Cultural Resource Management (CRM), with archaeologists discovering and evaluating sites that would be affected by proposed construction projects. If destruction of all or a portion of a site cannot be avoided, developers must pay for excavation of a sample of the site. Since the early 1980s, the majority of new archaeological data in New York has come from Cultural Resource Management projects.

Unfortunately, the mining of archaeological sites for artifacts by unscrupulous diggers or "pot hunters" further destroys sites. Once an artifact is removed from its context without proper recording of its location and association with other artifacts and features, information is lost. Since the target of these activities is often the removal of objects from rich sixteenth—and seventeenth-century graves, Native Americans are understandably outraged. Even well-meaning individuals interested in Iroquois culture indirectly encourage this activity by purchasing these objects, thereby creating a market that encourages further looting.

This situation is not unique to New York, which is why professional archaeological organizations such as the Society for American Archaeology and the Registry of Professional Archaeologists are on record as opposing the buying and selling of antiquities, whatever their provenance. In New York State, both the New York State Archaeological Association and the New York Archaeological Council have taken a similar position. While archaeologists do not view artifacts as animate objects in the way that their makers did, they do know that these objects have a story to tell, and that story may not be shared if an object is sitting on someone's mantle.

In the Southwest, the Archaeological Conservancy has been buying significant archaeological sites for years in an effort to protect them. Recently, the conservancy has established a regional office for the eastern United States and is now in the process of acquiring two important Seneca villages, the Tram site (c. A.D. 1580) and the Steele site (c. A.D. 1640–1655). Hopefully, Conservancy purchases of other Iroquois sites will follow.[5]

## The Native American Graves Protection and Repatriation Act (NAGPRA)

In 1632 Gabriel Sagard observed of the Huron, "nothing could give them greater offense than to ransack and remove anything in the tombs of their relatives" (Sagard-Théodat 1968, 209). This holds true for the Iroquois today. Removal of objects from graves is viewed by many as theft from the dead (Amato 2002, 7). In traditional belief, a soul continues to reside in the bones of a deceased individual (Thwaites 1896–1901, 10:287; Hall 1997, 30). To disturb human bones would disturb this individual's soul, and possibly cause difficulty for the living (Hamell 1988). "Iroquois people feel the pains and pleasures of their grandfathers" (Hill and Grinde 1975, 57).

Not surprisingly, Iroquois often view the excavation, study, and curation of skeletons of their ancestors in a negative light. In the past, there was often insensitivity to these concerns by many in the archaeological profession. Even Arthur C. Parker, a Seneca and crusader for Indian rights, was an active excavator of Iroquois

burials in his role as archaeologist with the New York State Museum.[6]

Since the early 1970s, professional archaeologists have responded to Native American concerns, and cemeteries in particular are no longer excavated for research. Today, professional archaeologists consult with Native Americans when human remains must be excavated because of construction activities.

In 1990, Congress passed the Native American Graves Protection and Repatriation Act (NAGPRA). As a result of this legislation, institutions receiving federal funds must consult with representatives of federally recognized Native American groups if they have human remains or sacred objects that pertain to these groups. In some cases, human remains and objects have been returned (repatriated) to these groups. Repatriated human remains and objects are customarily reburied. Museum personnel, scientists, and Native Americans are now engaged in a dialogue over the disposition of hundreds of human remains and associated objects from New York State.

While a variety of opinions exist regarding NAGPRA, disagreement is rooted in two opposing worldviews: one scientific and one traditional. Many Native Americans are angry over what they perceive as

---

5. The Archaeological Conservancy, 5301 Central Ave., Suite 1218, Albuquerque, NM 87108–1517. (505) 266–1540.

6. Parker later became director of what is now the Rochester Museum of Science Center, and in 1935 he was elected the first president of the Society for American Archaeology. See Sullivan (1992) and Funk (1997) for more on Parker's contribution to New York State Archaeology.

racist attitudes on the part of scientists and feel that the only proper disposition of skeletal material and associated objects is immediate reburial. Scientists point out the many kinds of information that may be gained from careful study of these ancient materials. Skeletons may yield information on age, gender, health status, and diet. New techniques, such as the ability to extract DNA from ancient bone, promise insights into human remains, which are saved for future study. Each skeleton or artifact has a story to tell, and these stories may be of particular interest to future generations of Native Americans.

Much potential information has already been lost by hasty reburial. Often, newly exposed remains and associated materials are reinterred without the opportunity for study, the bones mixed with those of others and buried at a private location. A minimum compromise in such situations would be the provision of adequate time and funding for removal and study of artifacts and skeletal material before reburial.

## The Past in the Present

Many museums across the state have Iroquois material on display. A particularly noteworthy exhibit is "At the Western Door: Seneca Indians, Europeans, and Americans in the Genesee Valley" at the Rochester Museum and Science Center. The New York State Museum in Albany features an excellent reconstructed longhouse. The Seneca-Iroquois National Museum is located on the Allegany Reservation in Salamanca, New York, and presents the prehistory, history, and contemporary culture of Seneca and other Iroquois. In a successful blending of old and new, the Iroquois Indian Museum near Schoharie exhibits both archaeological material and contemporary Iroquois artists.[7]

Those wishing to visit an actual village site may go to Ganondagan, now a state historic site. Ganondagan was the larger village of the eastern Seneca sequence occupied from approximately 1670 to 1687, when it was burned in advance of a French expedition led by the Marquis de Nonville. A longhouse was recently erected there.[8] Near Syracuse along the shores of Onondaga Lake there is a reconstruction of Fort Sainte Marie de Gannentaha, constructed by the French in 1656 and abandoned in 1658.

Membership in the New York State Ar-

7. Seneca-Iroquois National Museum
   Broad Street Extension
   Salamanca, N.Y. 14779

   Iroquois Indian Museum
   Box 7, Caverns Rd.
   Howes Cave, N.Y. 12092

   Rochester Museum & Science Center
   657 East Ave.
   Rochester, N.Y. 14607

   New York State Museum
   Cultural Education Center
   Albany, N.Y. 12230

8. Ganondagan
   1488 Victor-Holcomb Rd.
   Victor, N.Y. 14564

chaeological Association is open to anyone interested in archaeology. The NYSAA has chapters around the state. It publishes a journal, *The Bulletin,* conducts an annual meeting, and sponsors a scholarship in archaeology. The New York Archaeological Council (NYAC) is composed largely of professional archaeologists working in the state, and meetings focus on issues of importance to the conduct of cultural resource management. Both NYAC and NYSAA seek to learn more about and protect the state's archaeological heritage.

At a number of junctures, this study has referred to oral traditions to enrich archaeological interpretation. In a complementary fashion, archaeology can contribute to an understanding of cultural traditions. "Archaeology can uncover information no one thought to pass down in legend form" (Mithun 1984, 259). Na-

tionally, the Society for American Archaeology has established the Arthur C. Parker scholarship fund in honor of its first president. The scholarship makes funds available for Native American students to participate in archaeological field work. In New York, Professor Jordan Kerber of Colgate University has started the Oneida Indian Nation Summer Workshop in Archaeology in cooperation with the Oneida Indian Nation Youth Work Learn Program. This program introduces Oneida youth to the archaeology of Oneida sites on the nation's land (see fig. 70).
Hopefully, this program will become a model for other Iroquois nations. Archaeology can be a powerful tool with which to enrich one's heritage.

Iroquois nations emerged during a time of widespread conflict in the Eastern Woodlands. Neighbor fought neighbor.

Fig. 70. Oneida Indian Nation summer workshop in archaeology. Photo courtesy of Jordan Kerber.

The formation of larger communities and then alliances among these communities maintained peaceful relations among increasing numbers of people. This process culminated in the formation of the famous League of the Haudenosaunee, made possible by the efforts of the Peacemaker, along with Hiawatha and "individuals of good mind." The success of the Iroquois League was both military and spiritual.

Following the American Revolution, the Iroquois struggle for survival no longer followed a military path. The teachings of Handsome Lake provided spiritual renewal for a people whose land had been expropriated and altered, and whose way of life was consequently changed forever.

Today traditional Iroquois, like other native peoples, stress the importance of maintaining the proper relationship to the land and other living creatures. They are concerned about what this Earth will be like for the seventh generation. Such a long-term outlook is needed in the modern world.

The study of ecology demonstrates our interrelationship with both living and non-living aspects of the environment, while the structure of DNA shows us that at some level humans and all living beings are related. National boundaries divide us, but as Iroquois nations once did, we must find mechanisms for maintaining the appropriate balance among nations and in relation to the natural world in which we live.

# WORKS CITED

# INDEX

# WORKS CITED

Abel, Timothy J. and David N. Fuerst. 1999. "The Prehistory of the St. Lawrence Headwaters Region." *Archaeology of Eastern North America* 27:1–53.

Abler, Thomas S. 1970. "Longhouse and Palisade: Northeastern Iroquoian Villages of the Seventeenth Century." *Ontario History* 62:17–40.

———. 1987. "Dendrogram and Celestial Tree: Numerical Taxonomy and Variants of the Iroquoian Creation Myth." *The Canadian Journal of Native Studies* 7, no. 2:195–221.

———. 1989. "European Technology and the Art of War in Iroquoia." In *Cultures in Conflict: Current Archaeological Perspectives,* edited by Diana Claire Tkaczuk and Brian C. Vivian. Proceedings of the Twentieth Annual Cacmool Conference. Calgary: Archaeological Association of the Univ. of Calgary.

———. 1992. "Beavers and Muskets: Iroquois Military Fortunes in the Face of European Colonization." In *War in the Tribal Zone: Expanding States and Indigenous Warfare,* edited by R. Brian Ferguson and Neil L. Whitehead. 151–74. Santa Fe, New Mexico: School of American Research Press.

Abler, Thomas S., and Michael H. Logan. 1988. "The Florescence and Demise of Iroquoian Cannibalism: Human Sacrifice and Malinowski's Hypothesis." *Man in the Northeast* 35:1–26.

Abler, Thomas S., and Elisabeth Tooker. 1978. "Seneca." In *Handbook of North American Indians.* Vol. 15, *Northeast,* edited by Bruce Trigger. Washington, D.C.: Smithsonian Institution.

Abrams, George H. J. 1976. *The Seneca People.* Phoenix: Indian Tribal Series.

Allen, Kathleen. 1988. "Ceramic Style and Social Continuity in an Iroquoian Tribe." Ph.D. diss., SUNY/Buffalo.

———. 1992. "Iroquois Ceramic Production: A Case Study of Household-Level Organization." In *Ceramic Production and Distribution an Integrated Approach,* edited by G. J. Bey III and C. A. Pool. Boulder: Westview Press.

———. 1998. "Archaeology in the Cayuga Lake Region." Paper presented at the Northeast Archaeology Symposium, Cayuga Museum, Auburn, N.Y.

Allen, Kathleen, and Ezra Zubrow. 1989. "Environmental Factors in Ceramic Production: The Iroquois." *Ceramic Ecology, 1988: Current Research on Ceramic Materials,* edited by Charles C. Kolb. Oxford: BAR International Series 513.

Amato, Christopher A. 2002. "Digging Sacred Ground: Burial Site Disturbances and the Loss of New York's Native American Heritage." *Columbia Journal of Environmental Law* 27, no. 1:1–44.

Anderson, Lisa M. 1996. "Vine Valley Revisited." *A Golden Chronograph for Robert E. Funk,* edited by Chris Lindner and Edward V. Curtin. 155–61. Occasional Publications in Northeastern Anthropology, no. 15. Bethlehem, CT: Archaeological Services.

Axtell, James. 1981. *The European and the Indian: Essays in the Ethnohistory of Colonial North America.* New York: Oxford Univ. Press.

Bakker, P. 1990. "A Basque Etymology for the Word 'Iroquois.'" *Man in the Northeast* 40:89–93.

Bamann, Susan. 1993. "Settlement Nucleation in Mohawk Iroquois Prehistory: An Analysis of a Site Sequence in the Lower Otsquago Drainage of the Mohawk Valley." Ph.D. diss., State Univ. of New York at Albany.

Bamann, Susan, Robert Kuhn, James Molnar, and Dean Snow. 1992. "Iroquoian Archaeology." In *Annual Review of Anthropology* 21:435–60.

Bardwell, Kathryn. 1986. "The Case for an Aboriginal Origin of Northeast Indian Woodsplint Basketry." *Man in the Northeast* 31:49–67.

Barker, Alex W., Craig E. Skinner, M. Steven Shackley, Michael D. Glascock, and J. Daniel Rogers. 2002. "Mesoamerican Origin for an Obsidian Scraper from the Precolumbian Southeastern United States." *American Antiquity* 67, no. 1:103–8.

Barreiro, José. 1989. "Introduction—'A Season of Corn.'" *Northeast Indian Quarterly* (Spring/Summer):9–13.

Bartram, J. 1973. *A Journey from Pennsylvania to Onondaga in 1743,* edited by W. J. Bell, Jr. Barre, Massachusetts: Imprint Society.

Beauchamp, William M. 1892. *The Iroquois Trail, or Foot-prints of the Six Nations, in Customs, Traditions, and History, in Which Are Included David Cusick's Sketches of Ancient History of the Six Nations.* Fayetteville, N.C.: H. C. Beauchamp.

———. 1898. *Earthenware of the New York Aborigines.* New York State Museum Bulletin 5, n. 22. Albany: University of the State of New York.

———. 1905. *Aboriginal Use of Wood in New York.* New York State Museum Bulletin 89, Archaeology 11. Albany: New York State Education Dept.

———. 1916. *Moravian Journals Relating to Central New York, 1745–66.* Syracuse, N.Y.: Dehler Press.

———. 1922. *Iroquois Folk Lore: gathered from the Six Nations of New York.* Empire State Historical Publication 31. Reissued 1965. Port Washington, New York: Friedman, Kennikat Press.

Bigelow, Gerald, Connie Bodner, Gian Cervone, David Kieber, and Brain Nagel. 1987. *Stage III Mitigation Excavation at the Archbald Site (Ood 6–3) Oak Orchard Marine Park, Town of Carlton, Orleans County New York.* Prepared by Cultural Resource Survey Program, Research Division, Rochester Museum and Science Center.

Biggar, H. P. 1971. *The Works of Samuel De Champlain.* 6 vols. 1929. Reprint, Toronto: Univ. of Toronto Press.

Bilharz, Joy. 1998. *The Allegany Seneca and Kinzua Dam: Forced Relocation Through*

*Two Generations.* Lincoln: Univ. of Nebraska Press.

Black, F. L. 1992. "Why Did They Die?" *Science* 258:1739–40.

Blake, Leonard W. 1981. "Early Acceptance of Watermelon by Indians of the United States." *Journal of Ethnobiology* 1, no. 2:193–99.

Blanton, R. E. 1994. *Houses and Households.* New York: Plenum.

Blau, Harold. 1967. "Notes on the Onondaga Bowl Game." In *Iroquois Culture, History, and Prehistory: Proceedings of the 1965 Conference on Iroquois Research,* edited by Elisabeth Tooker. Albany: Univ. of the State of New York, the State Education Department, and the New York State Museum and Science Service.

Blau, Harold, Jack Campisi, and Elisabeth Tooker. 1978. "Onondaga." In *Handbook of North American Indians.* Vol. 15, *Northeast,* edited by Bruce Trigger. Washington, D.C.: Smithsonian Institution.

Blitz, John H. 1988. "Adoption of the Bow in Prehistoric North America." *North American Archaeologist* 9, no. 2:123–45.

Bodner, Connie Cox. 1999. "Sunflower in the Seneca Iroquois Region of Western New York." In *Current Northeast Paleoethnobotany,* edited by John P. Hart. New York State Museum Bulletin 494. Albany: New York State Education Department.

Bond, S. C. 1985. "The Relationship between Soils and Settlement Patterns in the Mohawk Valley." In *The Mohawk Valley Project: 1982 Field Season Report,* edited by D. R. Snow. Albany: The Institute for Northeast Anthropology, State Univ. of New York at Albany.

Boucher, P. 1883. "True and Genuine Description of New France, Commonly called Canada, and of the Manners and Customs and Productions of that Country." In *Canada in the Seventeenth Century,* by E. L. Montizambert. 1664. Reprint. Montreal: G. E. Desbarats.

Bradbury, Andrew P. 1997. "The Bow and Arrow in the Eastern Woodlands: Evidence for an Archaic Origin." *North American Archaeologist* 18, no. 3:207–33.

Bradley, James W. 1987. *Evolution of the Onondaga Iroquois.* Syracuse: Syracuse Univ. Press.

Bradley, James W., and S. T. Childs. 1991. "Basque Earrings and Panther's Tails: The Form of Cross-Cultural Contact in Sixteenth-Century Iroquoia." In *Metals in Society: Theory Beyond Analysis,* edited by R. M. Ehrenreich. MASCA. Philadelphia: The Univ. Museum, Univ. of Pennsylvania.

Brandão, Jose Antonio. 1997. *"Your fyre shall burn no more": Iroquois Policy toward New France and Its Native Allies to 1701.* Lincoln: Univ. of Nebraska Press.

Brashler, Janet G. 1987. "A Middle Sixteenth Century Susquehannock Village in Hampshire County, West Virginia." *The West Virginia Archeologist* 39, no. 2:1–30.

Brasser, T. J. 1975. *A Basketful of Indian Culture Change.* Canada Ethnology Division, Mercury Series, Archeological Survey of Canada, Paper no. 22. Ottawa: National Museum of Man.

———.1978a. "Early Indian-European Contacts." In *Handbook of North American Indians.* Vol. 15, *Northeast,* edited by Bruce Trigger. Washington, D.C.: Smithsonian Institution.

———. 1978b. "Mahican." In *Handbook of North American Indians.* Vol. 15, *North-*

*east,* edited by Bruce Trigger. Washington, D.C.: Smithsonian Institution.

———. 1980. "Self-Directed Pipe Effigies." *Man in the Northeast* 19:95–104.

Braun, David P. 1983. "Pots as Tools." In *Archaeological Hammers and Theories,* edited by Arthur S. Keene and James A. Moore. New York: Academic Press.

———. 1988. "The Social and Technological Roots of 'Late Woodland.' " In *Interpretations of Culture Change in the Eastern Woodlands during the Late Woodland Period,* edited by Richard Yerkes. Ohio State Univ. Occasional Papers in Anthropology no. 3.

Braun, David P., and Stephen Plog. 1982. "Evolution of 'Tribal' Social Networks: Theory and Prehistoric North American Evidence." *American Antiquity* 47, no. 3:504–25.

Brinkerhoff, John I. 1882. "Article on the Early Settlement of Cayuga County." Manuscript in the Cayuga County Historical Society, Auburn, N.Y.

Brown, Ian W. 1980. *Salt and the Eastern North American Indian: An Archaeological Study.* Lower Mississippi Survey Bulletin No. 6. Cambridge: Peabody Museum, Harvard.

Brown, James A. 1997. "The Archaeology of Ancient Religion in the Eastern Woodlands." *Annual Review of Anthropology* 26:465–85.

Brumbach, Hetty Jo. 1986. "Anadromous Fish and Fishing: A Synthesis of Data from the Hudson River Drainage." *Man in the Northeast* 32:35–66.

———. 1995. "Algonquian and Iroquoian Ceramics in the Upper Hudson River Drainage." *Northeast Anthropology* no. 49:55–66.

Campisi, Jack. 1978. "Oneida." In *Handbook of North American Indians.* Vol. 15, *Northeast,* edited by Bruce Trigger. Washington, D.C.: Smithsonian Institution.

Campisi, Jack, and Laurence M. Hauptman. 1988. *The Oneida Indian Experience.* Syracuse: Syracuse Univ. Press.

Cannon, Aubrey. 1991. "Gender, Status, and the Focus of Material Display." In *The Archaeology of Gender,* edited by Dale Walde and Noreen D. Willows. Calgary: Univ. of Calgary Archaeological Association.

Cantwell, Ann-Marie. 1980. "Middle Woodland Dog Ceremonialism." *Wisconsin Archaeologist* 61, no. 11:480–96.

Carneiro, Robert L. 1956. "Slash-and-Burn Agriculture: A Closer Look at Its Implications for Settlement Patterns." In *Man and Cultures, Selected Papers of the Fifth International Congress of Anthropological and Ethnological Sciences,* edited by A.F.C. Wallace. Philadelphia: Univ. of Pennsylvania Press.

Carr, Christopher, and Robert F. Maslowski. 1995. "Cordage and Fabrics: Relating Form, Technology, and Social Processes." In *Style, Society, and Person,* edited by Christopher Carr and Jill Neitzel. New York: Plenum Press.

Cassedy, Daniel F., Paul A. Webb, and James Bradley. 1996. "The Vanderwerken Site: A Protohistoric Iroquois Occupation on Schoharie Creek." *The Bulletin: Journal of the New York State Archaeological Association* nos. 111 and 112:21–34.

Ceci, Lynn. 1975. "Fish Fertilizer: A Native North American Practice?" *Science* 188:26–30.

———. 1978. "Watchers of the Pleiades: Ethnoastronomy Among Native Cultivators in Northeastern North America." *Ethnohistory* 24, no. 4:301–17.

———. 1989. "Tracing Wampum's Origins:

Shell Bead Evidence from Archaeological Sites in Western and Coastal New York." In *Proceedings of the 1986 Shell Bead Conference: Selected Papers.* General editor, Charles F. Hayes III. Research Records No. 20, Rochester Museum and Science Center.

Chafe, Wallace L. 1967. *Seneca Morphology and Dictionary.* Vol. 4 of *Smithsonian Contributions in Anthropology.* Washington. D.C.: Government Printing Office.

Chafe, Wallace L., and Michael K. Foster. 1981. "Prehistoric Divergences and Recontacts Between Cayuga, Seneca, and Other Northern Iroquoian Languages." *International Journal of American Linguistics* 47, no. 2:121–42.

Chapdelaine, C. 1993. "The Sedentarization of the Prehistoric Iroquoians: A Slow or Rapid Transformation?" *Journal of Anthropological Archaeology* 12:173–209.

Charlevoix, Pierre de. [1761] 1966. *Journal of a Voyage to North America.* 2 vols. Ann Arbor: Univ. Microfilms, Inc.

Chilton, Elizabeth S. 1998. "The Cultural Origins of Technical Choice: Unraveling Algonquian and Iroquoian Ceramic Traditions in the Northeast." In *The Archaeology of Social Boundaries,* edited by Miriam T. Stark. Washington: Smithsonian Institution.

Cleland, Charles E. 1982. "The Inland Shore Fishery of the Northern Great Lakes: Its Development and Importance in Prehistory." *American Antiquity* 47, no. 4:761–84.

Cohen, Ronald. 1978. "Ethnicity: Problem and Focus in Anthropology." *Annual Review of Anthropology* 7:379–403.

Cook, Katsi. 1997. "Women are the First Environment." *Native Americas* 14, no. 3:58–59.

Cook, Ramsay. 1993. *The Voyages of Jacques Cartier.* Toronto: Univ. of Toronto Press.

Cornplanter, Jesse J. 1963. *Legends of the Longhouse.* 1938. Reprint. Port Washington, N.Y.: Kennikat Press.

Coupland, Gary, and E. B. Banning. 1996. "Introduction: The Archaeology of Big Houses." In *People Who Lived in Big Houses: Archaeological Perspectives on Large Domestic Structures,* edited by Gary Coupland and E. B. Banning. 1–9. Monographs in World Archaeology no. 27. Madison, Wisconsin: Prehistory Press.

Cowan, C. Wesley. 1985. "Understanding the Evolution of Plant Husbandry in Eastern North America: Lessons from Botany, Ethnography and Archaeology." In *Prehistoric Food Production in North America,* edited by Richard Ford. Univ. of Michigan Anthropological Papers 75. Ann Arbor: Museum of Anthropology.

Crawford, Gary W., David G. Smith, and Vandy E. Bowyer. 1997. "Dating the Entry of Corn *(Zea mays)* into the Lower Great Lakes Region." *American Antiquity* 62, no. 1:112–19.

Crisell, Rob. 1999. "On the Brink of a Cultural Collapse." *American Archaeology* 3, no. 2:31.

Cronon, William. 1983. *Changes in the Land: Indians, Colonists, and the Ecology of New England.* New York: Hill and Wang.

Crosby, Alfred W. 1972. *The Columbian Exchange: Biological and Cultural Consequences of 1492.* Westport, Conn.: Greenwood.

Culin, Stewart. [1907] 1975. *Games of the North American Indians.* Reprint, New York: Dover.

Currie, Douglas R. 1994. "Micromorphology of a Native American Cornfield." *Archaeology of Eastern North America* 22:63–72.

Curtin, Jeremiah, and J. N. B. Hewitt. 1918.

"Seneca Fiction, Legends, and Myths." *Thirty-second Annual Report of the Bureau of American Ethnology,* 1910–1911. Edited by J. N. B. Hewitt. Washington: Government Printing Office.

Davies, Nigel. 1984. "Human Sacrifice in the Old World and the New: Some Similarities and Differences." In *Ritual Human Sacrifice in Mesoamerica,* edited by Elizabeth H. Boone. Washington, D.C.: Dumbarton Oaks Research Library and Collection.

Day, Gordon M. 1953. "The Indian as an Ecological Factor in the Northeastern Forest." *Ecology* 34, no. 2:329–46.

DeBoer, Warren R. 1988. "Subterranean Storage and the Organization of Surplus: The View from Eastern North America." *Southeastern Archaeology* 7, no. 1:1–20.

Deer, Alec Brian. 1998. "How the Condolence Ceremony Manifests Itself Today." Paper presented at the Annual Conference on Iroquois Research, Rensselaerville, N.Y.

Delcourt, Paul A., Hazel R. Delcourt, Cecil R. Ison, William E. Sharp, and Kristen J. Gremillion. 1998. "Prehistoric Human Use of Fire, the Eastern Agricultural Complex, and Appalachian Oak-Chestnut Forests: Paleoecology of Cliff Palace Pond, Kentucky." *American Antiquity* 63, no. 2:263–78.

Dennis, Matthew. 1993. *Cultivating a Landscape of Peace: Iroquois-European Encounters in Seventeenth-Century America.* Ithaca: Cornell Univ. Press.

DeOrio, Robert. 1980. "Perspectives on the Prehistoric Cayuga, Post Owasco Tradition, Through the Correlation of Ceramic Types with Area Development." In *Proceedings of the 1979 Iroquois Pottery Conference.* General editor, Charles F. Hayes III. Research Records No. 13. Rochester: Rochester Museum and Science Center.

———. 1998. "Cayuga Update." Paper presented at the Northeast Archaeology Symposium, Cayuga Museum, Auburn, N.Y.

Dincauze, Dena, and Robert Hasenstab. 1989. "Explaining the Iroquois: Tribalization on a Prehistoric Periphery." In *Comparative Studies in the Development of Complex Societies,* edited by T. Champion. Boston: Allen and Unwin.

Divale, William. 1984. *Matrilocal Residence in Pre-Literate Society.* Ann Arbor: UMI Research Press.

Dobyns, H. F. 1983. *Their Number Become Thinned.* Knoxville: Univ. of Tennessee Press.

Dodd, Christine. 1984. *Ontario Iroquois Tradition Longhouses.* Mercury Series, Archeological Survey of Canada, Paper no. 124. Ottawa: National Museum of Man.

Dodd, Christine, D. R. Poulton, P. A. Lennox, D. G. Smith, and G. A. Warrick. 1990. "The Middle Ontario Iroquoian Stage." In *The Archaeology of Southern Ontario to A.D. 1650,* edited by C. Ellis and N. Ferris. Occasional Publications of the London Chapter, Ontario Archaeological Society 5.

Doxtater, Michael. 1998. "Passing of an Elder: The Iroquoian Indigenous Epistemology of Chief Jacob Thomas." *Native Americas* 15, no. 4:48–55.

Dragoo, Don W. 1976. "Prehistoric Iroquoian Culture in the Upper Ohio Valley." In *The Late Prehistory of the Lake Erie Drainage Basin: A 1972 Symposium Revised,* edited by David S. Brose. Cleveland: Cleveland Museum of Natural History.

———. 1977. "Prehistoric Iroquoian Occupation in the Upper Ohio Valley." In *Current Perspectives in Northeastern Archaeology: Essays in Honor of William A. Ritchie,* edited by Robert E. Funk and Charles F. Hayes III.

*Researches and Transactions of the New York State Archaeological Association* 17, no. 1:41–47. Rochester and Albany.

Drooker, Penelope. 1997. *The View from Madisonville: Protohistoric Western Fort Ancient Interaction Patterns.* Memoirs of the Museum of Anthropology, Univ. of Michigan, no. 31. Ann Arbor, Michigan.

Einhorn, Arthur C. 1999. "Warriors of the Sky: The Iroquois Iron Workers." *European Review of Native American Studies* 13, no. 1:25–34.

Einhorn, Arthur C., and Thomas Abler. 1998. "Tattooed Bodies and Severed Auricles: Images of Native American Body Modification in the Art of Benjamin West." *American Indian Art Magazine* 23 no. 4:42–53, 116–17.

Ember, Carol R., and Melvin Ember. 1996. "What Have We Learned from Cross-Cultural Research?" *General Anthropology: Bulletin of the Council for General Anthropology* 2, no. 2:1, 5–7.

Engelbrecht, William. 1971. "A Stylistic Analysis of New York Iroquois Pottery." Ph.D. diss., Univ. of Michigan.

———. 1972. "The Reflection of Patterned Behavior in Iroquois Pottery Decoration." *Pennsylvania Archaeologist* 42, no. 3:1–15.

———. 1974a. "The Iroquois: Archaeological Patterning on the Tribal Level." *World Archaeology* 6, no. 1:52–65.

———. 1974b. "Cluster Analysis: A Method for the Study of Iroquois Prehistory." *Man in the Northeast* 7:57–70.

———. 1978. "Ceramic Patterning between New York Iroquois sites." In *The Spatial Organisation of Culture,* edited by Ian Hodder. London: Duckworth.

———. 1980. "Inferring Prehistoric Social Organization in the Northeast." *Proceedings of the Conference on Northeastern Archaeology,* edited by James A. Moore. Research Reports Number 19, Department of Anthropology. Amherst: Univ. of Massachusetts.

———. 1985. "New York Iroquois Political Development." In *Cultures in Contact: The European Impact on Native Cultural Institutions in Eastern North America,* A.D. *1000–1800,* edited by William Fitzhugh. Anthropological Society of Washington Series. Washington and London: Smithsonian Institution Press.

———. 1987. "Factors Maintaining Low Population Density among the Prehistoric New York Iroquois." *American Antiquity* 52, no. 1:13–27.

———. 1991. "Erie." *The Bulletin: Journal of the New York State Archaeological Association* no. 102:2–12.

———. 1994. "The Eaton Site: Preliminary Analysis of the Iroquoian Component." *The Bulletin: Journal of the New York State Archaeological Association* no. 107:1–8.

———. 1995. "The Case of the Disappearing Iroquoians: Early Contact Period Superpower Politics." *Northeast Anthropology* no. 50:35–59.

———. 1999. "Iroquoian Ethnicity and Archaeological Taxa." In *Taming the Taxonomy: Toward a New Understanding of Great Lakes Archaeology,* edited by Ronald F. Williamson and Christopher M. Watts. Toronto: eastendbooks in association with The Ontario Archaeological Society.

Engelbrecht, William, Earl Sidler, and Michael Walko. 1990. "The Jefferson County Iroquoians." *Man in The Northeast* 39:65–77.

Engelbrecht, William, and Lynne P. Sullivan. 1996. "Cultural Context." In *Reanalyzing the Ripley Site: Earthworks and Late Prehistory on the Lake Erie Plain,* edited by Lynne

P. Sullivan. New York State Museum Bulletin no. 489. Albany: Univ. of the State of New York, State Education Department.

Fecteau, R. D. 1985. *The Introduction and Diffusion of Cultivated Plants in Southern Ontario.* M.A. thesis, Department of Geography, York Univ.

Fenton, William N. 1940. "Problems Arising from the Northeastern Position of the Iroquois." *Smithsonian Miscellaneous Collections* 100:159–251.

———. 1950. "The Roll Call of the Iroquois Chiefs: A Study of a Mnemonic Cane from the Six Nations Reserve." *Smithsonian Miscellaneous Collections* 3(15):1–73. Washington, D.C.: Smithsonian Institution.

———. 1978. "Northern Iroquoian Culture Patterns." In *Handbook of North American Indians.* Vol. 15, *Northeast,* edited by Bruce Trigger. Washington, D.C.: Smithsonian Institution.

———. 1987. *False Faces of the Iroquois.* Norman: Univ. of Oklahoma Press.

———. 1998. *The Great Law and the Longhouse: A Political History of the Iroquois Confederacy.* Norman: Univ. of Oklahoma Press.

Fenton, William N., and Ernest Dodge. 1949. "An Elm Bark Canoe in the Peabody Museum of Salem." *American Neptune* 9, no. 3:185–206.

Fenton, William N., and Gertrude P. Kurath. 1951. "The Feast of the Dead, or Ghost Dance, at Six Nations Reserve, Canada." *Bureau of American Ethnology Bulletin* 149:139–65. Washington, D.C.

Fenton, William N., and Elisabeth Tooker. 1978. "Mohawk." In *Handbook of North American Indians.* Vol. 15, *Northeast,* edited by Bruce Trigger. Washington, D.C.: Smithsonian Institution.

Fiedel, Stuart J. 1987. *Prehistory of the Americas.* New York: Cambridge Univ. Press.

Finlayson, William D. 1985. *The 1975 and 1978 Rescue Excavations at the Draper Site: Introduction and Settlement Patterns.* Mercury Series, Archaeological Survey of Canada, Paper no. 130. Ottawa: National Museum of Man.

———. 1998. *Iroquoian Peoples of the Land of Rocks and Water, A.D. 1000–1650: A Study in Settlement Archaeology.* Vols. 1–4. London, Ontario: London Museum of Archaeology.

Fitzgerald, W. R., L. Turgeon, R. Holmes Whitehead, and J. W. Bradley. 1993. "Late Sixteenth-Century Basque Banded Copper Kettles." *Historical Archaeology* 27, no. 1:44–57.

Freilich, Morris. 1963. "Scientific Possibilities in Iroquoian Studies: An Example of Mohawk Past and Present." *Anthropus* 58, no. 2:171–86.

Fritz, Gayle J. 1999. "Gender and the Early Cultivation of Gourds in Eastern North America." *American Antiquity* 64, no. 3:417–29.

Funk, Robert E. 1967. "Garoga: A Late Prehistoric Iroquois Village in the Mohawk Valley." In *Iroquois Culture, History, and Prehistory: Proceedings of the 1965 Conference on Iroquois Research,* edited by Elisabeth Tooker. Albany: New York State Museum and Science Service.

———. 1992. "Some Major Wetlands in New York State: A Preliminary Assessment of their Biological and Cultural Potential." *Man in the Northeast* 43:25–41.

———. 1993. *Archaeological Investigations in the Upper Susquehanna Valley, New York State.* Buffalo: Persimmon Press Monographs in Archaeology.

————. 1997. "An Introduction to the History of Prehistoric Archaeology in New York State." *The Bulletin: Journal of the New York State Archaeological Association* no. 113:4–59.

Garbarino, Merwyn S., and Robert F. Sasso. 1994. *Native American Heritage.* Prospect Heights, Illinois: Waveland Press.

Gehring, Charles T., and William A. Starna. 1988. *A Journey into Mohawk and Oneida Country, 1634–1635: The Journal of Harmen Meyndertsz van den Bogaert.* Wordlist and Linguistic Notes by Gunther Michelson. Syracuse: Syracuse Univ. Press.

Galloway, Patricia. 1997. "Where Have All the Menstrual Huts Gone? The Invisibility of Menstrual Seclusion in the Late Prehistoric Southeast." In *Women in Prehistory: North America and Mesoamerica,* edited by Cheryl Claassen and Rosemary A. Joyce. Philadelphia: Univ. of Pennsylvania Press.

Gibson, Stanford J. 1971. "An Elevation Comparison of Iroquois Sites in Three Valleys of Central New York State." *Chenango Chapter NYSAA Bulletin* 12, no. 2.

Glassow, Michael A. 1972. "Changes in the Adaptations of Southwestern Basketmakers: A Systems Perspective." In *Contemporary Archaeology,* edited by Mark P. Leone. Carbondale and Edwardsville: Southern Illinois Univ. Press.

Goddard, Ives. 1984. "Agreskwe, A Northern Iroquoian Deity." In *Extending the Rafters: Interdisciplinary Approaches to Iroquoian Studies,* edited by Michael K. Foster, Jack Campisi, and Marianne Mithun. Albany: State Univ. of New York Press.

Gramly, Richard Michael. 1977. "Deerskins and Hunting Territories: Competition for a Scarce Resource." *American Antiquity* 42, no. 4:601–5.

————. 1988. "Conflict and Defense in the Eastern Woodlands." In *Interpretations of Culture Change in the Eastern Woodlands during the Late Woodland Period,* edited by Richard W. Yerkes. Ohio State Univ. Occasional Papers in Anthropology, no. 3.

Granger, Joseph. 1976. "The Orchid Site, Area B, Fort Erie, Ontario." *The Bulletin: Journal of the New York State Archeological Association* no. 67:1–39.

Grant, W. L. [1907] 1959. *Voyages of Samuel De Champlain: 1604–1618.* Reprint, New York: Barnes and Noble.

Green, William, and Lynne P. Sullivan. 1997. "Pits and Pitfalls: An Analysis of Pit Features and Site Function at the Ripley Site." *Northeast Anthropology* no. 53:1–22.

Griffin, James B. 1944. "The Iroquois in American Prehistory." *Papers of the Michigan Academy of Science, Arts, and Letters* 29:357–74.

Grim, John A., and Donald P. St. John. 1987. "The Northeast Woodlands." In *Native American Religions: North America,* edited by Lawrence E. Sullivan. New York: MacMillan.

Guilday, John E. 1973. "Vertebrate Remains from the Garoga Site, Fulton County, New York." In *Aboriginal Settlement Patterns in the Northeast* by William A. Ritchie and Robert E. Funk. Memoir 20, New York State Museum and Science Service. Albany: Univ. of the State of New York, State Education Department.

Guldenzopf, David. 1984. "Frontier Demography and Settlement Patterns of the Mohawk Iroquois." *Man in the Northeast* 27:79–94.

Hall, Robert L. 1977. "An Anthropocentric Perspective for Eastern United States Prehistory." *American Antiquity* 42, no. 4:499–518.

———. 1997. *An Archaeology of the Soul: North American Indian Belief and Ritual.* Urbana and Chicago: Univ. of Illinois Press.

———. 2000. "Sacrificed Foursomes and Green Corn Ceremonialism." *Mounds, Modoc, and Mesoamerica: Papers in Honor of Melvin L. Fowler,* edited by Steven R. Ahler. Illinois State Museum Scientific Papers Series, Vol. 28. Springfield: Illinois State Museum.

Hallowell, A. Irving. 1926. "Bear Ceremonialism in the Northern Hemisphere." *American Anthropologist* 28, no. 1:1–175.

Hamell, G. R. 1977. "Report on the Alhart Site Radiocarbon Dates." Ms. on file at the Rochester Museum and Science Center, Rochester, N.Y.

———. 1980. "Gannagaro State Historic Site: A Current Perspective." *Occasional Papers in Northeastern Anthropology* no. 6:91–108.

———. 1983. "Trading in Metaphors: The Magic of Beads." In *Proceedings of the 1982 Glass Trade Bead Conference,* edited by Charles F. Hayes III. Research Records no. 16. Rochester Museum and Science Center.

———. 1987. "Mythical Realities and European Contact in the Northeast during the Sixteenth and Seventeenth Centuries." *Man in the Northeast* 33:63–87.

———. 1988. "The Dragon of Discord, Village Relocation, and Ossuary Burial." Paper presented at the annual conference on Iroquois Research. Rensselaerville, N.Y.

———. 1992. "The Iroquois and the World's Rim: Speculations on Color, Culture, and Contact." *American Indian Quarterly* 16:451–69.

———. 1996. "Wampum." In *One Man's Trash Is Another Man's Treasure.* Williamsburg, Virginia: Jamestown Settlement Museum.

———. 1998. "Long-Tail: The Panther in Huron-Wyandot and Seneca Myth, Ritual, and Material Culture." In *Icons of Power: Feline Symbolism in the Americas,* edited by Nicholas J. Saunders. New York: Routledge.

———. n.d. "More on Lafitau's Hoes." Manuscript.

Hammond, L. M. 1872. *History of Madison County, State of New York.* Syracuse: Truair, Smith and Co.

Harrington, M. R. 1909. "The Last of the Iroquois Potters." New York State Museum Bulletin 133:222–27. Education Department Bulletin no. 453. Albany: Univ. of the State of New York.

———. 1977. "Ancient Shell Heaps Near New York City." *Readings in Long Island Archaeology and Ethnohistory* 1:1–15. Stony Brook, N.Y.: Suffolk County Archaeological Association. Reprinted from American Museum of Natural History *Anthropological Papers* 3, 1909.

Harris, Marvin. 1979. *Cultural Materialism: The Struggle for a Science of Culture.* New York: Random House.

Hart, John P. 1999a. "Dating Roundtop's Domesticates: Implications for Northeast Late Prehistory." In *Current Northeast Paleoethnobotany,* edited by John P. Hart. New York State Museum Bulletin 494. Albany: New York State Education Department.

———. 1999b. "Maize Agriculture Evolution in the Eastern Woodlands of North America: A Darwinian Perspective." *Journal of Archaeological Method and Theory* 6, no. 2:137–80.

———. 2000. "New Dates from Classic New York Sites: Just How Old Are Those Longhouses?" *Northeast Anthropology* 60:1–22.

———. 2001. "Maize, Matrilocality, Migration, and Northern Iroquoian Evolution."

*Journal of Archaeological Method and Theory* 8, no. 2:151–82.

Hart, John P., and C. Margaret Scarry. 1999. "The Age of Common Beans *(Phaseolus vulgaris)* in the Northeastern United States." *American Antiquity* 64, no. 4:653–58.

Hart, John P., and Nancy Asch Sidell. 1996. "Prehistoric Agricultural Systems in the West Branch of the Susquehanna River Basin, A.D. 800 to A.D. 1350." *Northeast Anthropology* no. 52:1–30.

———. 1997. "Additional Evidence for early Cucurbit Use in the Northern Eastern Woodlands East of the Allegheny Front." *American Antiquity* 62, no. 3:523–37.

Hart, John P., Robert G. Thompson, and Hetty Jo Brumbach. n.d. "Evidence for Seventh—and Eighth-Century A.D. Maize *(Zea mays* spp. *mays)* and Squash *(Cucurbita* sp.) in the Northern Finger Lakes Region of New York." Manuscript in preparation.

Hasenstab, Robert John. 1990. "Agriculture, Warfare, and Tribalization in the Iroquois Homeland of New York: A G.I.S. Analysis of Late Woodland Settlement." Ph.D. diss., Univ. of Massachusetts.

———. 1996. "Aboriginal Settlement Patterns in Late Woodland Upper New York State." *Journal of Middle Atlantic Archaeology* 12:17–26.

———. 2001. "Proto-Iroquois." *Encyclopedia of Prehistory.* Vol. 6, *North America,* edited by Peter N. Peregrine and Melvin Ember. New York: Kluwer Academic/Plenum Publishers.

———. n.d. "The Three Sisters: Staples of the Iroquois." In *Ethnobiology: Perspectives and Practices in the Northeastern United States and Eastern Canada,* edited by Connie Cox-Bodner. Research Records no. 24. Rochester Museum and Science Center.

Hayden, Brian. 1982. "Recognizing Intact Iroquoian Domestic Refuse: The Draper Case." *Ontario Archaeology* no. 28:3–16.

Hayes, Charles F., III. 1965. "A Regional Approach to Archaeology—A Cultural Sample from the Cornish Site." *Museum Service* 38, nos. 5–6:45–54. Bulletin of the Rochester Museum of Arts and Sciences.

———. 1966. "Excavating an Early Historic Seneca Longhouse." *Museum Service* 39, nos. 5–6:76–81. Bulletin of the Rochester Museum of Arts and Sciences.

Hayes, G. L., and D. E. Wonderly. 1998. "A Long Oneida Longhouse at Vaillancourt." Paper presented at The Northeast Archaeology Symposium, The Cayuga Museum, Auburn, N.Y.

Heidenreich, Conrad E. 1971. *Huronia: A History and Geography of the Huron Indians 1600–1650.* Toronto: McClelland and Stewart.

Herrick, James W. 1995. *Iroquois Medical Botany.* Syracuse: Syracuse Univ. Press.

Hewitt, J. N. B., 1903. "Iroquoian Cosmology: First Part." *Annual Report of the Bureau of American Ethnology for the Years 1899–1900* 21:127–339. Washington, D.C.: Smithsonian Institution.

———. 1928. "Iroquoian Cosmology, Second Part." *Annual Report of the Bureau of American Ethnology* 43:449–819. Washington, D.C.: Smithsonian Institution.

Hickerson, Harold. 1965. "The Virginia Deer and Intertribal Buffer Zones in the Upper Mississippi Valley." In *Man, Culture, and Animals,* edited by Anthony Leeds and Andrew Vayda. Washington D.C.: Publication no. 78 of the American Association for the Advancement of Science.

Hill, Richard. 1997. "Personal Reflections on the Meaning of the Longhouse." Paper presented at the Longhouse Conference, Rochester Museum and Science Center.

Hill, Richard, and Donald A. Grinde, Jr. 1975. "Problems in Prehistory and History of the Iroquois." *Ontario Archaeology* no. 25:57–59.

Hodder, I. 1979. "Economic and Social Stress and Material Culture Patterning." *American Antiquity* 44, no. 3:446–54.

Hosbach, Richard E. 1997. "The Architectural Changes in Oneida Iroquois Longhouse over Time." Paper presented at the Longhouse Conference, Rochester Museum and Science Center.

———. 1999. "Iroquois Pediatrics as Viewed in the Light of Twentieth-Century Medicine: Part 2." Paper presented at the 1999 annual meeting of the New York State Archaeological Association, Sparrowbush, N.Y.

Huey, Paul R. 1994. "Archaeological Testing for an Electrical Line at Ganondagan State Historic Site, July 12, 1994." *The Bulletin: Journal of the New York State Archaeological Association* no. 108:11–17.

Hultkrantz, A. 1979. *The Religions of the American Indians.* Berkeley: Univ. of California Press.

Hunt, George T. 1940. *The Wars of the Iroquois: A Study in Intertribal Trade Relations.* Madison: Univ. of Wisconsin Press.

Hunter, William A. 1978. "History of the Ohio Valley." In *Handbook of North American Indians.* Vol. 15, *Northeast,* edited by Bruce Trigger. Washington, D.C.: Smithsonian Institution.

Isaacs, Hope L. 1977. "*Orenda* and the Concept of Power among the Tonawanda Seneca." *The Anthropology of Power: Ethnographic Studies from Asia, Oceania, and the New World,* edited by Raymond D. Fogelson and Richard N. Adams. New York: Academic Press.

Jacobson, Jerome. 1980. *Burial Ridge: Archaeology at New York City's Largest Prehistoric Cemetery.* Staten Island Institute of Arts and Sciences.

Jamieson, J. B. 1990. "Trade and Warfare: The Disappearance of the Saint Lawrence Iroquoians." *Man in the Northeast* 39:79–86.

Jemison, G. Peter, and John White. 1997. "Ganondagan's Longhouse: Connecting the Past with the Future." Paper presented at the Longhouse Conference, Rochester Museum and Science Center.

Johansen, Bruce E. 1999. "Construction Workers at Akwesasne Casino Tap Toxic Pool Fouling Well Water." *Native Americas* Spring:7.

Jones, David, and Anne Jones. 1980. "The Defenses at Indian Fort Road, Tompkins County, New York." *Pennsylvania Archaeologist* 50, nos. 1–2:61–71.

Jordan, Kurt A. 1997a. "Seneca Settlement Pattern and Community Structure, 1677–1779." Paper presented at the Annual Conference on Iroquois Research, Rensselaerville, N.Y.

———. 1997b. "Pan-Iroquoian Trend or Mohawk Exceptionalism?: A Reconsideration of the Longhouse to Loghouse Transition, 1687–1779." Paper presented at the Longhouse Conference, Rochester Museum and Science Center.

———. 1998. "Excavations at the Townley-Read Site, an Eighteenth-Century Seneca Iroquois Community: A Progress Report." Paper presented at The Northeast Archaeology Symposium, Cayuga Museum, Auburn, N.Y.

———. n.d. "Seneca Iroquois Settlement Pattern, Community Structure, and Household Organization, 1677–1779." Manuscript.

Junker-Andersen, C. 1986. "Faunal Remains from the Jackson-Everson (NYSM 1213) Site." In *The Mohawk Valley Project: 1983 Jackson-Everson Excavations,* edited by Robert D. Kuhn and Dean R. Snow. Albany: Institute for Northeast Anthropology, State Univ. of New York at Albany.

Kaldy, M. S., A. Johnston, and D. B. Wilson. 1980. "Nutritional Value of Indian Breadroot, Squaw-root, and Jerusalem Artichoke." *Economic Botany* 34, no. 4:352–57.

Kalm, Peter. 1935. "Pehr Kalm's Description of Maize," translated by E. L. Larsen. *Agricultural History* 9, no. 2:98–117.

———. 1966. *The America of 1750: Peter Kalm's Travels in North America; The English Version of 1770,* edited by Adolph B. Benson. 2 vols. New York: Dover Publications.

Kapches, Mima. 1976. "The Internment of Infants of the Ontario Iroquois." *Ontario Archaeology* 27:29–39.

———. 1980. "Wall Trenches on Iroquoian Sites." *Archaeology of Eastern North America* 8:98–105.

———. 1984. "Cabins on Ontario Iroquois Sites." *North American Archaeologist* 5, no. 1:63–71.

———. 1990. "The Spatial Dynamics of Ontario Iroquoian Longhouses." *American Antiquity* 55, no. 1:49–67.

———. 1992. " 'Rude but Perfect' (Beauchamp 1899): A Study of Miniature Smoking Pipes in Iroquoia." In *Proceedings of the 1989 Smoking Pipe Conference: Selected Papers.* General editor, Charles F. Hayes III; associate editors, Connie Cox Bodner and Martha Sempowski. Research Records no. 22, Rochester Museum and Science Center.

———. 1993. "The Identification of an Iroquoian Unit of Measurement: Architectural and Social/Cultural Implications for the Longhouse." *Archaeology of Eastern North America* 21:137–62.

———. 1994a. "The Hill Site: A Possible Late Early Iroquoian Ceramic Firing Site in South-Central Ontario." *Northeast Anthropology* no. 48:91–102.

———. 1994b. "The Use of Space in Iroquois Longhouses: Insights from the Present and the Past." Paper presented at the Northeastern Anthropological Association Meetings, Geneseo, N.Y.

Kaplan, L. 1973. "Ethnobotanical and Nutritional Factors in the Domestication of American Beans." In *Man and His Foods: Studies in the Ethnobotany of Nutrition—Contemporary, Primitive, and Prehistoric Non-European Diets,* edited by C. Earle Smith, Jr. University, Alabama: Univ. of Alabama Press.

Katz, S. H., M. L. Hediger, and L. A. Valleroy. 1974. "Traditional Maize Processing Techniques in the New World." *Science* 184:765–73.

Katzenberg, A., H. P. Schwarcz, M. Knyf, and F. J. Melbye. 1995. "Stable Isotope Evidence for Maize Horticulture and Paleodiet in Southern Ontario, Canada." *American Antiquity* 60, no. 2:335–50.

Keeley, Lawrence H. 1996. *War Before Civilization.* New York: Oxford Univ. Press.

Keener, Craig, and Erica Kuhns. 1997. "The Impact of Iroquoian Populations on the Northern Distribution of Pawpaws in the Northeast." *North American Archaeologist* 18, no. 4:327–42.

Kent, Barry C. 1984. *Susquehanna's Indians.* Anthropological Series, no. 6. Harrisburg, Pa.: Pennsylvania Historical and Museum Commission.

Kenton, Edna. 1927. *The Indians of North America,* Vol. 1. New York: Harcourt, Brace.

Kenyon, I., and W. Fitzgerald. 1986. "Dutch Glass Beads in the Northeast: An Ontario Perspective." *Man in the Northeast* 32:1–34.

Kenyon, W. 1968. *The Miller Site.* Royal Ontario Museum, Art and Archaeology Division, Occasional Paper 14.

Kerber, Jordan E. 1997. "Native American Treatment of Dogs in Northeastern North America: Archaeological and Ethnohistorical Perspectives." *Archaeology of Eastern North America* 25:81–96.

Kinietz, W. Vernon. [1940] 1965. *The Indians of the Western Great Lakes 1615–1760.* Reprint, Ann Arbor: Ann Arbor Paperbacks, Univ. of Michigan Press.

Konrad, Victor. 1981. "An Iroquois Frontier: The North Shore of Lake Ontario during the Late Seventeenth Century." *Journal of Historical Geography* 7:129–44.

———. 1987. "The Iroquois Return to their Homeland: Military Retreat or Cultural Adjustment." In *A Cultural Geography of North American Indians,* edited by Thomas E. Ross and Tyrel G. Moore. Boulder: Westview Press.

Knowles, Nathaniel. 1940. "The Torture of Captives by the Indians of Eastern North America." *Proceedings of the American Philosophical Society* 82, no. 2:151–225. Philadelphia.

Kosse, K. 1990. "Group Size and Societal Complexity: Thresholds in the Long-term Memory." *Journal of Anthropological Archaeology* 9, no. 3:275–303.

Kraft, Herbert C. 1972. "Archaeological Evidence for a Possible Masking Complex among the Prehistoric Lenape in Northwestern New Jersey." *The Bulletin: Journal of the New York State Archeological Association* no. 56:1–11.

———. 1996. "Effigy Faces in Lenape Archaeology." *Journal of Middle Atlantic Archaeology* 12:81–93.

Krusche, Rolf. 1986. "The Origin of the Mask Concept in the Eastern Woodlands of North America." *Man in the Northeast* 31:1–47.

Kuhn, Robert. 1985. "Trade and Exchange among the Mohawk-Iroquois: A Trace Element Analysis of Ceramic Smoking Pipes." Ph.D. diss., Univ. at Albany, SUNY.

———. 1986. "Interaction Patterns in Eastern New York: A Trace Element Analysis of Iroquoian and Algonkian Ceramics." *The Bulletin and Journal of Archaeology for New York State* no. 92:9–21.

———. 1994a. "The Cromwell Site (NYSM 1121): Including a Brief Treatise on Early Seventeenth-Century Mohawk Pottery Trends." *The Bulletin: Journal of the New York State Archaeological Association* no. 108:29–38.

———. 1994b. "Recent CRM Contributions to Iroquoian Archeology in New York State." *Archaeology of Eastern North America* 22:73–88.

———. 1996. "A Comparison of Mohawk and Onondaga Projectile Point Assemblages." *Journal of Middle Atlantic Archaeology* 12:27–34.

Kuhn, Robert D., and Robert E. Funk. 1994. "Mohawk Interaction Patterns During the Late Sixteenth Century." In *Proceedings of the 1992 People to People Conference: Selected Papers.* General Editor: Charles F. Hayes III; Associate Editors: Connie Cox Bodner and

Lorraine P. Saunders. Research Records no. 23, Rochester Museum and Science Center.

Kuhn, Robert D., Robert E. Funk, and James F. Pendergast. 1993. "The Evidence for a Saint Lawrence Iroquoian Presence on Sixteenth-Century Mohawk Sites." *Man in the Northeast* 45:77–86.

Kuhn, Robert D., Dean Snow, and Robert Funk. 1997. "Mohawk Longhouse Patterns." Paper presented at the Longhouse Conference, Rochester Museum and Science Center.

Kuhn, Robert D., and Martha L. Sempowski. 2001 "A New Approach to Dating the League of the Iroquois." *American Antiquity* 66, no, 2:301–14.

Kupperman, Karen Ordahl. 2000. *Indians and English: Facing Off in Early America*. Ithaca, N.Y.: Cornell Univ. Press.

LaDuke, Winona. 1992. "Indigenous Environmental Perspectives: A North American Primer." *Akwe:kon Journal* 9, no. 2:52–71.

Laet, Johannes de. 1640. *L'histoire du Nouveau monde ou Description des Indes Occidentales contenant dix-huict liures . . .* Leyden: A. Leyde, Chez B., and A. Elseuiers.

Lafitau, Father Joseph François. 1974, 1977. *Customs of the American Indians Compared with the Customs of Primitive Times,* 2 vols. Edited and translated by William Fenton and Elizabeth Moore. [1724]. Toronto: The Champlain Society.

Lahontan, Baron de. 1970. *New Voyages to North-America,* 2 vols. Edited by Reuben G. Thwaites. [1703]. New York: Lenox Hill.

Latta, Martha A. 1985. "A 17th Century Attigneenongnahac Village: Settlement Patterns at the Auger Site (BdGw-3)." *Ontario Archaeology* no. 44:41–54.

———. 1991. "The Captive Bride Syndrome: Iroquoian Behavior or Archaeological

Myth?" In *The Archaeology of Gender,* edited by Dale Walde and Noreen D. Willows. Calgary: Univ. of Calgary Archaeological Association.

Lenig, Donald. 1965. *The Oak Hill Horizon and Its Relations to the Development of Five Nations Iroquois Culture*. Researches and Transactions of the New York State Archaeological Association 15, no. 1. Buffalo.

———. 1977. "Of Dutchmen, Beaver Hats and Iroquois." In *Current Perspectives in Northeastern Archeology: Essays in Honor of William A. Ritchie,* edited by R. E. Funk and C. F. Hayes III, 71–84. Researches and Transactions of the New York State Archaeological Association 17, no. 1.

Lenig, Wayne. 1999. "Patterns of Material Culture in the First Quarter Century of New Netherlands Trade." *Northeast Anthropology* 58: 47–74.

———. n.d. "Prehistoric Mohawk Studies: The Mohawk Valley Project and Beyond." Manuscript.

Lennox, Paul. 1984. *The Hood Site: A Historic Neutral Town of 1640 A.D.* National Museum of Man Mercury Series, Archaeological Survey of Canada, Paper 121. Ottawa.

Lennox, Paul, and William R. Fitzgerald. 1990. "The Culture History and Archaeology of the Neutral Iroquoians." *The Archaeology of Southern Ontario to A.D. 1650,* edited by Chris J. Ellis and Neal Ferris. 405–56. Occasional Publications of the London Chapter of the Ontario Archaeological Society, 5.

Lewis, Dennis M. 1994. "An Intact Prehistoric Ceramic Pot from Cumberland Bay, Lake Champlain." *The Bulletin: Journal of the New York State Archaeological Association* no. 107:25.

Lewis, Henry T. 1980. "Indian Fires of Spring." *Natural History* (January):76–83.

Lounsbury, Floyd G. 1960. *Iroquois Place-Names in the Champlain Valley*. Reprinted from Report of the New York-Vermont Interstate Commission on the Lake Champlain Basin, 1960, Legislative Document No. 9:23–66. Albany: The Univ. of the State of New York, The State Education Department.

———. 1978. "Iroquoian Languages." In *Handbook of North American Indians*. Vol. 15, *Northeast*, edited by Bruce Trigger. Washington, D.C.: Smithsonian Institution.

———. 1982. "Tawiskala." Paper delivered at the Annual Conference on Iroquoian Research, Rensselaerville, New York.

Lynch, James. 1985. "The Iroquois Confederacy, and the Adoption and Administration of Non-Iroquoian Individuals and Groups Prior to 1756." *Man in the Northeast* 30:83–99.

Macauley, James. 1825. *History of New York*. New York: Gould and Banks.

MacDonald, Robert I. 1988. "Ontario Iroquoian Sweat Lodges." *Ontario Archaeology*, no. 48:17–26.

Mackay, Gene. 1989. "A Selection of Drawings by Gene Mackay." *Proceedings of the 1986 Shell Bead Conference,* general editor Charles F. Hayes III, 46–61. Rochester Museum and Science Center, Research Records no. 20. Rochester, N.Y.

MacNeish, Richard. 1952. *Iroquois Pottery Types: A Technique for the Study of Iroquois Prehistory*. National Museum of Canada Bulletin 124.

Mandzy, Adrian O. 1990. "The Rogers Farm Site: A Seventeenth-Century Cayuga Site." *The Bulletin: Journal of the New York State Archaeological Association* no. 100:18–25.

———. 1994. "The Results of Interaction: Change in Cayuga Society During the Seventeenth Century." In *Proceedings of the 1992 People to People Conference: Selected Papers,* general editor: Charles F. Hayes III; associate editors: Connie Cox Bodner and Lorraine P. Saunders; 133–56. Research Records no. 23, Rochester Museum and Science Center.

Mathews, Zena P. 1976. "Huron Pipes and Iroquoian Shamanism." *Man in the Northeast* 12:15–31.

———. 1978. *The Relation of Seneca False Face Masks to Seneca and Ontario Archaeology*. New York: Garland Publishing, Inc.

———. 1980. "Seneca Figurines: A Case of Misplaced Modesty." *Occasional Papers in Northeast Anthropology* 6:71–90.

———. 1981. "Janus and other Multiple-Image Iroquoian Pipes." *Ontario Archaeology*, no. 35:3–22.

Megapolensis, Johannes, Jr. [1644] 1857. *A short sketch of the Mohawk Indians in New Netherland, their land, stature, dress, manners, and magistrates, written in the year 1644 . . .* In *Collections of the New-York Historical Society*. Second Series: Vol. 3, Part 1. New York: New-York Historical Society. Revised from the translation in Hazard's Historical Collections, with an introduction and notes by John Romeyn Brodhead.

Miller, Charles L. 1994. "Lamoka Phase Settlement Pattern in the Genesee River Valley." Ph.D. diss., SUNY at Buffalo.

Milner, George R., Eve Anderson, and Virginia G. Smith. 1991. "Warfare in Late Prehistoric West-Central Illinois." *American Antiquity* 56, no. 4:581–603.

Mithun, Marianne. 1984. "The Proto-Iroquoians: Cultural Reconstruction from Lexical Materials." In *Extending The Rafters: Interdisciplinary Approaches to Iroquoian Studies,* edited by Michael Foster, Jack

Campisi, and Marianne Mithun. 259–81. Albany: State Univ. of New York Press.

Moeller, Roger W. 1996. "Some Thoughts on Late Woodland Ecology." *Journal of Middle Atlantic Archaeology* 12:61–66.

Mohawk, John. 1994. "A View from Turtle Island: Chapters in Iroquois Mythology, History and Culture." Ph.D. diss., State University of New York at Buffalo.

Monckton, Stephen G. 1992. *Huron Paleoethnobotany.* Ontario Archaeological Reports 1. Toronto: Ontario Heritage Foundation

Moore, John. 1994. "Putting Anthropology Back Together Again: The Ethnogenetic Critique of Cladistic Theory." *American Anthropologist* 96, no. 4:925–48.

Morgan, Lewis Henry. 1962. *League of the Ho-De-No-Sau-Nee, Iroquois.* 1851. Reprint. New York: Corinth Books.

Moulton, Anne L., and Thomas S. Abler. 1991. "Lithic Beings and Lithic Technology: References from Northern Iroquoian Mythology." *Man in the Northeast* 42:1–7.

Mrozowski, Stephen A. 1994. "The Discovery of a Native American Cornfield on Cape Cod." *Archaeology of Eastern North America* 22:47–62.

Mt. Pleasant, Jane. 1989. "The Iroquois Sustainers: Practices of a Longterm Agriculture in the Northeast." In *Indian Corn of the Americas: Gift to the World,* edited by Jose Barreiro. Northeast Indian Quarterly 6, nos. 1–2:33–39. Ithaca: American Indian Program, Cornell Univ.

Munson, Patrick J. 1988. "Late Woodland Settlement and Subsistence in Temporal Perspective." In *Interpretations of Culture Change in the Eastern Woodlands During the Late Woodland Period,* edited by Richard Yerkes. Occasional Papers in Anthropology no. 3. Columbus,Ohio: Ohio State Univ.

Murphy, James L. 2001. "Pawpaws, Persimmons, and Possums: On the Natural Distribution of Pawpaws in the Northeast." *North American Archaeologist* 22, no. 2: 93–115.

Nabokov, Peter. 1981. *Indian Running: Native American History and Tradition.* Santa Fe, New Mexico: Ancient City Press.

Nassaney, Michael S., and Kendra Pyle. 1999. "The Adoption of the Bow and Arrow in Eastern North America: A View from Central Arkansas." *American Antiquity* 64, no. 2:243–63.

Neusius, Sarah W., Lynne P. Sullivan, Phillip D. Neusius, and Claire McHale Milner. 1998. "Fortified Village or Mortuary Site?" In *Ancient Earthen Enclosures of the Eastern Woodlands,* edited by Robert C. Mainfort, Jr., and Lynne P. Sullivan, 202–30. Gainesville: Univ. Press of Florida.

Niemczycki, Mary Ann Palmer. 1984. *The Origin and Development of the Seneca and Cayuga Tribes of New York State.* Research Records no. 17. Charles F. Hayes III, editor. Rochester, New York: Rochester Museum and Science Center.

———. 1986. "The Genesee Connection: The Origins of Iroquois Culture in West-Central New York." *North American Archaeologist* 7, no. 1:15–44.

———. 1991. "Cayuga Archaeology: Where Do We Go From Here?" *The Bulletin: Journal of the New York State Archaeological Association* no. 102:27–33.

———. 1995. "Ceramics and Ethnicity in West-Central New York: Exploring Owasco-Iroquois Connections." Northeast Anthropology no. 49:43–54.

Noble, William C. 1979. "Ontario Iroquois Effigy Pipes." *Canadian Journal of Archaeology* 3:69–90.

O'Callaghan, E. B. 1849–1851. *The Documentary History of the State of New York.* 4 vols. Albany: Weed, Parsons, and Co.

———. 1853–1887. *Documents Relative to the Colonial History of the State of New York.* 15 vols. Albany: Weed, Parsons, and Co.

Onion, Daniel K. 1964. "Corn in the Culture of the Mohawk Iroquois." *Economic Botany* 18 no. 1:60–66.

O'Shea, John. 1988. "Social Organization and Mortuary Behavior in the Late Woodland Period in Michigan." In *Interpretations of Culture Change in the Eastern Woodlands During the Late Woodland Period,* edited by Richard W. Yerkes, 68–85. Ohio State Univ. Occasional Papers in Anthropology no. 3.

———. 1989. "The Role of Wild Resources in Small-Scale Agricultural Systems: Tales from the Lakes and the Plains." In *Bad Year Economics: Cultural Responses to Risk and Uncertainty,* edited by Paul Halstead and John O'Shea, 57–67. New York: Cambridge Univ. Press.

Orlandini, John B. 1996. "The Passenger Pigeon: A Seasonal Native American Food Source." *Pennsylvania Archaeologist* 66, no. 2:71–77.

Otterbein, Keith F. 1964. "Why the Iroquois Won: An Analysis of Iroquois Military Tactics." *Ethnohistory* 11:56–63.

Owsley, Douglas W. and Richard L. Jantz. 2000. "Biography in the Bones." *Discovering Archaeology* 2, no. 1:56–58.

Paper, Jordan. 1992. "The Iroquoian and Pan-Indian Sacred Pipes: Comparative Ritual and Symbolism." In *Proceedings of the 1989 Smoking Pipe Conference: Selected Papers,* general editor, Charles F. Hayes III, associate editors: Connie Cox Bodner and Martha Sempowski, 163–69. Research Records no. 22, Rochester Museum and Science Center.

Parker, Arthur C. 1918. *A Prehistoric Iroquoian Site on the Reed Farm, Richmond Mills, Ontario County, N.Y.* Researches and Transactions of the New York State Archeological Association 1, no. 1. Rochester.

———. 1922. *The Archaeological History of New York.* 2 pts. Albany: New York State Museum Bulletin, 235–38.

———. 1923. *Seneca Myths and Folk Tales.* Buffalo Historical Society, Buffalo, New York.

———. 1967. *The History of the Seneca Indians.* 1926. Reprint. Port Washington, NY: Ira J. Friedman.

———. 1968. "Iroquois Uses of Maize and Other Food Plants." In *Parker on the Iroquois,* edited by William Fenton, 1–119. 1910. Reprint. Syracuse: Syracuse Univ. Press.

Parry, William J., and Robert Kelly. 1987. "Expedient Core Technology and Sedentism." In *The Organization of Core Technology.* Edited by Jay K. Johnson and Carol Morrow, 285–304. Boulder: Westview Press.

Pasternak, B., C. R. Ember, and M. Ember. 1976. "On the Conditions Favoring Extended Family Households." *Journal of Anthropological Research* 32, no. 2:109–23.

Peña, E. S. 1990. "Wampum Production in New Netherland and Colonial New York: The Historical and Archaeological Context." Ph.D. diss., Boston Univ..

Pendergast, James F. 1982. *The Origin of Maple Sugar.* Syllogeus no. 36. Ottawa: National Museums of Canada.

———. 1985. "Huron-St. Lawrence Iroquois Relations in the Terminal Prehistoric Period." *Ontario Archaeology* 44:23–39.

———. 1989. "The Significance of Some Marine Shell Excavated on Iroquoian Archaeological Sites in Ontario." In *Proceedings of the 1986 Shell Bead Conference, Selected Papers,* edited by Charles F. Hayes III, 97–112. Rochester Museum and Science Center, Research Records 20, Rochester, New York.

———. 1991a. *The Massawomeck: Raiders and Traders into the Chesapeake in the Seventeenth Century.* Philadelphia, Pennsylvania: Transactions of the American Philosophical Society 81, Pt. 2.

———. 1991b. "The St. Lawrence Iroquoians: Their Past, Present, and Immediate Future." *The Bulletin: Journal of the New York State Archaeological Association* 102:47–74.

———. 1992. "Susquehannock Trade Northward to New France Prior to A.D. 1608: A Popular Misconception." *Pennsylvania Archaeologist* 62, no. 1:1–11.

———. 1994. "Possible Botanical Indicators of St. Lawrence Iroquoian Archaeological Sites." Paper presented at the Ethnobiology Conference sponsored by the Rochester Museum and Science Center.

Pendergast, James F., and Bruce C. Trigger. 1972. *Cartier's Hochelaga and the Dawson Site.* Montreal: McGill-Queen's Univ. Press.

Perino, Gregory. 1973: "The Koster Mounds, Greene County, Illinois." In *Late Woodland Site Archaeology in Illinois I: Investigations in South-Central Illinois,* edited by J. A. Brown. 141–206. Illinois Archeology Survey Bulletin no. 9. Urbana: Univ. of Illinois.

Perkl, Bradley E. 1998. *"Cucurbita pepo* from King Coulee, Southeastern Minnesota." *American Antiquity* 63, no. 2:279–88.

Petersen, James B., and Nancy Asch Sidell. 1996. "Mid-Holocene Evidence of *Cucurbita* sp. from Central Maine." *American Antiquity* 61, no. 4:685–98.

Pfeiffer, Susan. 1980. "Spatial Distribution of Human Skeletal Material within an Iroquoian Ossuary." *Canadian Journal of Archaeology* 4:169–72.

Phillips, Philip, and James A. Brown. 1984. *Pre-Columbian Shell Engravings from the Craig Mound at Spiro, Oklahoma,* Pt 2. Cambridge: Peabody Museum Press of Harvard Univ..

Pratt, Marjorie K. 1991. "The St. Lawrence Iroquois of Northern New York." *The Bulletin: Journal of the New York State Archaeological Association* no. 102:43–46.

Pratt, Peter P. 1963. "A Heavily Stockaded Late Prehistoric Oneida Iroquois Settlement." *Pennsylvania Archaeologist* 33, nos. 1–2:56–92.

———. 1976. *Archaeology of the Oneida Iroquois.* Vol. 1. Occasional Publications in Northeastern Anthropology, no. 1. Rindge, New Hampshire: Man in the Northeast.

———. 1991. "Oneida Archaeology: The Last Quarter Century." *The Bulletin: Journal of the New York State Archaeological Association* no. 102:40–42.

———. 1977. "A Perspective on Oneida Archaeology." In *Current Perspectives in Northeastern Archaeology: Essays in Honor of William A. Ritchie, Researches and Transactions of the New York State Archaeological Association* 17, no. 1:51–69. Edited by Robert E. Funk and Charles F. Hayes III. Rochester and Albany.

Pratt, Peter P., and Marjorie K. Pratt. 1998. "The Evolution and Crystallization of the Iroquois Longhouse and the Identification of a People." Paper presented at the annual meeting of the New York State Archaeological Association. Alexandria Bay.

Prentice, G. 1986. "Origins of Plant Domestication in the Eastern United States: Promoting the Individual in Archaeological Theory." *Southeastern Archaeology* 5:103–19.

Prezzano, Susan C. 1988. "Spatial Analysis of Post Mold Patterns at the Sackett Site, Ontario County, New York." *Man in the Northeast* 35:27–45.

———. 1992. "Longhouse, Village, and Palisade: Community Patterns at the Iroquois Southern Door." Ph.D. diss., SUNY Binghamton.

———. 1996. "Household and Community: The Development of Iroquois Agricultural Village Life." *Journal of Middle Atlantic Archaeology* 12:7–16.

———. 1997. "Warfare, Women, and Households: The Development of Iroquois Culture." In *Women in Prehistory: North America and Mesoamerica,* edited by Cheryl Claassen and Rosemary A. Joyce, 88–99. Philadelphia: Univ. of Pennsylvania Press.

Prisch, Betty Coit. 1982. *Aspects of Change in Seneca Iroquois Ladles A.D. 1600–1900.* Charles F. Hayes III, general editor. Research Records no. 15. Rochester Museum and Science Center.

Quain, Buell. 1961. "The Iroquois." In *Cooperation and Competition among Primitive Peoples,* edited by Margaret Mead, 240–81. Boston: Beacon Press.

Quinn, D. B. 1979. *New American World: A Documentary History of North America to 1612.* 5 vols. New York: Arno Press and Hector Bye.

Ramsden, Peter G. 1990. "Saint Lawrence Iroquoians in the Upper Trent Valley." *Man in the Northeast* 39:87–95.

Rands, Robert L., and Carroll L. Riley. 1958. "Diffusion and Discontinuous Distribution." *American Anthropologist* 60:274–97.

Reid, C. S. Paddy. 1975. "Early Ontario Iroquois Tradition." *Ontario Archaeology* no. 25:7–20.

Richards, Cara E. 1967. "Huron and Iroquois Residence Patterns, 1600–1650." In *Iroquois Culture, History and Prehistory: Proceedings of the 1965 Conference on Iroquois Research,* edited by Elisabeth Tooker, 51–56. Albany: New York State Museum and Science Service.

Richter, Daniel K. 1987. "Ordeals of the Longhouse: The Five Nations in Early American History." In *Beyond the Covenant Chain: The Iroquois and Their Neighbors in Indian North America, 1600–1800,* edited by Daniel K. Richter and James H. Merrell, 11–28. Syracuse: Syracuse Univ. Press.

———. 1992. *The Ordeal of the Longhouse: The Peoples of the Iroquois League in the Era of European Colonization.* Chapel Hill: Univ. of North Carolina Press.

Ritchie, William. 1932. *The Lamoka Lake Site.* Researches and Transactions of the New York State Archeological Association 7, no. 2. Rochester.

———. 1936. *A Prehistoric Fortified Village Site at Canandaigua, Ontario County, New York.* Research Records of the Rochester Museum of Arts and Sciences no. 3. Rochester.

———. 1945. *An Early Site in Cayuga County, New York: Type Component of the Frontenac Focus, Archaic Pattern.* Researches and Transactions of the New York State Archaeological Association 10, no. 1. Rochester: Lewis H. Morgan Chapter.

———. 1947. *Archaeological Evidence for Ceremonialism in the Owasco Culture.* Researches and Transactions of the New York State Archeological Association 11, no. 2. Rochester: Lewis H. Morgan Chapter.

———. 1950. "Another Probable Case of Prehistoric Bear Ceremonialism in New York." *American Antiquity* 15, no. 3:247–49.

———. 1952. *The Chance Horizon, An Early Stage of Mohawk Iroquois Cultural Development.* New York State Museum, circular 29. Albany.

———. 1953. *Indian History of New York State:* Pt. 1, *Pre-Iroquoian Cultures.* New York State Museum Educational Leaflet Series no. 6. Albany.

———. 1954. *Dutch Hollow, an Early Historic Period Seneca Site in Livingstone County, New York.* Rochester Museum of Arts and Sciences, Research Records, no. 10. Rochester.

———. 1980. *The Archaeology of New York State.* Revised edition. Harrison, New York: Harbor Hill Books

Ritchie, William, and Robert Funk. 1973. *Aboriginal Settlement Patterns in the Northeast.* New York State Museum and Science Service, memoir 20. Albany: The State Univ. of New York, The State Education Department.

Rogers, Edward H. 1935. "A Double Burial from Niantic." *Bulletin of the Archaeological Society of Connecticut* no. 1:2–3. New Haven: Peabody Museum.

Rousseau, Jacques. 1966. "Movement of Plants under the Influence of Man." In *The Evolution of Canada's Flora,* edited by Roy L. Taylor and R. A. Ludwig, 81–99. Toronto: Univ. of Toronto Press.

Rowlands, M. 1972. "Defence: A Factor in the Organization of Settlements." In *Man, Settlement and Urbanism,* edited by Peter J. Ucko, Ruth Tringham, and G. W. Dimbleby. 447–62. London: Duckworth.

Rumrill, Donald A. 1985. "An Interpretation and Analysis of the Seventeenth Century Mohawk Nation: Its Chronology and Move-

ments." *The Bulletin and Journal of Archaeology for New York State* no. 90:1–39.

———. 1988. "Art Form or Artifact Type?" *The Bulletin: Journal of the New York State Archaeological Association* no. 96:19–25.

Russell, Emily. 1983. "Indian-Set Fires in the Forests of the Northeastern United States." *Ecology* 64, no. 1:78–88.

Sagard-Théodat, G. 1968. *Sagard's Long Journey to the Country of the Hurons (1632),* edited by G. M. Wrong. New York: Greenwood Press.

Salisbury, Neal. 1996. "Native People and European Settlers in Eastern North America, 1600–1783." In *The Cambridge History of the Native Peoples of the Americas: North America,* vol. 1, pt 1. Edited by Bruce G. Trigger and Wilcomb E. Washburn, 399–460. New York: Cambridge Univ. Press.

Sauer, Carl O. 1971. *Sixteenth Century North America: The Land and the People as Seen by the Europeans.* Berkeley: Univ. of California Press.

Saunders, Lorraine P. 1986. "Biological Affinities Among Historic Seneca Groups and Possible Precursive Populations." Ph.D. diss. Univ. of Texas: Austin.

———. 1996. "Orbital Pitting: Diet or Cooking Utensil?" *Journal of Middle Atlantic Archaeology* 12:35–41.

Saunders, Lorraine P., and Martha L. Sempowski. 1991. "The Seneca Site Sequence and Chronology: The Baby or the Bathwater?" *The Bulletin: Journal of the New York State Archaeological Association* no. 102:13–26.

Saunders, Nicholas J. 1998. "Stealers of Light, Traders in Brilliance: Amerindian Metaphysics in the Mirror of Conquest." *Res 33* (Spring):225–52.

Scheele, Raymond. 1950. "Warfare of the Iroquois and Their Northern Neighbors." Ph.D. diss., Columbia.

Schiffer, Michael B. 1987. *Formation Processes of the Archaeological Record.* Albuquerque: Univ. of New Mexico Press.

Schock, Jack M. 1974. "The Chautauqua Phase and Other Late Woodland Sites in Southwestern New York." Ph.D. diss., State Univ. of New York at Buffalo.

———. 1976. "Southwestern New York: The Chautauqua Phase and Other Late Woodland Occupation." In *The Late Prehistory of the Lake Erie Drainage Basin: A 1972 Symposium Revised,* edited by David S. Brose, 89–109. Cleveland: Cleveland Museum of Natural History.

Schoolcraft, H. R. 1847. *Notes on the Iroquois.* Albany: E. H. Pease.

Schwarcz, Henry P., Jerry Melbye, M. Anne Katzenberg, and Martin Knyf. 1985. "Stable Isotopes in Human Skeletons of Southern Ontario: Reconstructing Palaeodiet." *Journal of Archaeological Science* 12:187–206.

Schwartz, Marion. 1997. *A History of Dogs in the Early Americas.* New Haven, CT: Yale Univ. Press.

Seabrook, John. 1998. "The Gathering of the Tribes: Preppies vs. Indians on an old American playing field." *The New Yorker* Sept.7:30–36.

Seaver, James. F. 1975. *A Narrative of the Life of Mrs. Mary Jemison.* [1824]. New York: Corinth Books Inc.

Seeman, Mark F. 1992. "The Bow and Arrow, The Intrusive Mound Complex, and a Late Woodland Jack's Reef Horizon in the Mid-Ohio Valley." In *Cultural Variability in Context: Woodland Settlements of the Mid-Ohio Valley,* edited by Mark F. Seeman.

41–51. MCJA Special Paper no. 7. Kent, Ohio: Kent State Univ. Press.

Sempowski, Martha J. 1989. "Fluctuations Through Time in the Use of Marine Shell at Seneca Iroquois Sites. *Proceedings of the 1986 Shell Bead Conference, Selected Papers,* edited by Charles F. Hayes III, 81–96. Rochester Museum and Science Center, Research Records 20. Rochester, New York.

———. 1994. "Early Historic Exchange Between the Seneca and the Susquehannock." In *Proceedings of the 1992 People to People Conference: Selected Papers,* general editor, Charles F. Hayes III, associate editors, Connie Cox Bodner and Lorraine P. Saunders. 51–64. Research Records no. 23. Rochester Museum and Science Center.

———. 1997. "The Metaphor of the Iroquois Longhouse: Its Role in the Expansion of the League of the Iroquois." Paper presented at the Long House Conference, Rochester Museum and Science Center.

Sempowski, Martha. n.d. "Supernatural Transformation: As Reflected in Late Prehistoric Human Effigy Pipes from Western New York." Paper presented at the 2002 annual meeting of the New York State Archaeological Association, Norwich, N.Y.

Sempowski, Martha L., and Annette Nohe. 1998. "Classification and Analysis of Glass Beads from three early Seventeenth-Century Seneca Iroquois Sites: Warren, Cornish, and Bosley Mills." Paper presented at The Northeast Archaeology Symposium, the Cayuga Museum, Auburn, N.Y.

Sempowski, Martha L., and Lorraine P. Saunders. In Press. *Dutch Hollow and Factory Hollow: The Advent of Dutch Trade Among The Seneca.* Charles F. Wray Series in Seneca Archaeology, vol. 3, Research Records no. 24, Rochester Museum and Science Center.

Sempowski, Martha L., Lorraine P. Saunders, and Gian Carlo Cervone. 1988. "The Adams and Culbertson Sites: A Hypothesis for Village Formation." *Man in the Northeast* 35:95–108.

Shen, Chen. 1997. "Towards a Comprehensive Understanding of the Lithic Production System of the Princess Point Complex, Southwestern Ontario." Ph.D. diss., Univ. of Toronto.

Shimony, Annemarie. 1961. *Conservatism Among the Iroquois at the Six Nations Reserve.* New Haven, Connecticut: Yale Univ. Publications in Anthropology 65.

Skinner, Alanson. 1909. "The Lenape Indians of Staten Island." *Anthropological Papers of the American Museum of Natural History* 3:14–16.

Slayman, A. 1997. "A Battle Over Bones." *Archaeology* 50 (Jan./Feb.):16–20.

Smith, Bruce D. 1989. "Origins of Agriculture in Eastern North America." *Science* 246:1566–71.

Smith, David Gray. 1987. "Archaeological Systematics and the Analysis of Iroquoian Ceramics: A Case Study from the Crawford Lake Area, Ontario." Ph.D. diss., McGill Univ..

Smith, David G., and Gary W. Crawford. 1997. "Recent Developments in the Archaeology of the Princess Point Complex in Southern Ontario." *Canadian Journal of Archaeology* 21:9–32.

Snow, Dean R. 1980. *The Archaeology of New England.* Academic Press.

———. 1984. "Iroquois Prehistory." In *Extending The Rafters: Interdisciplinary Approaches to Iroquoian Studies,* edited by Michael Foster, Jack Campisi, and Marianne Mithun, 241–57. Albany: State Univ. of New York Press.

———. 1991. "Mohawk." *The Bulletin: Journal of the New York State Archaeological Association* no. 102:34–39.

———. 1994a. "Iroquoians and Europeans: Disunited Nations in the Early Contact Period." In *Proceedings of the 1992 People to People Conference: Selected Papers,* general editor, Charles F. Hayes III, associate editors, Connie Cox Bodner and Lorraine P. Saunders. 1–5. Research Records no. 23, Rochester Museum and Science Center.

———. 1994b. *The Iroquois.* Cambridge: Blackwell Publishers.

———. 1995a. *Mohawk Valley Archaeology: The Sites.* The Institute For Archaeological Studies, Univ. at Albany, SUNY.

———. 1995b. "Migration in Prehistory: The Northern Iroquoian Case." *American Antiquity* 60, no. 1:59–79.

———. 1995c. "Population Movements During the Woodland Period: The Intrusion of Iroquoian Peoples." In *Origins of the People of the Longhouse,* edited by Andre Bekerman and Gary Warrick, 5–8. North York, Ontario: The Ontario Archaeological Society.

———. 1996. "Mohawk Demography and the Effects of Exogenous Epidemics on American Indian Populations." *Journal of Anthropological Archaeology* 15:160–82.

———. 1997. "The Architecture of Iroquois Longhouses." *Northeast Anthropology* no. 53:61–84.

Snow, Dean R., Charles T. Gehring, and William A. Starna. 1996. *In Mohawk Country: Early Narratives about a Native People.* Syracuse: Syracuse Univ. Press.

Snow, Dean R., and David B. Guldenzopf.

1998. "The Mohawk Upper Castle Historic District National Historic Landmark." *The Bulletin, Journal of the New York State Archaeological Association* no. 114:32–44.

Snow, Dean R., and K. M. Lamphear. 1988. "European Contact and Indian Depopulation in the Northeast: The Timing of the First Epidemics." *Ethnohistory* 35, no. 1:15–33.

Snow, Dean R., and William A. Starna. 1989. "Sixteenth-Century Depopulation: A View from the Mohawk Valley." *American Anthropologist* 91:142–49.

Snyderman, George. 1961. "The Functions of Wampum in Iroquois Religion." *American Philosophical Society Proceedings* 105:571–605.

Socci, Mary Catherine. 1995. "The Zooarchaeology of the Mohawk Valley." Ph.D. diss., Yale.

Sohrweide, Gregory A. 1997. "Onondaga Longhouses in the Late Seventeenth Century on the Weston Site." Paper presented at the Longhouse Conference, Rochester Museum and Science Center.

———. 2001. "Onondaga Longhouses in the Late Seventeenth Century on the Weston Site." *The Bulletin: Journal of the New York State Archaeological Association* no. 117:1–24.

———. n.d. "Experimental Archaeology: A Preliminary Report on Iroquois Wall Architecture." Paper presented at the 1999 Northeast Archaeology Symposium, Auburn, New York.

Soffer, Olga, James M. Adovasio, David C. Hyland, Boshwslav Klima, and Jiri Svoboda. 1998. "Perishable Technologies and the Genesis of the Eastern Gravettian." *Anthropologie* 36, nos. 1–2:43–68.

Soper, James H., and Margaret L. Heimburger. 1982. "Shrubs of Ontario." *Life Sciences Miscellaneous Publication*. Toronto: Royal Ontario Museum.

Speck, Frank G. 1925. "Dogs of the Labrador Indians." *Natural History* 25:58–64.

———. 1931. *A Study of the Delaware Indian Big House Ceremony*. Harrisburg: Pennsylvania Historical Commission.

———. 1955. *The Iroquois: A Study in Cultural Evolution*. 2d ed. Bloomfield Hills, Michigan: Cranbrook Institute of Science.

Speth, John. 1983. *Bison Kills and Bone Counts: Decision-making by Ancient Hunters*. Chicago: Univ. of Chicago Press.

Squier, Ephraim G. 1851. *Antiquities of the State of New York*. Buffalo: George Derby.

Stahle, David W., Malcolm K. Cleaveland, Dennis B. Blanton, Matthew D. Therrell, and David A. Gay. 1998. "The Lost Colony and Jamestown Droughts." *Science* 280:564–67.

Starna, William A. 1988. "The Oneida Homeland in the Seventeenth Century." In *The Oneida Indian Experience,* edited by Jack Campisi and Laurence M. Hauptman. 9–22. Syracuse: Syracuse Univ. Press.

Starna, William A., and Robert E. Funk. 1994. "The Place of the In Situ Hypothesis in Iroquoian Archaeology." *Northeast Anthropology,* no. 47:45–54.

Starna, William A., George R. Hamell, and William L. Butts. 1984. "Northern Iroquois Horticulture and Insect Infestation: A Cause for Village Removal." *Ethnohistory* 31, no. 3:197–207.

Starna, William A., and R. Watkins. 1991. "Northern Iroquoian Warfare and Slavery: A Hypothesis." *Ethnohistory* 38, no. 1:34–57.

Steckley, J. L. 1985. "A Tale of Two Peoples." *Arch Notes: Newsletter of the Ontario Archaeological Society* (July/August):9–15.

———. 1987. "An Ethnolinguistic Look at the Huron Longhouse." *Ontario Archaeology*, no. 47:19–32.

St. John, Donald P. 1987. "Iroquois." In *Native American Religions: North America*, edited by Lawrence E. Sullivan. 133–38. New York: MacMillan.

Stothers, David. 1977. *The Princess Point Complex*. Mercury Series, Archeological Survey of Canada, Paper no. 58. Ottawa: National Museum of Man.

Stothers, David, and Timothy Abel. 1989. "The Position of the 'Pearson Complex' in the Late Prehistory of Ohio." *Archaeology of Eastern North America* 17:109–41.

Strong, John A. 1985. "Late Woodland Dog Ceremonialism on Long Island in Comparative and Temporal Perspective." *The Bulletin and Journal of Archaeology for New York State* no. 91:32–38.

Stutzman, Tracy S. 1998. "Recent Investigations at the Parker Farm Site—A Cayuga Iroquois Village." Paper presented at The Northeast Archaeology Symposium, The Cayuga Museum, Auburn, N.Y.

Sublett, Audrey J., and Charles F. Wray. 1970. "Some Examples of Accidental and Deliberate Human Skeletal Modification in the Northeast." *The Bulletin: Journal of the New York State Archaeological Association* no. 50:14–26.

Sullivan, Lynne P. 1992. "Arthur C. Parker's Contributions to New York State Archaeology." *The Bulletin: Journal of the New York State Archaeological Association* no. 104:3–8.

Swan, Frederick R. Jr. 1970. "Post-Fire Response of Four Plant Communities in South-Central New York State." *Ecology* 51:1074–82.

Sykes, Clark M. 1980. "Swidden Horticulture and Iroquoian Settlement." *Archaeology of Eastern North America* 8:45–52.

Taliman, Valerie. 2002. "Mohawk Ironworkers at Ground Zero." *National Museum of the American Indian* 3, no. 1: 14–20. Washington, D.C.: Smithsonian Institution.

Taylor, Walter P., ed. 1956. *The Deer of North America*. Harrisburg: Stackpole Books.

Thibaudeau, Paul A. 2002. "Use-Wear Analysis on Cuprous Materials: Method and Theory." Ph.D. diss., University of Toronto.

Thomas, Chief Jacob. 1994. *Teachings from the Longhouse*. With Terry Boyle. Toronto: Stoddart Publishing Co.

Thomas, Stephen C. 1997. "Interior-Exterior Distribution of Activities at the Hubbert Site: An Early Fifteenth Century Iroquoian Village near Barrie, Ontario." Paper presented at the Longhouse Conference, Rochester Museum and Science Center.

Thwaites, Reuben Gold, ed. 1896–1901. *The Jesuit Relations and Allied Documents: Travels and Explorations of the Jesuit Missionaries in New France, 1610–1791*. 73 vols. Cleveland: Burrows Brothers.

Tooker, Elisabeth. 1960. "Three Aspects of Northern Iroquoian Culture Change." *Pennsylvania Archaeologist* 30, no. 2:65–71.

———. 1964. *An Ethnography of the Huron Indians, 1615–1649*. Smithsonian Institution, Bureau of American Ethnology, Bulletin 190. Washington: U.S. Government Printing Office.

———. 1965. "The Iroquois White Dog Sacrifice in the Latter Part of the Eighteenth Century." *Ethnohistory* 12, no. 2:129–40.

———. 1970. *The Iroquois Ceremonial of Midwinter*. Syracuse: Syracuse Univ. Press.

———. 1978. "Iroquois since 1820." In *Handbook of North American Indians*. Vol.

15, *Northeast,* edited by Bruce Trigger. Washington, D.C.: Smithsonian Institution.

Tremblay, Roland. 1998. Review of "Enfants du Néant et Mangeurs D'Âmes: Guerre, Culture et Société en Iroquoisie Ancienne by Roland Viau." *Northeast Anthropology,* no. 55:73–75.

Trigger, Bruce G. 1967. "Settlement Archaeology: Its Goals and Promise." *American Antiquity* 32:149–60.

———. 1976. *The Children of Aatensic: A History of the Huron People to 1660.* 2 vols. Montreal: McGill-Queen's Univ. Press.

———. 1978a. "Early Iroquoian Contacts with Europeans." In *Handbook of North American Indians.* Vol. 15, *Northeast,* edited by Bruce Trigger. Washington, D.C.: Smithsonian Institution.

———. 1978b. "Cultural Unity and Diversity." In *Handbook of North American Indians.* Vol. 15, *Northeast,* edited by Bruce Trigger. Washington, D.C.: Smithsonian Institution.

———. 1978c. "Iroquoian Matriliny." *Pennsylvania Archaeologist* 48, nos. 1–2:55–65.

———. 1981. "Prehistoric Social and Political Organization: An Iroquoian Case Study." In *Foundations of Northeast Archaeology,* edited by Dean Snow. 1–50. New York: Academic Press.

———. 1985. *Natives and Newcomers: Canada's "Heroic Age" Reconsidered.* Montreal: McGill-Queen's Univ. Press.

———. 1987. "Introduction to Papers on the Beginnings of the Fur Trade." *Man in the Northeast* 33:27–30.

———. 1990a. "Maintaining Economic Equality in Opposition to Complexity: An Iroquoian Case Study." In *The Evolution of Political Systems: Sociopolitics in Small-Scale*

*Sedentary Societies,* edited by Steadman Upham. 119–45. New York: Cambridge Univ. Press.

———. 1990b. *The Huron: Farmers of the North.* New York: Holt, Rinehart, and Winston. 2d edition.

Trigger, Bruce G., and William R. Swagerty. 1996. "Entertaining Strangers: North America in the Sixteenth Century." In *The Cambridge History of the Native Peoples of the Americas: North America.* Vol. 1, part 1. Edited by Bruce G. Trigger and Wilcomb E. Washburn. 325–98. New York: Cambridge Univ. Press.

Trubowitz, Neal. 1978. "The Persistence of Settlement Pattern in a Cultivated Field." In *Essays in Northeastern Anthropology in Memory of Marian E. White,* edited by William Engelbrecht and Donald Grayson. 41–66. Occasional Publications in Northeastern Anthropology no. 5. Rindge, New Hampshire: Man in the Northeast.

Tuck, James A. 1971. *Onondaga Iroquois Prehistory: A Study in Settlement Archaeology.* Syracuse: Syracuse Univ. Press.

———. 1978. "Northern Iroquoian Prehistory." In *Handbook of North American Indians.* Vol. 15, *Northeast,* edited by Bruce Trigger. Washington, D.C.: Smithsonian Institution.

Turgeon, Laurier. 1990. "Basque-Amerindian Trade in the St. Lawrence During the Sixteenth Century: New Documents, New Perspective." *Man in the Northeast* 40:81–87.

Turton, Charles, Mel Brown, and William Finlayson. 1998. "Purslane Use: A Cultural Practice by Ontario Iroquoians near Crawford Lake A.D. 1000–1650, Evidence from Pollen and Macrofossil Studies of Lake Sediments in Southern Ontario, Canada." In *Iroquoian Peoples of the Land of Rocks and Water, A.D. 1000–1650: A Study in Settlement Archaeology,* by William Finlayson, 1:115–120. London, Ontario: London Museum of Archaeology.

Vandrei, Charles. 1987. "Observations on Seneca Settlement in the Early Historic Period." *The Bulletin: Journal of the New York State Archaeological Association* no. 95:8–17.

Vennum, Thomas Jr. 1994. *American Indian Lacrosse: Little Brother of War.* Washington: Smithsonian Institution Press.

Viau, Roland. 1997. *Enfants du Néant et Mangeurs D'Âmes: Guerre, Culture et Société en Iroquoisie Ancienne.* Montreal: Editions du Boreal.

Vogel, J. C., and Nikolaas J. van der Merwe. 1977. "Isotopic Evidence for Early Maize Cultivation in New York State." *American Antiquity* 42, no. 2:238–42.

Von Gernet, Alexander. 1992. "Hallucinogens and the Origins of the Iroquoian Pipe/Tobacco/Smoking Complex." In *Proceedings of the 1989 Smoking Pipe Conference: Selected Papers,* general editor, Charles F. Hayes III, associate editors, Connie Cox Bodner and Martha L. Sempowski. 171–85. Research Records no. 22, Rochester Museum and Science Center.

Von Gernet, Alexander, and Peter Timmins. 1987. "Pipes and Parakeets: Constructing Meaning in an Early Iroquoian Context." In *Archaeology as Long-Term History,* edited by Ian Hodder. 31–42. Cambridge: Cambridge Univ. Press.

Wagner, Gail, and Gayle Fritz. n.d. "Up in Smoke? Reassessment of Early Eastern Tobacco." Paper presented at the 2002 annual meeting of the Society for American Archaeology. Denver.

Wagner, Norman E., Lawrence Toombs, and Eduard R. Riegert. 1973. *The Moyer Site: A Prehistoric Village in Waterloo Country.* Waterloo, Ontario: Wilfrid Laurier Univ. Press.

Wallace, Anthony F. C. 1958. "Dreams and the Wishes of the Soul: A Type of Psychoanalytic Theory among the Seventeenth Century Iroquois." *American Anthropologist* 60:234–48.

———. 1972. *The Death and Rebirth of the Seneca.* 1969. Reprint, New York: Vintage Books.

Warrick, Gary A. 1984. *Reconstructing Ontario Iroquoian Village Organization.* Mercury Series, Archeological Survey of Canada, Paper no. 124:1–180. Ottawa: National Museum of Man.

———. 1988. "Estimating Ontario Iroquoian Village Duration." *Man in the Northeast* 36:21–60.

———. 1996. "Evolution of the Iroquoian Longhouse." In *People Who Lived in Big Houses: Archaeological Perspectives on Large Domestic Structures,* edited by Gary Coupland and E. B. Banning. 11–26. Monographs in World Archaeology no. 27. Madison, Wisconsin: Prehistory Press.

Washburn, Wilcomb E. 1996. "The Native American Renaissance, 1960–1995." In *The Cambridge History of the Native Peoples of the Americas: North America.* Vol. 1, part 2. Edited by Bruce G. Trigger and Wilcomb E. Washburn. 401–73. New York: Cambridge Univ. Press.

Watson, Patty Jo. 1988. "Prehistoric Gardening and Agriculture in the Midwest and Midsouth. In *Interpretations of Culture*

*Change in the Eastern Woodlands During the Late Woodland Period,* edited by Richard W. Yerkes. 39–67. Ohio State Univ. Occasional Papers in Anthropology, no. 3.

Waugh, F. W. 1973. *Iroquois Foods and Food Preparation.* Anthropological Series 12, Memoirs of the Canadian Geological Survey 86. 1916. Reprint. Ottawa: Government Printing Bureau.

Weber, C. J. 1971. "Types and Attributes in Iroquois Pipes." *Man in the Northeast* 2:51–65.

Wedel, Waldo R. 1936. *An Introduction to Pawnee Archaeology.* Smithsonian Institution, Bureau of American Ethnology, Bulletin 112.

Weeden, William B. 1884. *Indian Money as a Factor in New England Civilization.* Johns Hopkins Univ. Studies in Historical and Political Science, 2nd ser., vols. 8–9. Baltimore.

Weiskotten, Daniel H. 1988. "Origins of the Oneida Iroquois: Fact and Fallacy—Past and Present." *Bulletin, Chenango Chapter, New York State Archaeological Association* 22, no. 4:1–20.

———. 1995. "Sizing up the Oneida, Keeping Pace with Harmen Myndertz van den Bogaert." Paper presented at the annual meeting of the New York State Archaeological Association. Syracuse.

Weltfish, Gene. 1965. *The Lost Universe.* New York: Basic Books.

Whallon, Robert. 1968. "Investigations of Late Prehistoric Social Organization in New York State." In *New Perspectives in Archeology,* edited by Sally R. Binford and Lewis R. Binford. 223–44. Chicago: Aldine Publishing Co.

White, Marian E. 1961. *Iroquois Culture History in the Niagara Frontier Area of New York State.* Anthropological Papers, Museum of Anthropology, Univ. of Michigan, no. 16. Ann Arbor.

———. 1963. "Settlement Pattern Change and the Development of Horticulture in the New York-Ontario Area." *Pennsylvania Archaeologist* 23, nos. 1–2:1–12.

———. 1978. "Neutral and Wenro." In *Handbook of North American Indians.* Vol. 15, *Northeast,* edited by Bruce Trigger. Washington, D.C.: Smithsonian Institution.

White, Marian E., William Engelbrecht, and Elisabeth Tooker. 1978. "Cayuga." In *Handbook of North American Indians.* Vol. 15, *Northeast,* edited by Bruce Trigger. Washington, D.C.: Smithsonian Institution.

White, Richard. 1984. "Native Americans and the Environment." In *Scholars and the Indian Experience,* edited by W.R. Swagerty. 179–204. Bloomington: Indiana Univ. Press.

White, Richard, and William Cronon. 1988. "Ecological Change and Indian-White Relations." In *Handbook of North American Indians.* Vol 4, *History of Indian-White Relations,* edited by Wilcomb E. Washburn. 417–29. Washington: Smithsonian Institution.

Whitney, Theodore. 1970. "The Buyea Site OND 13-3." *The Bulletin: New York State Archaeological Association* no. 50:1–14.

———. 1974. "Aboriginal Art and Ritual Objects." *Chenango Chapter Bulletin* 15, no. 1.

Wilk, R. R., and W. L. Rathje. 1982. "Household Archaeology." *American Behavioral Scientist* 25, no. 6:617–39.

Williamson, Ronald F. 1986. "The Miller Stream Cluster: The Other Side of the Coin." In *Studies in Southwestern Ontario Archaeology,* edited by William A. Fox.

25–31. Occasional Publications of the London Chapter, Ontario Archaeological Society, no. 1.

Williamson, Ronald F., and David A. Robertson. 1994. "Peer Polities Beyond the Periphery: Early and Middle Iroquoian Regional Interaction." *Ontario Archaeology* 58:27–44.

Wilson, Edmund. 1959. *Apologies to the Iroquois.* New York: Farrar, Straus and Cudahy.

Wissler, Clark, and Herbert J. Spinden. 1916. "The Pawnee Human Sacrifice to the Morningstar." *The American Museum Journal* 16, no. 1:49–55.

Witthoft, John. 1949. *Green Corn Ceremonialism in the Eastern Woodlands.* Occasional Contributions from the Museum of Anthropology of the Univ. of Michigan, no. 13. Ann Arbor: Univ. of Michigan Press.

———. 1953. "The American Indian as Hunter." *Pennsylvania Game News* 24, no. 4:8–13.

———. 1959. "Ancestry of the Susquehannocks." In *Susquehannock Miscellany,* edited by John Witthoft and W. F. Kinsey III. 19–60. Harrisburg: The Pennsylvania Historical and Museum Commission.

———. 1961. "Eastern Woodlands Community Typology and Acculturation." *Symposium on Cherokee and Iroquois Culture.* Smithsonian Institution, Bureau of American Ethnology, Bulletin 180:67–76. Washington: U.S. Government Printing Office.

Wolf, Eric R. 1982. *Europe and the People Without History.* Berkeley: Univ. of California Press.

Wonderley, Anthony. 1999. "Oneida Ceramic Effigies: A Question of Meaning." Paper presented at the Northeast Archaeological Symposium, Auburn, N.Y.

Woodbury, Hanni. 1992. *Concerning the League: the Iroquois Tradition as Dictated by John Arthur Gibson.* Winnipeg: Algonquian and Iroquoian Linguistics. Memoir 9.

Wray, Charles F. 1963. "Ornamental Hair Combs of the Seneca Iroquois." *Pennsylvania Archaeologist* 33, nos. 1–2:35–50.

———. 1973. *Manual For Seneca Iroquois Archeology.* Rochester: Cultures Primitive, Inc.

Wray, Charles F., and Harry L. Schoff. 1953. "A Preliminary Report on the Seneca Sequence in Western New York, 1550–1687." *Pennsylvania Archaeologist* 23, no. 2:53–63.

Wray, Charles F., Martha Sempowski, Lorraine Saunders, and Gian Carlo Cervone. 1987. *The Adams and Culbertson Sites.* Charles F. Wray Series in Seneca Archaeology. Vol. 1. Charles F. Hayes III, general editor. Research Records no. 19. Rochester Museum and Science Center.

Wray, Charles F., Martha Sempowski, and Lorraine Saunders. 1991. *Tram and Cameron: Two Early Contact Era Seneca Sites.* Charles F. Wray Series in Seneca Archaeology. Vol. 2. Charles F. Hayes III, general editor. Research Records No. 21. Rochester Museum and Science Center.

Wright, Gordon K. 1950. "The Long Point Site." *Pennsylvania Archaeologist* 20, nos. 3–4:75–86.

Wright, J. V. 1966. *The Ontario Iroquois Tradition.* National Museum of Canada, Bulletin 210. Ottawa.

———. 1974. *The Nodwell Site.* Mercury Series, Archaeological Survey of Canada, Paper no. 22. Ottawa: National Museum of Man.

———. 1979. *Quebec Prehistory.* Toronto: Van Nostrand Reinhold.

———. 1994. "The Prehistoric Transportation of Goods in the St. Lawrence River Basin." In *Prehistoric Exchange Systems in North America,* edited by Timothy G. Baugh and Jonathon E. Ericson. 47–71. New York: Plenum Press.

———. 1995. "Three Dimensional Reconstructions of Iroquoian Longhouses: A Comment." *Archaeology of Eastern North America* 23:9–21.

———. 1998. Foreword to *Iroquoian Peoples of the Land of Rocks and Water,* A.D. *1000–1650: A Study in Settlement Archaeology,* by William Finlayson. Vol. 1:xi–xvi. London, Ontario: London Museum of Archaeology.

Wright, J. V., and D. M. Wright. 1993. "Iroquoian Archaeology: Its the Pits." In *Essays in St. Lawrence Iroquoian Archaeology,* edited by James F. Pendergast and Claude Chapdelaine. 1–7. Dundas, Ontario: Copetown Press.

Wright, Phillip J. 1980. "Prehistoric Ceramics from the Red Horse Lake Portage Site (BdGa–12) Eastern Ontario." *Archaeology of Eastern North America* 8:53–70.

Wright, Roy A. 1974. "The People of the Panther—A Long Erie Tale." *Papers in Linguistics from the 1972 Conference on Iroquoian Research,* edited by Michael K. Foster. 47–118. Mercury Series, Ethnology Division, Paper no. 10. Ottawa: National Museum of Man.

Wykoff, William M. 1988. "Iroquoian Prehistory and Climate Change: Notes for Empirical Studies of the Eastern Woodlands." Ph.D. diss., Cornell Univ.

———. 1991. "Black Walnut on Iroquoian Landscapes." *Northeast Indian Quarterly* 8, no. 2:4–17. Phoenix: Indian Tribal Series.

Zenkert, Charles A. 1934. *The Flora of the Niagara Frontier Region: Ferns and Flowering Plants of Buffalo, N.Y. and Vicinity.* Bulletin of the Buffalo Museum of Natural Sciences. Vol. 16. Buffalo: Buffalo Museum of Science.

# INDEX

Italic page number denotes illustration.